# WORKING FOR CHILDREN ON THE CHILD PROTECTION REGISTER

To Janet, whose love and support have motivated me to complete this task. To Liam, Adam and Laura, who will never be forgotten, and to my mum and dad for giving me the best foundation from which to build. To Stacy Laura, born 15 February 1998. This book is as much theirs as it is mine.

MARTIN C. CALDER

To Baz, Kate and Rachell for giving me encouragement and support when it was most needed.

JAN HORWATH

# Working for Children on the Child Protection Register

## An inter-agency practice guide

*Edited by*
Martin C. Calder
Jan Horwath



**Ashgate**
ARENA
Aldershot • Brookfield USA • Singapore • Sydney

Published by
Ashgate Publishing Ltd
Gower House
Croft Road
Aldershot
Hants GU11 3HR
England

Ashgate Publishing Company
Old Post Road
Brookfield
Vermont 05036
USA

**British Library Cataloguing in Publication Data**
Working for children on the Child Protection Register : an inter-agency practice guide
1. Abused children — Services for — Great Britain 2. Child abuse — Great Britain
I. Calder, Martin C. II. Horwath, Jan
362.7'6'0941

**Library of Congress Cataloging-in-Publication Data**
Working for children on the child protection register : an inter-agency practice guide / edited by Martin C. Calder, Jan Horwath.
p. cm.
ISBN 1-85742-367-4 (hc.)
1. Abused children—Services for—Great Britain. 2. Child welfare —Great Britain. 3. Social work with children—Great Britain.
I. Calder, Martin C. II. Horwath, Jan.
HV751.A6W66 1998
362.76'8'0941—dc21 98-35471
CIP

ISBN 1 85742 367 4

Printed in Great Britain

# Contents

# List of figures

# List of tables

# Acknowledgements

We would like to thank those who were involved in planning and participating in the National Conference core groups, 'Central to Child Protection Myth or Reality?', particularly Barbara Hayes and Margaret Bissell. It was as a consequence of the needs identified at the conference that this book was written.

Thanks are also due to the Leigh library staff, for seeking and finding some obscure references and to Joanne Crossland, who patiently typed the final script, coping with our indecipherable handwriting.

# Notes on the contributors

**Jane Appleton** is Principal Lecturer in the Department of Nursing and Paramedic Sciences at the University of Hertfordshire where she was formerly a senior lecturer in nursing. She trained and worked as a nurse in Sheffield, before moving to London to undertake her health visitor training. Jane worked full-time as health visitor for Harrow Community NHS Trust until October 1992 and has subsequently been employed as a health visitor for West Hertfordshire Community (NHS) Trust. Her research interests focus on health visitors' child protection work and use of professional judgements in identifying families needing increased support/interventions. Jane is currently a part-time doctoral student at King's College, London University and has published a number of research papers on health visiting and contributed to professional publications.

**Elaine Baxter** is an independent social work consultant and trainer. She delivers training on a range of child care subjects to professionals who work with children. She also undertakes assessments in connection with legal proceedings. Elaine works as a guardian *ad Litem* and is editor of the journal of the National Association of Guardians ad Litem and Reporting Officers.

**Martin C. Calder** is a child protection coordinator with City of Salford Community and Social Services Directorate. He has interests in developing inter-agency post-registration practice, especially core groups, and working with juveniles who sexually abuse and with adult sex offenders. He has published extensively in these fields and was recently invited to join a panel of experts on child abuse in Auckland, New Zealand.

**Alastair Christie** has been employed as a social worker and social work manager in England and Canada. He is currently employed as a lecturer in the Department of Applied Social Studies at University College Cork and is an Honorary Research Fellow in the Department of Applied Social Science at Lancaster University.

**Jill Clemerson** was formerly a nurse adviser (child protection) with the City and East London Family and Community Studies (CELFACS) project in Tower Hamlets, London. She has been actively involved in training and writing about child protection matters for the Health Visitors Association.

**Sharon Anne Cooke** is Team Leader, Children and Families, Barnsley Metropolitan Borough Council. After gaining a BA (Hons) degree, she was employed in residential social work for 12 months before taking the Certificate of Qualification in Social Work (CQSW) and Diploma in Social Work at University College, Cardiff. She qualified in 1986 and gained employment with Barnsley Metropolitan Borough Council, working in child care/child protection. She was appointed to the post of Team Leader in 1992. She gained a Diploma in Child Protection in 1993 and is currently undertaking a Post Graduate Diploma in Management.

**Barbara Firth** is a freelance trainer, researcher and consultant, as well as a member of the Professional Development Group at the University of Nottingham. She has had extensive work experience in statutory and voluntary social work agencies as a practitioner and a manager. Her current interests include all aspects of child protection and child welfare, assessment, team building, group work and interprofessional training.

**Jan Horwath** is a lecturer in social work studies. She undertakes research, consultancy and training for Area Child Protection Committees, social services departments and health trusts. Her professional and research interests include training and professional development, child protection practice and the management of child protection services. She has written books and articles in these fields.

**Helle Mittler** is a freelance trainer, consultant and researcher. She has many years' experience, first as a psychiatric social worker/team leader in the Manchester schools psychological and child guidance service and then as a trainer and staff development officer in a social services department. She has written extensively about working with parents and families of disabled children and adults and in the field of child protection. She has conducted workshops and lectured in many countries in Europe, Asia and South America.

**Tony Morrison** is an independent social care trainer and consultant. He works with staff and managers in social services, health, probation and other agencies. His main areas of work are supervision, inter-agency collaboration, risk management and motivational interviewing. He has written *Supervision in Social Care* (Pavillion, 1993) and (with Jan Horwath) *Effective Staff Training in Social Care: From Theory to Practice* (Routledge, 1998).

**Michael Murphy** is the coordinator of Bolton ACPC's staff resource, where he works as a trainer and a counsellor. Michael is the author of *Working Together in Child Protection* (Arena, 1995) and *The Child Protection Unit* (Avebury, 1996). He is also a founder member of the Stress in Social Work group.

**Anne Peake** has worked as a psychologist since 1976 in both education and social services, in Liverpool, Haringey, and now in Oxfordshire. Her main area of professional interest is child protection work. She has run a Child Sexual Abuse Consultation Service, groups for children and for mothers, and offered a regular service to child protection investigation teams in Oxfordshire.

**Bobbie Print** is a social worker who has worked in the child protection field for 25 years. Since 1986, she has specialised in work with children and young people who have been sexually abused or who have sexually abused others. She is currently Programme Director of G-MAP, a therapeutic programme based in Manchester that works with young people who have had sexual behaviour problems.

**Barry Raynes** is the managing director of Reconstruct. He has 20 years of varied social work experience, mostly with children and families. He works with social services departments as a trainer of staff and a consultant with senior managers allowing him to see the effect of change at all levels of the organisation.

**Christine Samra-Tibbetts** has 22 years' experience in child care and child protection, in both the voluntary and the statutory sectors. For the past six years, she has been an independent trainer and consultant working in many local authorities, health authorities and voluntary organisations around the country. She is currently undertaking work with local authorities who are developing assessment formats and family support services.

**Julie Turner** qualified as a teacher in 1978. She worked for a year as a chef and then began work in Banbury School in 1980. She trained to work with children with emotional and behavioural difficulties, which became an area of focus for her work. She currently works as a school counsellor and as the designated teacher for child protection. She trains teachers, both primary and secondary, in child protection. She has run groups in school and recently initiated peer counselling.

# Introduction

Much has been written in recent years about child protection practice, so what is the benefit of yet another book? This book is unique inasmuch as it addresses an area of practice that has received little attention in terms of research and post-registration practice development. The book seeks to provide a resource for those workers and their managers who are working with children and families where the child has been formally identified as being abused or at significant risk of abuse.

Before we can explore post-registration practice in any detail we consider it is important to set the book in context, in terms of defining terms, identifying some of the key issues and outlining ways in which those who have contributed to the book address these issues.

## What is post-registration child protection practice?

Post-registration practice covers a whole range of interventions that occur once a child is formally perceived to be at risk of future harm and their name is placed on the child protection register. Post-registration practice has been interpreted in a number of ways (Farmer and Owen, 1995: 71). At one end of the spectrum it describes the reactive involvement of child protection workers, who focus on the initial causes for concern regarding the child and attempt to address these. At the other end of the spectrum it is perceived as proactive, planned interventions, that effect positive change for the child and the family and promote and enhance the child's welfare. At this end of the spectrum the work is undertaken in partnership between a range of child protection professionals and the child and their carers. Other practitioners will provide services that fall between the two extremes: for example, addressing the immediate causes for concern and undertaking some work to promote the child's development and potential. The diversity of activity can be attributed to the lack of guidance at both national and local level which often leaves practitioners with no clear framework or understanding regarding the purpose of post-registration practice.

## Lack of guidance

Historically, post-registration work has been a neglected area of child protection practice. The primary focus of child protection, since the death of Maria Colwell in 1974, has been on the recognition, reporting and investigation of child abuse and neglect. This focus has been mirrored in policy and guidance at both national and local level. For example, the concept of the child protection register was introduced in 1974 as a means of identifying children at risk of abuse or neglect who require professional intervention to protect them from further harm; since then there has been no substantial guidance issued about ways in which professionals should work with each other to meet the needs of those children and their families.

It is ironic that so much time and energy and so many resources are invested in following procedures, up to and including the registration of the child on the child protection register, but that once this has occurred guidance becomes hazy, with the post-registration phase being marked by a lack of inter-agency activity (Hallett, 1995). Whilst we accept this in the field of child protection, investigation alone would not be accepted in other areas. For example, if our car breaks down, we would expect a mechanic to undertake an investigation to find the fault. Once the fault is identified, we do not expect the mechanic to walk away. We would expect the investigation to be the beginning of the process by which the fault to the car is rectified. Yet, in the case of child protection, we often identify what harm has occurred or is likely to occur to the child but, once this has been identified, we have little prescriptive guidance enabling us to put right the damage.

In the absence of any substantial national guidance regarding post-registration practice, many practitioners and managers look towards their local Area Child Protection Committee (ACPC) for guidance. This is because the ACPC is responsible for coordinating child protection work at a local level. However, a national study of post-registration practice, which was completed in 1996 (Calder and Horwath, 1996) highlighted the fact that only 3 per cent of ACPCs had developed policies, procedures and practice guidance compared to 24 per cent who had none. Within the sample, 63 per cent reported having procedures alone and 10 per cent did not respond to this question. Whilst 58 per cent had written statements regarding the purpose and tasks of the core group, a significant number (42 per cent) had no common reference point with respect to their function. This is important, as no common understanding of purpose can lead to different professionals working with different agendas and expectations of themselves and each other. Those committees that had developed policies and procedures noted immediate benefits in terms of promoting inter-agency cooperation and working in partnership with families and other professionals. Those authorities which had produced some kind of guidance had focused on contextualising the core group within the system at the expense of providing the core group with operational tools, such as agendas or recording formats.

This lack of guidance has resulted in diversity of practice with local responses developing in an ad hoc, uncoordinated fashion that has consistently defied any attempts at consolidation. Respondents in the 1996 research noted: 'There is no detailed guidance on how [post-registration practice] might operate. It is left to the discretion of managers/social workers'; 'Problems [regarding post-registration practice] appear to arise from social services keyworkers feeling overburdened by the responsibilities and other agencies reluctant to share the tasks'; 'There are many differences between area teams.' The Social Services Inspectorate (SSI) reported that this area of practice was marked by 'lack of inter-agency planning, lack of inter-agency intervention and often only monitoring visits by social workers' (SSI, 1994: 32).

The reasons for the lack of commitment and diversity of practice would seem to be twofold. Firstly, Hallett (1995) found that policies and procedures are helpful as a way of structuring and organising work, in clarifying professional roles and in resolving inter-agency difficulties. Without a framework, it is difficult to establish a common understanding of what is expected of those who should be working together to meet the needs of children and their carers. Secondly, child protection practice has tended to be procedure-driven, with practitioners utilising procedures as their guide to action. If procedures do not exist, there can be a reluctance to act, fuelled by the belief that if there are no procedures, the work is of low priority (Horwath and Calder, 1998).

Not only do practitioners have little guidance regarding *what* they should be doing during the post-registration phase, but there is also a lack of literature and guidance regarding *how* they should be working with children and their carers. There is a wealth of literature regarding therapeutic interventions for children who have been abused, but these texts are aimed at those professionals with a specialist brief, such as psychologists and therapists. There is little available for professionals who have a broader brief and are expected to assess and meet the needs of children on the child protection register. The only practical advice offered by central government is in the form of a few tools to utilise when undertaking a comprehensive assessment, which are set out in the 'Orange Book' (DoH, 1988).

## Working in a climate of change

Guidance is particularly important in times of change and uncertainty. Child protection practitioners are currently placed in a situation where they are having to manage in a world of shifting child welfare priorities with little guidance regarding the priority that should be given to post-registration practice. At a national level, there has been a shift in emphasis in terms of child welfare priorities. The 1980s and early 1990s were dominated by a need to get things right at the 'hard end' of the child welfare spectrum, which resulted in an emphasis on developing child protection practice. In 1994, the publication of the Audit Commission Report, *Seen but not Heard* (Audit Commission, 1994) and, in 1995, the publication of the *Messages from Research* (DoH, 1995) resulted in a shift in thinking, which questioned whether there needed to be a refocusing away from emphasis solely on child protection, towards a more balanced approach to child welfare and a greater recognition of children in need. This has resulted, at local level, in confusion, loss of focus and a blurring of boundaries, as child protection merges into a wider picture of services for children (Armstrong, 1996). This has resulted in many agencies questioning the priority their workers should give to child protection work.

The Department of Health has recognised the confusion caused by advocating an approach which places child protection in the context of all services for children. As a result of this confusion it has decided to draw up new guidance to 'break down barriers and to promote a wider, more holistic view of the needs of children and their families' (Paul Boateng, in a letter accompanying the consultation document *Working Together to Safeguard Children* (DoH, 1998). At the time of writing, a consultation document *Working Together to Safeguard Children: New Government Proposals for Inter-agency Co-operation* (DoH, 1998) has been circulated with the intention of seeking the views and opinions of those engaged in child protection research and practice. The results of this consultation will lead to new guidance to replace the current 'Working Together' (DoH, 1991) Although the consultation paper stresses that the emphasis will shift to looking more widely at the needs of the more vulnerable families in society the government is also committed to 'reinforcing the best elements of the existing child protection system and have no intention of de-stabilising those elements we know work well' (DoH, 1998: 1V). It is clear from the consultation document that the systems and structures referred to within the present volume will continue to provide the framework for post-registration practice.

In addition to the impact of the national changes at local level, there have been major changes affecting local agencies engaged in child protection practice. Most organisations involved in child protection have felt the impact of restricted budgets and changes in organisational structures. Health services have grappled with the impact of an internal market and the subsequent change in the roles and responsibilities of health professionals. Education services have witnessed a devolution of control, with local management of schools conducted by their governing bodies. This greater independence makes an integrated approach towards child protection difficult to achieve. Social service departments have also been subject to change. Most departments have moved to a split between the provision for children and adult services. As a result of this, specialist knowledge has become compartmentalised: if you work in children's services your focus is the child and if you work within adult services the focus is the adult's needs.

The police have become increasingly engaged in child protection activity over the last 20 years. In 1976, a government circular (DHSS, 1976) recommended a 'low key' approach to police involvement in child protection. By the late 1980s, the police were identified as one of three major investigating agencies, along with social services and the NSPCC (DoH, 1991). The introduction of 'The Memorandum of Good Practice' (Home Office and DoH, 1992) has given them a pivotal role and has also resulted in their increased involvement with the child and family once the child has been placed on the child protection register. However, the refocusing debate raises questions about their future role within the child welfare arena.

The editors of the present volume, a child protection coordinator within a Community and Social Services Directorate and a social work educator and training consultant, became aware in the course of their work that practitioners and their managers are being placed in a difficult situation regarding work with children who are on the child protection register. Not only is there a lack of policy and procedures but there is lack of clarity regarding the contributions that can be made by different professionals in terms of their changing roles and responsibilities. It was as a result of identifying the lack of framework, guidance and available tools to undertake the task that they decided to edit this book embracing contributions from key agency personnel, academics and trainers.

## The aims and structure of the book

The central concern of this book is to identify how best to enable practitioners and their managers to work with children and their families in this post-registration phase of the child protection process. We hope to explore ways in which to maximise practitioners' interventions in terms of effecting positive change and enhancing the child's welfare. The book covers four major themes which we feel form the key components for effective post-registration practice: (1) a framework for practice, (2) effective methods of professional intervention, (3) the interface between professionals and the family, and (4) understanding and valuing the contributions of different disciplines.

## A framework for practice

As identified above, what is lacking in post-registration practice is any clear framework to inform policy and practice. The first two chapters of the book offer a framework that can be utilised and adapted by Area Child Protection Committees. Chapter 1 begins by exploring the context for current post-registration practice and shows why there are gaps and ambiguities in national guidance. The current system for post-registration practice is described and consideration is given to the tensions and dilemmas faced by managers and practitioners working within this system. The chapter concludes with a framework for developing post-registration practice at a local level.

Chapter 2 develops the framework, considering the key components of post-registration practice such as the core group, the child protection plan and the child protection review. Based on the findings of a national study of post-registration practice, attention is given to the details which should be considered when designing policy, procedure and practice guidance at a local level.

These first two chapters provide an overview of post-registration practice. In addition, the key components for effective policy and practice are designed to meet the needs of managers who wish to develop a local inter-agency structure for post-registration practice.

## Effective methods of professional intervention

The next three chapters take as their themes some of the key tasks involved in post-registration practice and consider ways in which they can be achieved. Chapter 3 concentrates on assessment and planning. The authors, Christine Samra-Tibbetts and Barry Raynes, utilise their practice and training experience to identify the different approaches that can be taken to a post-registration comprehensive assessment. The limitations of the government guidance in *Protecting Children. A Guide For Social Workers Undertaking a Comprehensive Assessment* (DoH, 1988) are outlined and a structure, tools and techniques to enhance the comprehensive assessment are identified. The authors provide a model to collate the information from the assessment to inform the planning, intervention and subsequent evaluation of the assessment itself. In Chapter 4, Barbara Firth explores the complex tasks undertaken by the social services keyworker. On the basis of her research, she identifies the tensions and dilemmas encountered by the keyworker and considers strategies for managing the multiple roles assigned to the keyworker. Chapter 5 considers ways in which the keyworker and the other professionals work together, with the family, as members of the core group. Elaine Baxter and Bobbie Print utilise their knowledge of group work and core groups to identify some of the problems associated with running multi-agency groups. They provide practical suggestions for managing difficulties that can arise when a diverse range of individuals with different values and expectations are expected to work together.

## The interface between professionals and the family

The following three chapters focus on the interface between the professionals and the family. Alastair Christie and Helle Mittler use their knowledge of working in partnership with children and families to consider ways in which partnership can be achieved during the post-registration phase. They identify three different models of partnership and apply them to a case study, highlighting the need for practitioners to assess, on a case-by-case basis, what level of partnership can be achieved that empowers the family yet safeguards the child's welfare. In Chapter 7, Martin Calder considers ways in which workers and agencies can begin to formulate an anti-oppressive response to minority groups in the post-registration arena. He considers the way in which the current system is designed to focus on carers' weaknesses and describes ways in which workers can identify and work with family strengths, while continuing to protect the child. Chapter 8 centres upon a key task for post-registration work: that is, to create the conditions in which change can occur that will meet the needs of the child. Tony Morrison, drawing on counselling literature, explains how a model of change and motivational interviewing techniques can be applied to post-registration practice. Using the model and research from child protection, he highlights the conditions required for creating change and ways in which workers can make assessments regarding the carers' commitment and ability to change. He also considers ways in which workers can facilitate and sustain carers' motivation for change.

## Understanding and valuing the contributions of different disciplines

Studies by Birchall and Hallett (1995) and Hallett (1995) found that practitioners are often confused regarding their own and other workers' child protection roles and responsibilities. In this section we try to provide some clarity. We consider the contributions of a range of professionals who have a role in participating and supporting post-registration practice. Chapter 9 is written by Sharon Cooke (a manager in a social service department) who describes the key components for effective supervision of post-registration practice. Consideration is also given to the role of the social services manager in terms of supporting the keyworker and managing conflict that cannot be resolved by the multidisciplinary group working with the family. In Chapter 10, Jane Appleton (a principal lecturer in community nursing) and Jill Clemerson (a nurse adviser for child protection) consider the current roles and responsibilities of health personnel who are likely to be working with children on the child protection register. They also identify some of the misconceptions which prevail amongst other disciplines regarding the responsibilities of health service staff in this area of work. In Chapter 11 Anne Peake (an educational psychologist) and Julie Turner (a teacher counsellor) outline the roles and responsibilities of teachers within the post-registration arena. They describe some of the dilemmas encountered by teachers in working with children who are on the child protection register and offer an insight into the difficulties teachers face when working in an inter-agency arena.

Finally, the role of training in supporting post-registration practice is considered. In Chapter 12, Michael Murphy (an inter-agency training coordinator) identifies ways in which inter-agency training can promote effective post-registration practice by developing the knowledge and skills of workers. He also describes how some of the inter-agency conflicts played out through post-registration practice are often mirrored in training. He considers ways in which trainers can manage these situations.

We feel that child protection practice should be informed by theory and research. Each author has consequently attempted to include the latest research findings and to utilise up-to-date analyses of practice issues. We hope this will enable the reader to reflect and apply the learning from this book to their own practice. Our commitment to writing this book grew out of a recognition of the tensions and dilemmas faced by practitioners and managers, on a daily basis, as they attempt to meet the needs of the most vulnerable groups of children within our communities. We hope that this publication will meet the needs of those who are actively engaged in post-registration practice and will assist educators and trainers to develop practice within this area.

# References

Armstrong, H. (1996) 'Annual Reports of Area Child Protection Committees', No. 2, Department of Health: ACPC series.

Audit Commission (1994) *Seen but not Heard – Co-ordinating Community Health and Social Services for Children in Need*, London: HMSO.

Birchall, E. and Hallett, C. (1995) *Working Together in Child Protection*, London: HMSO.

Calder, M.C. and Horwath, J. (1996) 'National Care Group Sample: Analysis of Questionnaire Responses', unpublished MS, Salford ACPC/University of Sheffield.

Department of Health (1988) *Protecting Children: A Guide for Social Workers Undertaking a Comprehensive Assessment*, London: HMSO.

Department of Health (1991) *Working Together under the Children Act 1989: A guide to arrangements for inter-agency co-operation for the protection of children from abuse*, London: HMSO.

Department of Health (1995) *Child Protection: Messages from Research Studies in Child Protection*, London: HMSO.

Department of Health (1998) *Working Together to Safeguard Children: New Government Proposals for Inter-agency Co-operation. Consultation Paper*, London: HMSO.

Department of Health and Social Security (1976) 'Non-accidental Injury to Children: The Police and Case Conferences', *ASSL*, **76**, (26).

Farmer, E. and Owen, M. (1995) *Child Protection Practice: Private Risks and Public Remedies. Decision-making, Intervention and Outcome in Child Protection Work*, London: HMSO.

Hallett, C. (1995) *Inter-Agency Co-ordination in Child Protection*, London: HMSO.

Home Office and Department of Health (1992) 'Memorandum of Good Practice'; on video, recorded interviews with child witnesses for criminal proceedings.

Horwath, J. and Calder, M.C. (1998) 'Working Together To Protect Children on The Child Protection Register: Myth or Reality?', *British Journal of Social Work*, **28**, 6: 879–95.

SSI (1994) *Evaluating Child Protection Services*, London: HMSO.

# 1 The background and current context of post-registration practice

*Jan Horwath and Martin C. Calder*

In this chapter consideration is given to the following:

- the historical development of child protection practice over the last 25 years;
- the current framework for post-registration practice;
- research findings: the implications for practice development;
- issues and tensions faced by managers and practitioners working within the current child protection system; and
- a conceptual framework for developing post-registration practice at a local level.

## Introduction

Anyone currently working in the area of child protection needs no reminding of the emotional stresses and strains of this kind of work. The very nature of the task, which involves intervening in situations where a child may have been abused, is complex and can be distressing. However, the situation is exacerbated by a lack of guidance, which can result in a lack of clarity regarding the task and the roles and responsibilities of the different professionals. In addition, a climate of continual change is a fact of life for all those working in social care settings. Changes are occurring at a local level in terms of reorganisation regarding arrangements for the commissioning and delivery of services. A change in philosophy is also taking place at both a national and local level as those working in the area of child protection are being asked to refocus – balancing the needs of children who have been abused with children in need. It is against this backcloth that professionals are working with children and families where the children have been suffering, or there is concern that they are likely to suffer, significant harm and the children's names have consequently been placed on the child protection register.

In this chapter we consider the impact of the national and local frameworks for post-registration practice on the way in which professionals work together to protect children on the register. We identify ways in which practice could be improved and offer a conceptual framework enabling ACPCs to develop a response that meets local needs and addresses local problems.

## The evolution of working together in child protection

To begin to understand current post-registration practice frameworks it is necessary to consider ways in which child protection practice has evolved. Although government circulars dating back to 1945 encouraged more inter-agency collaboration in cases of child abuse, the first actual guidance in England and Wales, on inter-agency post-registration practice, emerged in 1974 (DHSS, 1974), when the current child protection system was established in embryonic form. At this juncture, the emphasis remained on the recognition, diagnosis and initial management of cases. However, the guidance stated that professionals at the initial conference should formulate a future plan for each child placed on the child protection register as being at risk of abuse. A subsequent DHSS circular (DHSS, 1980) extended the earlier guidance, broadening the criteria for registration and thus entry into the child protection system. It emphasised the need for professionals to monitor and review the plan of intervention for the family. The circular offered no guidance as to how the monitoring of the effectiveness of the plan should be achieved. However, it was clearly seen as a task for professionals, as parents were not allowed to attend either the initial or the review conference.

By the late 1970s, several child deaths linked to neglect and physical injury were brought to public and professional attention. A government review into these deaths (DHSS, 1982) highlighted a worrying combination of failings in the inter-agency system: information scattered between a number of agencies, meaning that information remained uncollated, a lack of clarity of respective roles and responsibilities and a lack of focus in terms of case planning. One of the recommendations of the review was the notion of a 'small group' which should be responsible for the formulation and implementation of a plan of action to protect a child from further abuse. It was intended that the plan should be based on an assessment of the needs of the child. The notion of a 'core group' to promote interdisciplinary practice was beginning to emerge.

In response to the identified failings of the existing system, the government issued a draft guide on arrangements for inter-agency cooperation (DHSS, 1986). Whilst this maintained a principal focus on the reporting and initial management of child abuse cases, it did give some consideration to the post-registration phase, clarifying the purpose of the child protection register: 'providing a record of all children who are currently the subject of an inter-agency protection plan and to ensure that the plans are formally reviewed at least every six months' (ibid.: 20). The guide distinguished between short-term plans (devised for the immediate protection of the child based on information from the investigation and tabled at a conference) and longer-term protection plans (based on an assessment of need that should be undertaken while the short-term plan was being implemented). The processing of the longer-term plans was the responsibility of the core group of professionals who were expected to work together to implement and review the plan (ibid.: 16). The core group remit was extended beyond a professional forum to, 'meet as a group with the parents from time to time in the course of their work with the family' (ibid.: 19).

The guidance regarding the child protection review was also made more specific. A Social Services Inspectorate report had expressed concerns about the vague and imprecise goals set by reviews (SSI, 1986). This was addressed in the guidance, which stated that a task for the review was to evaluate critically plans tabled by the core group, rather than uncritically endorsing them. Members of the review were also expected to make recommendations about alternative options regarding the focus of work with the child and family.

Under the 1980 guidance, the criteria for registration were broadened to include sexual abuse, resulting in an increase in the number of children placed on the child protection register and a subsequent increase in post-registration work. However, events in Cleveland concerning the management of cases of child sexual abuse resulted in the draft guidance (DHSS, 1986) remaining in its draft form for two years, waiting for the recommendations of the Cleveland Inquiry (Butler-Sloss, 1988). This inquiry was established to explore the management of allegations of sexual abuse, the invasion of family privacy, the lack of consultation with parents and different (polarised) professional perspectives (Calder, 1995). It also had to consider why there was so much emphasis on immediate protective strategies at the expense of current and planned interventions. *Working Together* (DHSS, 1988a), influenced by the recommendations of the Cleveland Inquiry, was finally issued and represented a significant shift in thinking about family involvement at all stages of the child protection process, with parents being included in part of the conference and in core groups. Even where parents were excluded from, or chose not to attend, meetings there was an expectation that they would receive written confirmation of the inter-agency action plan, setting out the reasons for the plan, the services to be provided for the family and the professional and family expectations of each other. Acting on the increase in isolated practice as reflected in child abuse enquiries, this guidance strongly reinforced the principle that child protection was the responsibility of all the agencies, and simultaneous guidance was issued to schools (DoE, 1988), doctors (DHSS, 1988b), and senior nurses, health visitors and midwives (DHSS, 1988c). This signified a move from emphasis on systems to emphasis on professional roles and responsibilities.

The 1988 guidance acknowledged that no child's name should be added to the child protection register simply because the criteria were met. There was a second threshold to cross: that there was a demonstrable need for an inter-agency child protection plan. This was an important development as it acknowledged the need to gatekeep, or actively restrict, the increasing numbers of registered cases. The initial conference, having deemed registration appropriate, now delegated the responsibility for conducting the assessment and formulating the child protection plan to the core group. Although the thrust of the guidance was to advocate collective responsibility, this was offset by a clear acknowledgement that social services (through the keyworker) were responsible for coordinating the contributions of all the agencies to the identified work. The guidance changed the positioning of short- and long-term plans within the system in order to accommodate the findings of a 'comprehensive social, medical and developmental assessment' in the equation. The core group was expected to translate the recommendations of the initial conference into a short-term written child protection plan whose remit extended to the commissioning of assessments. Upon completion of these pieces of work, the core group resubmitted its findings to the child protection review which was responsible for formulating the 'longer-term' plan and then for reviewing it at significant points in its implementation. The review was being established as the forum where plans were critically evaluated to measure whether the objectives of the plan were being achieved and to reformulate them if necessary.

In response to the increase in multidisciplinary assessments that professionals were expected to undertake, the government issued a guide for social workers undertaking a comprehensive assessment for children on the child protection register (DoH, 1988). The guide, known as the 'Orange Book', was influenced by a range of different models of assessment, including the observation and assessment methods used by residential social workers (Katz, 1997). The guide sets out 167 questions organised around several key areas, not to establish whether a child has been abused but to 'understand the child's and family's situation more fully in order to provide a sound basis for decisions about future actions' (DoH, 1988: 21).

Although the guidance provided a new structural framework for post-registration child protection practice, it failed to provide any guidance on the way the tasks within this phase should be completed. However, the guiding principles for inter-agency collaboration in post-registration practice, established in 1986, have remained in force to the present day.

## Working together under the Children Act 1989: the current framework for post-registration practice

The Children Act 1989 was introduced onto the statute books on 14 October 1991, accompanied by guidance designed to act as a means of providing more detail about specific areas of child care practice. The guidance most relevant to post-registration child protection practice was *Working Together under the Children Act* (DoH, 1991). This guidance provides the current framework for child protection practice in England and Wales. It describes the ways in which agencies should work together throughout the child protection process. Unfortunately, as with earlier guidance, much of the emphasis is on the role of professionals identifying and investigating potential cases of child abuse and neglect under section 47 of The Children Act 1989. The guidance does, however, outline the structure, process and content of post-registration practice, as shown in Figure 1.1. The child protection process is described below, with emphasis on the post-registration phase.

### The child protection process

#### *Pre-conference phase*

This phase describes the referral of a potential case of child abuse to one of the investigating child protection agencies, namely the police, social services or the NSPCC. The investigating agencies have a duty to investigate under section 47 of The Children Act 1989. The type of investigation will vary according to the nature of the allegations. It may be completed by one agency or, in cases of serious allegations, may be undertaken as a joint investigation between the police and social workers.

The investigation includes gathering and collating information regarding the child and their carers. This information should come initially from professionals, and then from the child and the family. The aim is to ascertain whether the child has suffered, or is likely to suffer, from significant harm. At any stage of the investigation process, for example through discussion with other professionals, it may be decided by the investigating agency that there is no cause for concern and no further action is required. In these situations,

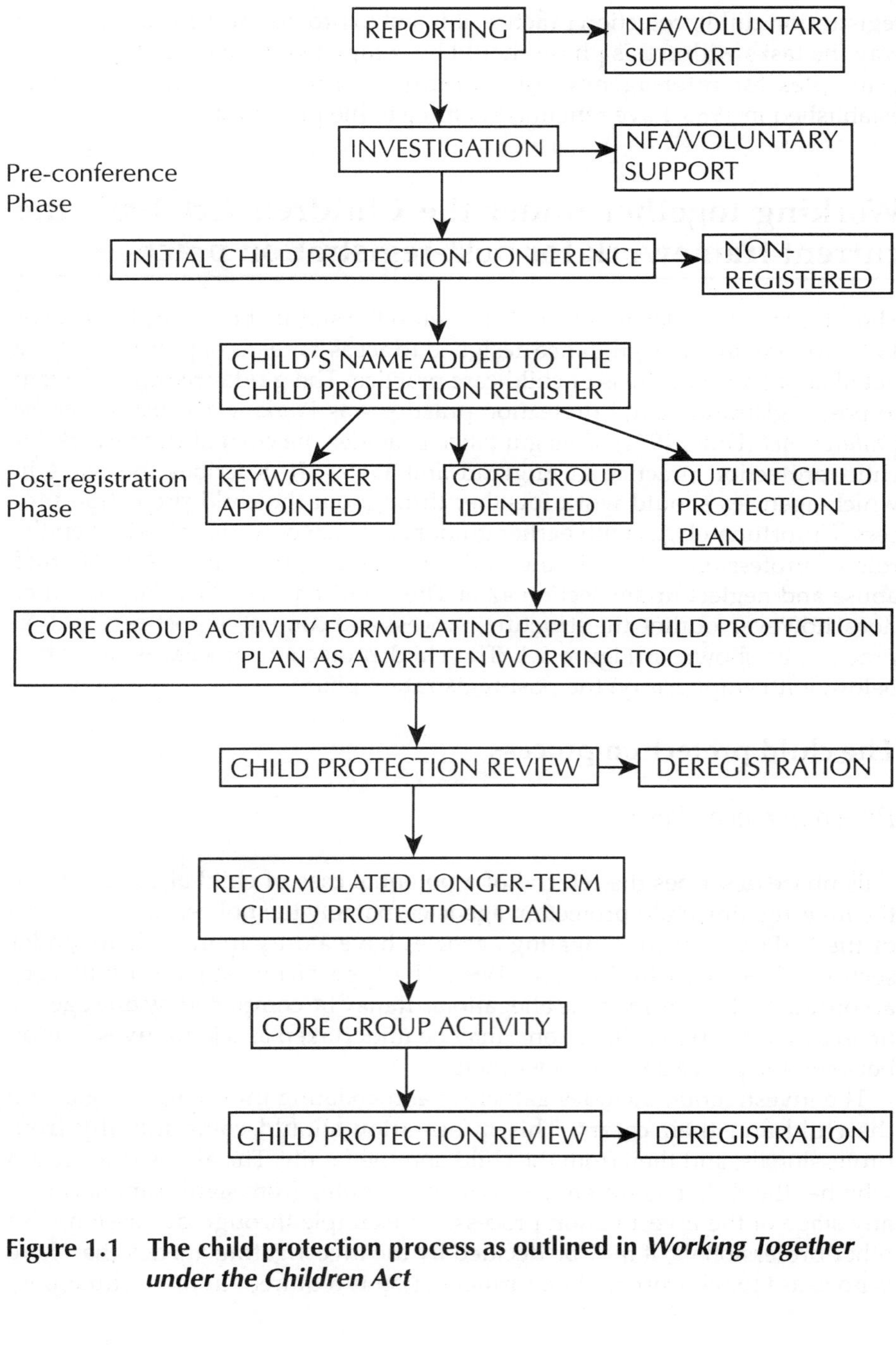


**Figure 1.1 The child protection process as outlined in *Working Together under the Children Act***

the family may not be aware of the referral. Alternatively, the investigation may indicate that the child has needs that are not necessarily child protection issues, but these needs can be met by offering family support services. If, however, as a result of the investigation, the investigating agencies have concerns that the child may be in immediate danger, court action can be taken to protect the child by removal from the home for a limited period of time. If future protection is the concern and the child is not in immediate danger, the case will be considered at an initial child protection conference.

## *The initial child protection conference phase*

A child protection conference should take place within eight to 15 days of the investigation. The conference is the forum where professionals and the family meet 'to share information and concerns, analyse and weigh up levels of risk to the children and make recommendations for action' (DoH, 1991: 31). The initial conference must come to a decision, based on the information available, as to whether to add the child's name to the child protection register. There are specific criteria laid down in *Working Together* which have to be met. These are listed below.

## *Criteria for registration*

There are two strands to the decision on registration of any child. First, there must be demonstrable evidence that the child fits into one of the following categories:

1 Physical injury: actual or likely physical injury to a child, or failure to prevent physical injury (or suffering) to a child, including deliberate poisoning, suffocation and Munchausen's Syndrome by Proxy.
2 Neglect: the persistent or severe neglect of a child, or the failure to protect a child from exposure to any kind of danger, including cold or starvation, or extreme failure to carry out important aspects of care, resulting in the significant impairment of the child's health or development, including non-organic failure to thrive.
3 Emotional abuse: actual or likely severe adverse affects on the emotional and behavioural development of a child caused by persistent or severe emotional ill-treatment. This category should be used where it is the main or sole form of abuse.
4 Sexual abuse: actual or likely sexual exploitation of a child or adolescent. The child may be dependent and/or developmentally immature.

Second, the conference must then be satisfied that there is a continuing risk to the child which justifies the construction of an inter-agency child protection plan. The evidence will normally be derived from one of the following: (1) there have been one or more identifiable incidents which have adversely affected the child and professional judgement indicates that further incidents are likely; (2) significant harm is considered likely on the basis of professional judgement and the findings of the investigation and assessment.

## *Action at the point of registration*

Once a decision has been made to add a child's name to the child protection register, the conference must attend to a series of recommendations which include the following:

1 the appointment of a keyworker, who is usually a social worker with the local authority but could be someone from the NSPCC, and who becomes responsible for coordinating the work of the professionals, engaging the parents, undertaking the social work tasks, instituting any legal proceedings and managing the core group;
2 the identification of a core group of professionals and the family charged with the tasks of carrying out any commissioned work;
3 a proposed 'plan of action', which should include a comprehensive assessment comprising social, environmental, medical and developmental circumstances; and
4 agreeing when the child protection review will meet (at intervals not exceeding six months, but often more frequently, such as every four months).

## *The post-registration phase*

*The child protection plan* The *Working Together* guidance indicates very clearly that the prototype plan devised at the initial child protection conference is not the operational working tool. The task of converting the plan into a working tool is the task of the core group which assumes the lead responsibility for planning. Once the full plan has been constructed by the core group, it is the responsibility of the individual agencies to implement the parts of the plan relating to them and to communicate with the keyworker and others as necessary. Whilst it is up to each agency representative to decide whether to accept the recommendations for action and their part in the plan, there is a clear expectation that there should be a locally agreed procedure for confirming that these recommendations will be acted upon. It is clearly better to construct plans based on offers from agencies that are realistic than to pursue a corporate approach that will never materialise in practice (Calder and Barratt, 1997).

*The written agreement* The written agreement is the contract that is negotiated between the child, the family and the professionals regarding the implementation of the plan. The purpose of the agreement is to ensure that the family are clear about the causes of concern which resulted in the child's name being placed on the child protection register and what is expected of them in terms of the child protection plan (Calder, 1990). Consideration should be given to ways in which professionals will monitor the outcomes of the plan. The agreement should also clarify the roles and responsibilities of the various agency representatives in terms of implementing the plan.

*The core group* It is ironic that no substantial operational guidance was issued on core groups after they were positioned as the control-room of inter-agency operations (Calder, 1995b) and as the principal forum for child protection planning. It is clear that, whilst key professionals and the family come together to process the plan, the ultimate responsibility for action remains with the keyworker, who retains the sole responsibility for pulling together and coordinating the contributions of different agencies, while also making recommendations to the child protection review. The principal reference on the core group in the *Working Together* guidance comes on the final page, when it requires the composition of the core group to be held on the child protection register (DoH, 1991: 107).

*The child protection review* The guidance sees the first review as the appropriate venue for the core group to table the proposed longer-term child protection plan following the completion of the commissioned assessment(s). The role of the members of the review is to rigorously evaluate the findings of the assessment and to reformulate the plan in light of the assessment. The core group is then delegated the continuing responsibility for implementing the plan, subject to regular, periodic reviews.

*Deregistration* The guidance sets out clear criteria for deregistration which should be seriously considered at each review:

1 A child has remained at home but abuse or the risk of abuse has been reduced by work with the family and through the protection plan.
2 A child has been placed away from home and there is no longer access to the abusing adult; or
3 Access to the abusing adult is no longer considered to present a risk to the child.

4 The abusing adult is no longer a member of the same household as the child and there is no contact, or such contact as occurs is no longer considered to be a risk to the child.
5 The completion of the comprehensive assessment and a detailed analysis of risk has shown that registration is no longer required and the child protection plan is not necessary.
6 The child and family have moved permanently to another area and that area has accepted responsibility for the future management of the case.
7 The child is no longer a child in the eyes of the law: the child has reached 18 years of age, has married or has died.

Normally, the decision to remove a child's name from the register will follow the achievement of the objectives set out in the inter-agency protection plan. However, there may be circumstances under which such a decision is appropriate even though some or all of the objectives have not been fully achieved: for example, there is an inability to secure the effective participation of family members and the risk of significant harm does not justify legal intervention at this point. The local authority's duty to safeguard and promote the welfare of children in need exists quite independently of its child protection responsibilities and the maintenance of a child's name on the register as a means of securing services cannot be considered acceptable once the risk of significant harm is no longer present.

## Subsequent informal guidance

Since the introduction of *Working Together* in 1991, there have been a number of government publications or commentaries which have arguably given some implicit direction to post-registration practice. The key documents are the SSI standards for evaluating quality performance in child protection (SSI, 1993) and *The Challenge of Partnership in Child Protection* (DoH, 1995b).

### Evaluating performance in child protection

The SSI publication demonstrated a move towards providing local authorities with a framework for self-regulation of their child protection services. It sets out in some detail the expected standards for practice following registration. Emphasis in the standards is on the core group acting as a forum where the keyworker can seek specialist advice about the construction of the protection plan, rather than highlighting the responsibility of the core group as a whole to construct the plan.

Additional guidance was issued on the child protection plan. The standards highlight the importance of clarifying the primary purpose of the plan. The emphasis is on the plan protecting the child as well as promoting their physical, emotional and intellectual health and development, and bringing about the necessary changes in the family system. Emphasis is also placed on outcomes for abused children. This document states that the plans should specify clear and measurable objectives for change which can be used to evaluate progress. These should include questions designed to explore whether the welfare of the child has been enhanced, whether the child is safer now than before the intervention took place and whether the family functioning has improved. In essence, a change in focus within planning is advocated to ensure that interventions are specific and planned.

### The challenge of partnership in child protection

The DoH publication sets out the reasons for working in partnership with families during the child protection process and attempts to provide practical advice on ways in which partnership can be used to ensure the appropriate protection for children. It is one of the first documents published by the Department of Health that recognises the importance of post-registration activity, acknowledging that professional interest in the welfare of the child frequently begins to 'wane' during the post-registration phase: 'this diminution of interest is often inexplicable to families because this is the very moment at which they expect to receive additional help and support' (DoH, 1995b: 83).

The practice guide offers workers some useful advice regarding the way in which they should work in partnership with families during the preparation of the comprehensive assessment. As with the SSI document, attention is paid to the child protection plan, and emphasis is laid on the importance of clearly defined, realistic goals to be achieved within specific time scales. The content of the plan and ways in which this should be negotiated with family members are also considered. The guide also stresses the role of the review as being more than a rubber stamp for the core group but one which 'requires as much commitment, careful management and preparation as the initial conference' (ibid.: 84).

The *Challenge to Partnership* developed ideas based on best practice in England and Wales. The publication also emphasised the importance of referring to research as a way of informing and developing practice.

## From guidance to practice: messages from research

Limited national guidance regarding post-registration practice can result in situations where at best each ACPC will make its own interpretation of what is good practice and, at worst, each professional will make their individual interpretation. This diversity of practice has been noted in a number of studies which were undertaken in the early and mid-1990s. The findings from these studies are useful in terms of highlighting areas which need to be considered when promoting and developing post-registration practice. We will focus on three studies in particular.

First are the Department of Health Studies. In the same year that *The Challenge to Partnership* was produced, the Department of Health also published *Messages from Research* (DoH, 1995a), a series of 20 studies which explored the impact of the Children Act 1989 and *Working Together* on child protection processes. While most of the studies were completed in the late 1980s and early 1990s, when the concepts of the core group and child protection plans were embryonic in nature, there are a number of key findings which can inform the development of post-registration practice at practitioner, managerial and organisational levels. The studies we will primarily refer to were completed by Farmer and Owen (1995), Gibbons *et al.* (1995), Hallett (1995) and Thoburn *et al.* (1995).

Second, there are the findings from SSI inspections. In 1997, the SSI produced an overview report of child protection inspections conducted in England and Wales. This report considered trends in practice that were noted through inspections carried out by the SSI between 1992 and 1996. Their findings are useful inasmuch as they provide an opportunity to identify ways in which practice has changed since the Department of Health studies were completed.

Third is *A national study of core group practice*. In 1996, the present authors completed a study to identify what response , if any, had been made by ACPCs to the lack of central guidance on post-registration practice (Calder and Horwath, 1996). We also wanted to identify strategies developed at a local level that promoted good practice. A postal questionnaire was sent to the child protection coordinators in all the local authorities in England and Wales. The questions asked focused on organisational policy, practice issues and family participation. There was a 53 per cent response rate, covering a broad cross-section of local authorities.

The key findings from these studies will be considered under a number of headings: the initial child protection conference, child protection core groups, child protection plans, assessments, professional roles and responsibilities, child protection reviews, outcomes, and child and family participation.

## The initial child protection conference

The Department of Health studies in general noted that investigative activity and the initial conference process had a major impact on any subsequent work.

For example, Farmer and Owen (1995) found that post-registration resistance was often influenced by families' feelings regarding the way in which the investigation was managed. They found that many assessments and decisions made by social workers before initial conferences were simply endorsed at the initial conference without critical appraisal. This may be allied to the reality that a quarter of all professionals routinely failed to attend initial conferences, with general practitioners (GPs) being the poorest attendees (Hallett, 1995). Farmer and Owen (1995) found that assessing risk and agonising about registration elbowed aside plans for action, so that deciding what to do by way of the child protection plan was pushed to the end of the meeting, lasting only nine minutes.

The research highlighted several shortcomings relating to the plan outlined by the initial conference.

1 In one-third of the plans studied, important aspects of the child's future protection were overlooked and in half of these cases the child was subsequently re-abused (Farmer and Owen, 1995).
2 While the conference recommendations listed components of the plan, there was rarely any understanding of how they related to the identified risks. In particular, there was rarely any statement in the initial conference minutes which articulated the unresolved child protection issues that made an inter-agency plan necessary (Gibbons *et al.*, 1995).
3 There was a high degree of debate over the plans, particularly where social workers entered the initial conference with a prototype, predetermined plan, which other agencies felt unable to challenge (Hallett, 1995).
4 Some 10 per cent of professionals argued that the conference did not assist in planning their own interventions with the family (Birchall and Hallett, 1995).
5 Plans did not set out clearly the roles and responsibilities of those professionals with routine contact with children (Hallett, 1995).
6 Where the objective of intervention and the minimum levels of required change were less clearly articulated in the plans, the task of monitoring their implementation and the assessment of the consequences and non-compliance for the continued protection of the child became problematic (Hallett, 1995).
7 Where plans were recommended in the absence of parents they were idealistic, not realistic. Thoburn *et al.* (1995) found that only 43 per cent of parents felt that they had contributed to the structuring of child protection plans.
8 In 40 per cent of plans, no other agency besides social services was mentioned, thus leaving some doubt about an inter-agency approach (Birchall and Hallett, 1995).

9 Plans may not be produced at the end of a lengthy conference (Hallett, 1995).

Calder (1996) found that there was a direct correlation between the number of recommendations made from a conference and the subsequent detail within the child protection plans formulated by the group. Hallett (1995) found that core groups were only established at the initial conference in 12 per cent of cases, leaving no forum to engage professionals or the family in the planning process. Despite these limitations, she did find that initial conferences were helpful in planning interventions, helping case assessments and managing professionals.

The SSI noted that, over the four years since the DoH studies were completed, there was progress in the conduct of initial conferences inasmuch as parents and children were more actively engaged. However, where families were unhappy with the way in which the child protection investigation had been managed, it seemed that they were not always provided with the information required to make an appeal or complaint. Most authorities used independent chairmen, but the actual independence and quality of chairing remained issues for some authorities. It was felt that the processes for registration, review and deregistration had improved over the four years and many authorities carried out analyses of registration figures.

## Child protection core groups

The core group, when established, tended to reflect a concentration of current work in the hands of a small group: predominantly social workers, health visitors and, in Hallett's primary school-aged sample, teachers and school nurses (Hallett, 1995). This is reinforced by an overemphasis on social services as the primary agent for child protection planning. Hallett found that the core group was often unsuccessful in sustaining continued cooperation, only retaining a core membership of three or four professionals in 10 per cent of cases. Unlike Hallett, the present authors found a range of professionals were involved in core groups, for example family centre staff, foster-carers and school nurses. However, it was not possible to ascertain whether this involvement was sustained. The core group was clearly seen in our study (Calder and Horwath, 1996) as a practitioner forum, with only a few ACPCs reporting managers' attendance.

Only 58 per cent of ACPCs in our study had written statements defining the purpose and tasks for the core group. The lack of a written statement can result in confusion regarding roles and the relationship between the keyworker and other professionals. Lack of consistency was noted in terms of both recording and establishing time scales. While 83 per cent of the ACPCs in the study recorded core group decisions, only 60 per cent took minutes and only 35 per cent had a standardised recording format. Full and consistent recording would seem to be crucial in an inter-agency arena with parents and children present, where there is great potential for misunderstandings and breakdown in communication. Farmer and Owen (1995) noted the confusion and frustration of families who expected active and prompt involvement from professionals following registration and who found they were often not contacted for lengthy periods of time. This could be occurring because only 48 per cent of respondents had devised guidance regarding fixing a date for the first core group meeting. We also noted wide variation in guidance regarding the frequency of core group meetings, with 14 ACPCs recommending meeting monthly, while 11 suggested meeting as infrequently as every three months. This raises issues as to how the group can monitor, intervene and work collaboratively. It also prevents families from engaging fully in the process as well as making the alteration and reformulation of plans to reflect changing circumstances very difficult.

## Child protection plans

Hallett (1995) found problems in the implementation of child protection plans, with variation in the amount of detail included in the plans and the resources available for their implementation. She observed that the complexity and change of pace of family circumstances were not reflected in flexible plans. Social workers struggled to implement any plans which they disagreed with, although, where parents contributed to, and agreed with plans, there was a direct correlation with improved outcomes for the child concerned. Social workers had significant difficulties regarding the roles and responsibilities of other agencies in constructing the plan, and this problem was more acute for families who did not understand the roles of the different professionals. Few plans articulated the minimum levels of required change, thus making it difficult to motivate people and evaluate progress. Farmer and Owen (1995) noted that the constructed plans varied significantly in the focus of attention: some considered the child alone, whilst others attempted to meet the needs of the carers.

By 1996, systems were in place in most authorities for checking plans and ensuring they were utilised in work with families. These systems included more rigorous monitoring at child protection reviews. However, a lack of consistency within authorities was noted by the SSI, resulting in varying quality of plans. Although a wide range of resources was deployed to implement plans, it was noted that social service departments tended to provide the main input, with lack of access to other agency resources becoming an increasing issue.

Wide variations were also noted regarding the purpose and implementation of the child protection plan, with a number of respondents referring indiscriminately to the written agreement and the plan as one and the same thing. Calder and Horwath (1996) found that 13 ACPCs devised the broad outline of the plan at the initial child protection conference, expecting the core group to undertake more specific planning and assessment. What is concerning, however, is that 18 respondents indicated that planning took place outside the core group and conference arena. For example, the key-worker and their manager constructed the plan together in some areas. There was also great diversity regarding time scales for the implementation of the plan: 31 per cent of ACPCs expected the plan to be implemented immediately after the conference, which is a matter for concern if the plan has not been fully negotiated by the core group members. In 60 per cent of ACPCs, the core group reviewed the plan, with 10 per cent of these reviewing registration itself, which is clearly the remit of the review only.

## Assessments

Hallett (1995) found that in only 10 per cent of cases was a comprehensive assessment completed. Whilst assessments require the varying skills and resources of many agencies to organise the necessary information effectively and interpret it competently, the Department of Health found that agencies detached themselves from any assessment that they did not consider necessary (particularly child sexual abuse) and many professional groups lacked any experience of assessment or ongoing work.

Inconsistency was noted by the SSI in the way in which assessments were completed, recorded and utilised. This was the case even when guidance on the completion of a comprehensive assessment was provided by the authority.

Calder (1996) found that there was a need for the initial conference to explicitly set out the kind of assessment needed by the core group as, otherwise, they would conduct an 'orange book' assessment that has defined deficits in certain cases, such as child sexual abuse. The core group also often needs very clear additional material to focus on the assessment being commissioned – for example, where issues of a non-abusing parent require further assessment, the materials of Gerrilyn Smith (1994, 1995, 1996) are essential. If assessing a case where a young person has sexually abused, you should refer to the detailed materials provided by Calder (1997 and 1999a) and in assessing sex offenders Calder (1999b) is an excellent sourcebook.

## Professional roles and responsibilities

Hallett (1995) found pervasive confusion among many agencies about their own roles and responsibilities as well as those of others. She found that most professionals were 'fairly clear' about the roles of social workers, the police and paediatricians, although 50 per cent reported being unclear about the keyworker's role and one-third were unclear about the role of the police. Only one-third of professionals was clear about the health visiting role and one-quarter was clear about the roles of school nurses and education welfare officers. Among teachers and GPs, 20 per cent were unclear about their own role in child protection, compared with 70 per cent of social workers who were unclear about the roles of these two groups.

Findings from the Calder and Horwath (1996) study indicated confusion regarding the role of the keyworker, which can result in their undertaking a multiplicity of roles. Over half the respondents indicated that the keyworker is expected to chair the core group and is frequently responsible for the minute taking. Thus the keyworker not only holds responsibility for coordinating post-registration work but is also responsible for managing the process. Calder and Barratt (1997) found that the keyworkers often felt that other agencies were quick to ask for additional core groups to share their anxieties, rather than the work completed, yet they did not assume any responsibility for chairing, convening, minuting or circulating the meeting or the minutes. Many workers felt that they attended the meeting to share the work that they had done, rather than collectively considering work completed and outstanding.

## Child protection reviews

Farmer and Owen (1995) found that reviews tended to endorse rather than adapt plans, even where they were deficient. Many of the reviews were not held within the prescribed time scale, often delaying deregistration, and this was an extension of their inability to support continued inter-agency coordination (Birchall and Hallett 1995). It was concerning that some 10 per cent of deregistrations occurred because the initial registration was considered counterproductive and help could be better offered without it. Clearly, more active restriction is needed at the point of registration to exclude these cases from the system.

## Outcomes

The Department of Health research overview noted that between a third and a quarter of children were known to have been re-abused after they came to the attention of child protection agencies. Most of this re-abuse occurred within two years of registration, a statistic only tempered by the low incidence of serious re-abuse. It is significant that the recurrence of abuse was less common in those families where some agreement had been reached between the professionals and the family members about the legitimacy of the enquiry and the solutions being proposed, and where attention was paid to meeting the needs of the carer as well as the child (Farmer and Owen, 1995).

## Child and family participation

Thoburn *et al.* (1995) examined the extent of family involvement in the first six months following registration. They noted that work after the conference was not truly multidisciplinary and there was a danger of confusion for families concerning the different forms of meeting and help being provided. Family members stressed the importance of being recognised as individuals. They could appreciate that professionals had a job to do and that procedures were necessary, but they strongly objected to workers who did not appear to listen, did not show warmth or who were not prepared to help. They were particularly irritated by professionals who were 'only interested in doing their job properly', for example by ensuring they were prepared for meetings about the family, rather than working with them.

The findings of Calder and Horwath (1996) indicated a high level of commitment to parental participation, with 69 per cent of ACPCs inviting parents to core groups; 77 per cent of these indicated that some arrangements were made to help parents to attend, although the majority of these stemmed from a parental request rather than a departmental offer. Any assistance appeared to be left to the keyworker to agree to and facilitate. What is concerning is the lack of attention paid to child participation. Only 8 per cent of ACPCs always invited children and young people to core groups, whilst 5 per cent never invited them. A general rule of practice emerged that children over the age of 14 were considered appropriate to invite to core groups. Those between 10 and 14 were occasionally invited if it was felt they were mature enough to participate, but it was generally felt that children under 10 were too young. No ACPC actively promoted a young person's attendance at the core group, although a number stated that, if a young person wanted to attend, consideration would be given to ways in which this could be supported. The present writers' view was that ACPCs in general had paid little attention to child participation and, where it did occur, it was a reactive rather than proactive response.

## Summary of research findings

Overall, there appears to be a confused and variable response across England and Wales to post-registration practice. All the studies noted that (1) there was a lack of clarity over respective professional roles and responsibilities;

(2) the remit of the initial child protection conference, core group and child protection review were often unclear; (3) the purpose of the child protection plan and the construction, operationalisation, recording and reviewing of the plan varied greatly; and (4) family participation tended to be a reactive rather than proactive activity.

# A conceptual framework for developing post-registration practice

Messages from research indicate that inter-agency practice has become an accepted way of working. However, as described above, the quality and commitment vary considerably. This can be partly attributed to the lack of guidance that clearly exists in many areas. A major issue for many ACPCs is creating a framework that can be sufficiently flexible to operate effectively in a climate of continual change. As Armstrong notes, ACPCs are in a position of having constantly to 'reassess and revise procedures to reflect policy shifts consequent on research, often in response to local case reviews or reorganisation' (Armstrong, 1997: 6).

In this climate it is essential that any framework allows for local and national change. This means that the framework should never be regarded as set in stone, rather, it represents a distillation of what is believed to be best practice at a given point in time. As the knowledge base expands, so it becomes necessary to re-evaluate established policies and practices in order to ensure that they continue to be relevant and appropriate and to make best use of available resources (Hampson, 1993). This requires a cyclical approach that recognises the need for flexibility and accommodates change. (See Figure 1.2.) Each component of this model will be considered in the context of post-registration practice.

## Aim: the foundation for post-registration practice

A major failing of *Working Together* is that it acknowledges the role of the ACPC in developing policies but does not consider that this cannot occur unless the purpose of the activity is clarified at a local level. This was evident in the information received from various respondents in our (1996) study. They sent us policies and procedures which presumed a common understanding of the purpose of post-registration practice, but none of the policies had explicit aims. A shared understanding of the purpose is at the core of effective post-registration practice. If this does not exist, different professionals may interpret the reasons for procedures in very different ways. With this in mind, it is essential that senior members of each child protection agency collaborate and agree on a common purpose so that individual agency decisions can be made within this framework.

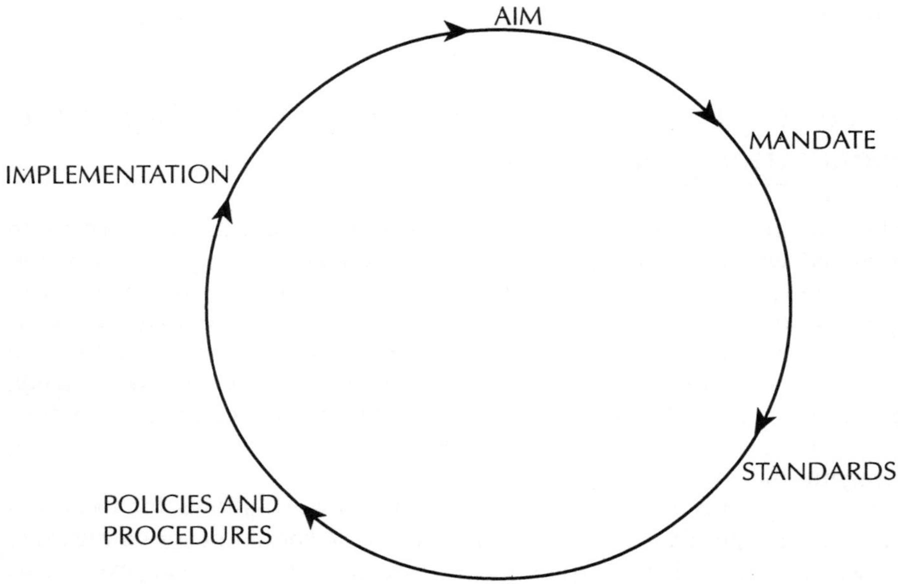


**Figure 1.2 A model for developing post-registration practice**

The fundamental question that needs to be considered when defining the purpose is whether post-registration practice is about protecting the child from further risk of abuse or, in addition to this, promoting the child's health and development, or not only meeting the needs of the child but meeting the needs of the carer(s) in order to promote the welfare of the child.

## Mandate, standards and resources

Once a common understanding of purpose has been agreed by the senior managers of the various agencies involved in child protection, a commitment towards achieving this is required. This commitment or mandate needs to be specified in terms of legislative and/or professional grounds (Morrison, 1996), ensuring that no agency can deny its roles and responsibilities.

Consideration also needs to be given to standards, as they provide the benchmark against which both agency and professional performance can be measured. Standards offer the baseline for quality assurance, audit and inspection (Hendry and Glennie, 1995) enabling the ACPC to have some measure to ensure that the resources committed to post-registration practice result in effective and high-quality services. The SSI emphasise that 'standards cannot be fixed, particularly in the child protection field, where different approaches to policy and practice are continually being developed and evaluated' (SSI, 1993: 5).

The standards for post-registration practice, according to the SSI, should be derived from legislation, regulations and guidance from central government, research and professional experience of what contributes to effective social work practice and management of services, and knowledge of what constitutes high-quality service delivery (SSI, 1993). The establishment of standards also requires an acknowledgement of resources available. Both practitioners and managers can be placed in untenable positions if they are expected to work to unrealistic standards. For example, one ACPC set as a standard that all core group minutes would be typed and circulated within a week of the core group meeting. Social services personnel were unable to meet this standard as their department had a centralised typing pool and it took a week for typing to be completed and returned to the worker.

## Policies, procedures and guidance

Clearly defined policies, procedures and practice guidance supported by senior representatives of each agency provide front-line practitioners and managers with a clear remit. We differentiate between policies, procedures and guidance in the following way. *Policies* are the principles or recommended course of action based on the mandate and standards agreed by senior managers. Policies focus on contextualising the task. *Procedures* offer a structural framework for practice based on policies. The procedures focus on processes. *Practice guidance* provides a mechanism for converting the policy and procedures into a working tool. Together they provide a framework to guide actions and clarify individual professional roles and responsibilities.

Policy and procedures need to reflect the desired standards of practice. For example, if it is anticipated that members of the core group will meet to develop the child protection plan within ten working days of the initial child protection conference, this should be included in the procedures. The inter-agency guidelines and procedures should be an adaptation of central government guidance that take into consideration local conditions rather than simply acting as an avenue through which the government implements its guidance without critical analysis (Evans and Miller, 1993). In addition, inter-agency procedures should complement internal agency policies, enabling workers to appreciate what is expected not only of themselves but also of other professionals.

Findings from the Calder and Horwath (1996) study highlighted that, where procedures existed, they were often concerned purely with administrative issues such as frequency of meetings and core group composition. Other process issues, such as strategies to work in partnership with the family, were often ignored. No procedures gave any indication of ways in which to work with carers with specific needs such as learning disabilities or mental health problems. Only two ACPCs in this study provided practice guidelines. As inter-agency post-registration practice can be a confusing area of work, guidelines could have a very useful role in making explicit exactly what is expected of the keyworker and other professionals.

In summary, if systems of policies, procedures and practice guidelines are to be effective they need to be clear, realistic, congruent, resourced, monitored and owned at a senior inter-agency level, so ensuring that accountability is unambiguous (Horwath and Morrison, 1998).

Box 1.1 lists areas that Calder and Horwath (1996) identified as requiring consideration when designing policy, procedure and practice guidance.

**Box 1.1 Designing Policy, Procedure and Guidance**

*The child protection conference*
Members' role in identifying core group members.
Contribution of conference members to designing the child protection plan.
Specifying when the core group should meet.
Setting out the circumstances when they should return to review.
Clarifying the type of assessment needed to assess risks.
Identifying ways of facilitating carer and child participation.

*The core group*
The purpose and function of the core group.
Possible attendees.
Should there be more than one core group?
Promoting family and child participation, including consideration of specific needs: for example, carers with learning disabilities.
Managing problems of inter-agency cooperation.
Reporting to the child protection review.
Management of process issues: frequency of meetings, chairing, minute taking, and so on.

*The child protection plan*
When, where and by whom is the plan constructed in outline and detail?
Procedures for major and minor alterations to the plan in relation to the child protection review's brief.
Time scales for implementation.

Procedure for managing professionals not completing tasks as written in the plan.
The written agreement and engaging the child and family.

*The keyworker*
Their role in terms of:

- co-ordination of the core group,
- working with the family,
- managing inter-agency difficulties,
- reporting back to the child protection review.

*The child protection review*
Consideration of the remit of the review.
Authority to delegate decision making to the core group.
Reporting to the child protection review.
Process for assessment of deregistration or continuing registration.

## Implementation

Not only do practitioners require a clear framework for post-registration practice but they also need opportunities to reflect on the way they are practising through supervision. Effective child protection practice requires agencies to understand the importance of supervision and make the appropriate investment. Supervision should provide workers with structured opportunities to reflect on practice, judgements, feelings and prejudices (Morrison, 1993).

If workers do not receive appropriate supervision, policy and procedures can become used as a checklist. Workers can be placed in situations where they process clients through the system with little opportunity to stand back and consider the individual needs of each client in an objective way. One of the key roles of the supervisor in terms of post-registration practice is to ensure that practitioners offer a service that meets the needs of the service user, that is the child. This means that managers should monitor individual practice to ensure that the work is child-focused and that assessments and interventions are objective and aimed at protecting the child.

In Chapter 9 the role of the social services manager is explored in detail and ways of promoting post-registration practice are considered. However, managers within other agencies also have responsibilities to ensure that supervision takes place. This can be a problem. For example, some health visitors may be supervised by supervisors with little knowledge of child protection. When considering ways in which policies and practice guidance will be implemented, senior managers need to identify ways in which their staff will be provided with opportunities to reflect on and develop their practice.

## Outcomes

Child care, particularly child protection, has received little attention in terms of measuring outcomes as part of general practice. Decisions are made to deregister children, but the criteria for this decision are based on whether the child is safe from further abuse, rather than identifying exactly what has been achieved. Outcome measures are important, enabling workers to become aware of the impact of their actions and decisions on others (Parker *et al.*, 1991).

Outcomes in child protection work do not lend themselves to a clear link between cause and effect. For example, is it possible to link improvements in quality of care to professional intervention? It is therefore necessary to look for appropriate approaches to measuring post-registration outcomes. One way to do this is to identify performance indicators. These can be linked to practice standards, so providing a framework enabling the worker to appreciate exactly what is expected and a measure to determine whether this has been achieved. Frost and Summerhill (1994) successfully linked standards and outcomes for one ACPC by getting managers and practitioners to identify the key activities involved in core groups before, during and after the core groups met. These core activities reflected policy and procedures. They identified 20 core activities which could be developed into standards. The participants were then asked to identify the results of these activities, which became the projected outcomes and performance indicators (see the appendix to this chapter). For example: *activity* – preparing parents/carers for the core group; *standard* – parents/carers should be prepared for the core group in a manner that takes into account their specific needs, such as disability or language; *outcome or performance indicator* – parents/carers understand the role of the core group. The parent/carer feels able to participate in the core group.

## Evaluation

The components outlined above form the foundation of post-registration practice. However, as identified earlier, practice is not static: systems need to be in place that enable the ACPC continually to evaluate ways in which changes are occurring. For example, research findings or measurements of local outcomes may influence the aims, which in turn may have an effect on each part of the cycle. In our view, the only way that ACPCs can manage a child protection system in a climate of continual change is through a continuing process of evaluation. As can be seen from Figure 1.3, evaluation forms the outer ring of the model as set out earlier in Figure 1.2. It cannot be included in the cycle as a single component, as each part of the model needs to be evaluated.

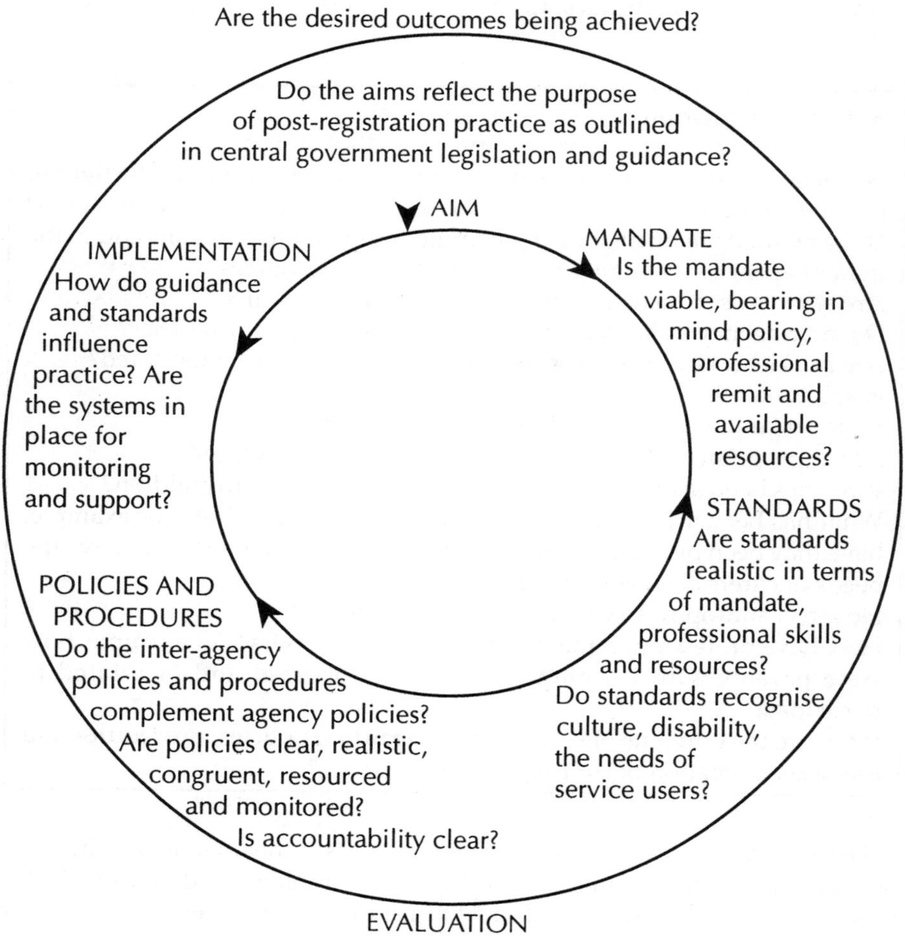


**Figure 1.3 The link between policy, practice and evaluation**

As Everitt and Hardiker (1996) have noted:

> evaluation involves processes of dialogue and practice and policy change. The structures and processes through which apparently objective facts and subjective

> experiences are generated and filtered need to be interrogated. Furthermore, the purpose of evaluation is not merely to provide better or more realistic accounts of phenomena, but to place a value on them and to change situations, practice and people's circumstances accordingly. (Everitt and Hardiker, 1996: 12)

To enable this to take place, the questions in Box 1.2 need to be part of the evaluation.

**Box 1.2 Evaluation**

Do the aims reflect the purpose of post-registration practice in the light of national guidance and local policy, for example the children's service plan?
Is the mandate relevant, bearing in mind the evaluation of aims and in the light of agencies' changing remit and available resources?
Are standards realistic in terms of mandate and resources?
Do inter-agency policies complement individual agency policies?
Are policies specific, realistic, congruent, resourced and monitored?
Is accountability clear?
How do guidance and standards influence practice?
Are appropriate support and monitoring systems in place?
What has been achieved in terms of services provided to children?
What has been achieved in terms of outcomes for children: for example, have they been protected; has their development been enhanced; have the needs of carers been addressed?
How has anti-oppressive practice been promoted?
How have professionals met the needs of service users? For example, how were parents with learning disabilities supported and facilitated to participate?
What are the opinions of service users regarding policies, procedures and the implementation of post-registration practice?

The message for ACPCs is a difficult and costly one. Gone are the days when a set of policies could be developed and implemented and the ACPC was able to move on to the next task. Policies and practice need to be regularly monitored and adjusted to accommodate both local and national changes.

## Training and staff development

Most workers in child protection think of training as being aimed at practitioners, yet training has an important role in terms of meeting the needs of middle and senior managers. 'Training should help policy makers and practitioners critically evaluate the developing body of knowledge and discuss and implement relevant changes. It should contribute to their knowledge of good policy and practice' (DOH, 1993: 10). It is for this reason that training forms another structure that supports the whole post-registration framework, as shown in Figure 1.4. Training is an encompassing structure as it influences every part of the cycle. It can become the vehicle whereby senior managers are given an opportunity to consider the aims of post-registration practice and discuss and debate their mandate and desired standards for practice. Once these have been considered in the light of research practice and organisational developments, policies and procedures can be devised. Once these are in place, training serves a purpose in terms of preparing first line and middle managers to supervise groups of staff involved in post-registration work. These managers need to have knowledge of policy, standards and their role in terms of promoting high quality practice. It is only when these managers have been trained that it is appropriate to train practitioners. In Chapter 12, Murphy describes in detail the suggested content of these training programmes.

Although training has an important role in terms of providing opportunities to reflect, develop and evaluate practice, it cannot be undertaken in isolation. Promoting and developing inter-agency post-registration practice requires a commitment to the following aims as well: ownership by senior managers, adequate staffing, relevant resources, support and supervision for the workforce, a positive working climate, and user involvement (Horwath and Morrison, 1998).

Training may emphasise the need to follow guidelines and procedures but it is ineffective if professionals do not know how to access them or if training is seen as a vehicle to compensate for any lack of procedures (Calder, 1998). Training is a key for promoting and modelling inter-professional work, desirable inter-professional behaviour and collective responsibility (Leathard, 1994). Those who attend inter-agency training often express fewer concerns over occupational rivalries and power struggles (Birchall and Hallett, 1995). Training is also pivotal in developing a workforce with appropriate knowledge, values and skills (Calder, 1998).

## Summary

Historically, emphasis has been placed on investigating child abuse at the expense of work with children and families where abuse has occurred or the child is considered likely to be at risk of abuse. This has resulted in a situation where professionals are working with children and their families on the child protection register with little guidance or a clear practice framework.

AIM
Raise awareness of senior managers to current research, control government guidance and professional issues
MANDATE
Raise awareness of senior managers regarding roles, responsibilities and different professionals
IMPLEMENTATION
Training for the workforce regarding best practice within the framework agreed by ACPC
TRAINING ROLE
TRAINING
FACILITATION ROLE
POLICIES AND PROCEDURES
Training for middle and front-line managers regarding the implementation of policies, procedures and standards; training regarding the manager's role in terms of monitoring, supporting and developing post-registration practice
STANDARDS
Raise awareness of senior managers to research and professional experience of what contributes to effective practice and the management of post-registration work

**Figure 1.4 Training and staff development**

Existing central guidance is vague, leading to a huge variation in local practice. Whilst the findings from the SSI and *Messages from Research* have uncovered failing and ineffectual post-registration practice and systems, national research in Calder and Horwath (1996) did uncover some pockets of innovative practice, policy and procedure which can be used as the building blocks for future developments.

Whilst central guidance has reinforced the need for professionals to work together, the current climate of organisational change is leading to local individual agencies reviewing their child protection roles and responsibilities, which makes a national approach towards post-registration practice difficult to achieve. The model developed for post-registration practice and provided in this chapter attempts to identify and address these issues and seeks to provide a framework for promoting and developing local practice, bearing in mind the climate of continuing local and national change. In the next chapter, we go on to provide a micro-level framework for post-registration core group practice and with it ideas for procedures and practice guidance.

## References

Armstrong, H. (1997) *Annual Report of Area Child Protection Committee 1995/6*, London: HMSO.
Birchall, E. and Hallett, C. (1995) *Working Together in Child Protection*, London: HMSO.
Butler-Sloss, E. (1988) *Report of the Inquiry into Child Abuse in Cleveland*, London: HMSO.
Calder, M.C. (1990) 'Child Protection Core Groups: Participation not Partnership', *Child Abuse Review*, **4** (2): 12–15.
Calder, M.C. (1995a) 'Child Protection: Balancing Paternalism and Partnership', *British Journal of Social Work*, **25** (6): 749–66.
Calder, M.C. (1995b) 'Towards Good Practice in Child Protection', Keynote presentation to the National Conference, 'Core Group: Central to Child Protection – Myth or Reality?' Manchester Town Hall, 14 July.
Calder, M.C. (1996) 'Inter-Agency Working in Child Protection: A Review of Local Arrangements in Salford', *Report to ACPC*, March.
Calder, M.C. (1998) 'Understanding and Unlocking the Potential of Core Groups', Keynote presentation to Wigan ACPC Development Day, Haigh Hall, 8 May.
Calder, M.C. (ed.) (1999a) *Young People who Sexually Abuse: New Pieces of the Jigsaw Puzzle*, Dorset: Russell House Publishing.
Calder, M.C. (1999b) *Assessing Risk in Adult Males who Sexually Abuse Children: A Practical Guide*, Dorset: Russell House Publishing.
Calder, M.C. and Barratt, M. (1997) 'Inter-agency Perspectives on Core Group Practice', *Children and Society*, **11** (4): 209–21.
Calder, M.C. and Horwath, J. (1996) 'National core group sample: analysis of questionnaire responses', unpublished manuscript, Salford ACPC/University of Sheffield.
Department of Education (1988) 'Working Together for the Protection of Children from Abuse: Procedures within the Education Service', Circular no. 4/88.
Department of Health (1988) *Protecting Children : A Guide for Social Workers Undertaking a Comprehensive Assessment*, London: HMSO.
Department of Health (1991) *Working Together under the Children Act 1989: A Guide to Arrangements for Inter-agency Co-operation for the Protection of Children from Abuse*, London: HMSO.
Department of Health (1993) *Working with Child Sexual Abuse: Guidelines for Trainers and Managers in Social Services Departments*, London: HMSO.
Department of Health (1995a) *Child Protection: Messages from Research*, London: HMSO.
Department of Health (1995b) *The Challenge of Partnership in Child Protection: practice guide*, London: HMSO.
Department of Health and Social Security (1974) 'Non-accidental Injury to Children', *LASSL*, **74** (13), London: HMSO.
Department of Health and Social Security (1980) 'Child Abuse: Central Register Systems', *LASSL*, **80** (4), London: HMSO.
Department of Health and Social Security (1982) *Child Abuse: A Study of Inquiry Reports 1974–1981*, London: HMSO.

Department of Health and Social Security (1986) *Child Abuse – Working Together: A draft guide for arrangements for inter-agency co-operation for the protection of children*, London: HMSO.

Department of Health and Social Security (1988a) *Working Together: A guide for inter-agency co-operation for the protection of children from abuse*, London: HMSO.

Department of Health and Social Security (1988b) *Diagnosis of Child Sexual Abuse: guidance for doctors*, London: HMSO.

Department of Health and Social Security (1988c) *Child Protection: Guidance for Senior Nurses, Health Visitors and Midwives*, London: HMSO.

Evans, M. and Miller, C. (1993) *Partnership in Child Protection: The Strategic Management Response*, London: NISW.

Everitt, A. and Hardiker, P. (1996) *Evaluating for Good Practice*, London: Macmillan.

Farmer, E. and Owen, M. (1995) *Child Protection Practice: Private Risks and Public Remedies. Decision-making, Intervention and Outcome in Child Protection Work*, London: HMSO.

Gibbons, J., Conroy, S. and Bell, C. (1995) *Operating the Child Protection System*, London: HMSO.

Hallett, C. (1995) *Inter-Agency Co-ordination in Child Protection*, London: HMSO.

Hampson A. (1993) 'Annual Report of the Principal Officer – child protection', City of Salford SSD.

Hendry, E. and Glennie, G. (1995) *Promoting Quality Standards for Inter-agency Child Protection Training*, London: NSPCC/PIAT.

Horwath, J. and Morrison, T. (1998) *Effective Staff Training in Social Care: From Theory to Practice*, London: Routledge.

Katz, I. (1997) *Current Issues in Comprehensive Assessments*, London: NSPCC.

Morrison, T. (1993) *Staff Supervision in Social Care*, London: Longman.

Morrison, T. (1996) 'Partnership and Collaboration Rhetoric and Reality', *Child Abuse and Neglect*, **20** (2): 127–40.

Parker, R., Ward, H., Jackson, S., Aldergate, J. and Wedge, P. (1991) *Looking after Children: Assessing Outcomes in Child Care*, London: HMSO.

Smith, G. (1994) 'Parent, Partner, Protector: Conflicting Role Demands for Mothers of Sexually Abused Children', in T. Morrison, M. Eroorga and R. Beckett (eds) *Sexual Offending Against Children: Assessment and Treatment of Male Abusers*, London: Routledge: 55–79.

Smith, G. (1995) 'Assessing 'Protectiveness in Cases of Child Sexual Abuse', in P. Reder and C. Lacey (eds) *Assessment of Parenting*, London: Routledge, 87–101.

Smith, G. (1996) 'Reassessing Protectiveness', in D. Batty and D. Cullen (eds) *Child Protection: The Therapeutic Option*, London: BAAF.

Social Services Inspectorate (1986) *Inspection of the Supervision of Social Workers in the Assessment and Monitoring of Cases of Child Abuse when Children, Subject to a Court Order, have been Returned Home*, London: SSI.

Social Services Inspectorate (1993) *Inspecting for Quality: Evaluating Performance in Child Protection. A Framework for the Inspection of Local Authority Social Services Practice and Systems*, London: HMSO.

Social Services Inspectorate (1997) *Messages from Inspections: Child Protection Inspections 1992/1996*, London: HMSO.

Summerhill, J. and Frost, N. (1994) *The Operation of Core Groups in the Wakefield Child Protection Committee Area: An Evaluation*, Leeds: Department of Adult Continuing Education.

Thoburn, J., Lewis, A. and Shemmings, D. (1995) *Paternalism or Partnership? Family Involvement in the Child Protection Process*, London: HMSO.

## Appendix: The outcome exercise

| ACTIVITY | OUTCOME |
|---|---|
| PARENTS/CARERS ARE PREPARED FOR THE CORE GROUP. | A. PARENTS/CARERS UNDERSTAND THE ROLE OF THE CORE GROUP.<br>B. PARENTS/CARERS FEEL ABLE TO PARTICIPATE IN THE CORE GROUP. |
| A SUITABLE/ACCESSIBLE/ FRIENDLY VENUE IS FOUND FOR THE MEETING. | C. ALL PARTICIPANTS FEEL ABLE TO TAKE PART IN THE MEETING. |
| TRANSPORT/CHILD CARE ARRANGEMENTS ARE IN PLACE FOR THE PARENTS/ CARERS/CHILDREN. | D. PARENTS/CARERS ARE ABLE TO ATTEND WHEREVER POSSIBLE. |
| THE MEETING IS CONVENED AT A CONVENIENT TIME/ DATE. | E. THE MAXIMUM NUMBER OF IDENTIFIED PARTICIPANTS ARE ABLE TO ATTEND. |
| MEMBERSHIP OF THE CORE GROUP IS DECIDED. | F. APPROPRIATE PEOPLE ATTEND THE CORE GROUP. |
| THE CHAIR EXPLAINS THE PURPOSE OF THE MEETING. THE CHAIR INTRODUCES PARTICIPANTS, WHERE APPROPRIATE. | G. ALL PARTICIPANTS FEEL CLEAR ABOUT THE PURPOSE OF THE MEETING.<br>H. ALL PARTICIPANTS ARE AWARE WHO THE OTHER PARTICIPANTS ARE. |
| THE CONFIDENTIALITY POLICY IS EXPLAINED BY THE CHAIR. | I. ALL PARTICIPANTS FEEL SAFE AND ABLE TO CONTRIBUTE. |
| THE CHAIR GOES THROUGH PREVIOUSLY IDENTIFIED TASKS (UNLESS INITIAL CORE GROUP). | J. ALL PARTICIPANTS ARE CLEAR IF PREVIOUS DECISIONS HAVE BEEN ACTED UPON. PARTICIPANTS ARE ABLE TO SHARE PERCEPTIONS OF EVENTS. |

| | |
|---|---|
| THERE IS AN OPEN SHARING OF INFORMATION. | K. TO ENSURE THAT ALL RELEVANT INFORMATION IS AVAILABLE TO THOSE WHO NEED TO KNOW.<br>L. PARENT/CARER FEELS ABLE TO CHALLENGE FALSE OR INAPPROPRIATE INFORMATION. |
| GOALS AND OBJECTIVES ARE SHARED AND AGREED. | M. ALL PARTICIPANTS ARE WORKING TOGETHER WHEREVER POSSIBLE.<br>N. A CLEAR/WRITTEN/AGREED PLAN/CONTRACT IS PRODUCED.<br>O. ALL PARTIES FEEL FULLY INVOLVED IN THE PROCESS. |
| AGREE WHO DOES WHAT AND WHEN. | P. ALL PARTICIPANTS ARE CLEAR ABOUT THEIR TASKS.<br>Q. ALL PARTICIPANTS ARE CLEAR ABOUT DECISIONS. |
| A CONTRACT IS ESTABLISHED. | R. AS 'N' ABOVE.<br>S. ALL PARTICIPANTS HAVE A COPY OF THE CONTRACT. |
| THE CHAIR CLARIFIES THE BASIS OF ANY DISAGREEMENTS. | T. INDIVIDUAL PERSPECTIVES ARE APPRECIATED AND RECOGNISED. |
| THE CORE GROUP RETAINS A FOCUS ON THE WELFARE AND PROTECTION OF THE CHILD. | U. THE OUTCOME OF THE MEETING IS POSITIVE FOR THE CHILD. |
| THE CORE GROUP GIVES FEEDBACK, POSITIVE OR NEGATIVE, TO THE PARENT/CARER. | V. PARENT/CARER FEELS THEY ARE TREATED WITH RESPECT, AND AWARE OF ANY NEED TO CHANGE. |
| MINUTES OF THE CORE GROUP ARE WRITTEN UP AND DISTRIBUTED. | W. ALL PARTICIPANTS HAVE A WRITTEN RECORD OF THE MEETING. |

| | |
|---|---|
| TO ESTABLISH CLEAR LINE OF COMMUNICATION BETWEEN THE MEETINGS. | X. ALL PARTICIPANTS ARE CLEAR HOW TO COMMUNICATE BETWEEN MEETINGS. |
| WORKER DISCUSSES CORE GROUP IN SUPERVISION. | Y. WORKER FEELS SUPPORTED.<br>Z. MANAGER IS AWARE OF EVENTS/ISSUES. |
| ALL DECISIONS ARE PUT INTO ACTION. | AA. ALL PARTICIPANTS UNDERTAKE AGREED TASKS IN AN AGREED AND COORDINATED MANNER. |
| CORE GROUP DECIDES RECOMMENDATION/REPORT TO CPC. | AB. ENSURES THAT INFORMED DECISIONS ARE TAKEN BY THE CPC.<br>THE PROCESS OF THE CPC IS STREAMLINED. |
| DATE(S) OF FUTURE MEETINGS ARE AGREED. | AC. ALL PARTIES ARE CLEAR ABOUT THE DATES OF FUTURE MEETINGS. |

*Source*: Summerhill and Frost (1994). Reproduced with permission from Wakefield ACPC.

# 2 Policies and procedures: developing a framework for working together

*Martin C. Calder and Jan Horwath*

In this chapter we consider:

- the key components of post-registration practice;
- the initial child protection conference – setting the scene for post-registration practice;
- the tasks for the core group;
- managing the core group process;
- a core group protocol; and
- the child protection review.

## Introduction

Policies, procedures and guidelines provide a framework enabling practitioners and managers to define aims and objectives, identify methods of intervention and clarify roles and responsibilities. As discussed in Chapter 1, post-registration practice in England and Wales is marked by lack of policy and guidance at both national and local level. Yet the findings from a national study we completed on post-registration practice indicated that a number of ACPCs have acknowledged the need to develop a framework for practice, utilising policies and procedures (Calder and Horwath, 1996; Horwath and Calder, 1998). This appears to have arisen for a number of reasons. Firstly, the research commissioned by the Department of Health (1995) highlighted the fact that practice needed structuring and developing in this area. Secondly, the Audit Commission Report, *Seen but not Heard* (Audit Commission, 1994) raised the profile of children's service plans and alerted ACPCs to the need for policies, as Local Authority Circular (LAC, 92: 18) advises agencies to make explicit their policies regarding children within the service plans (Horwath, 1997).

In this chapter we review the key components that should be considered when developing post-registration policies and procedures. Utilising the findings from our study and the work of other researchers (Calder and Horwath, 1996; Horwath and Calder, 1998), we attempt to identify areas where there is lack of clarity regarding roles and responsibilities and consider areas of practice which are open to misinterpretation. Having identified these areas, we explore ways in which explicit guidance could result in greater clarification regarding the tasks and the ways in which these should be managed, for professionals, children and families.

Post-registration practice is the work that takes place within three different arenas: the initial child protection conference, the core group and the child protection review. We will consider each of these in turn.

## The initial child protection conference

The post-registration phase starts at the initial child protection conference and the work undertaken here is likely to influence subsequent interventions. Indeed, it is clear that, where the conference fails to effectively discharge its tasks, then it sets the core group, and the work needed, up for failure (Calder, 1996). *Working Together* (DoH, 1991) is clear about the tasks that should be completed at the initial conference. Whilst the evidence available suggests that they have not been translated into practice (Calder, 1996), the chairman of the conference should be satisfied that the criteria for registration are met, the need for an inter-agency child protection plan should also be clearly identified. It is only when these two conditions have been achieved that a child's name should be placed on the child protection register.

Where the primary registration criteria are met, the conference will need to consider whether registration is appropriate to the circumstances of the particular case. In doing so the following factors will need to be taken into account:

Are there any outstanding child protection issues; that is, is there a continuing risk of harm?
How high is the probability of harm?
Is there likely to be continuing contact with the perpetrator of the original incident of abuse?

Is there likely to be contact with a person previously implicated in the abuse of other children?
Is there a lack of certainty with regard to the non-abusing carer's capacity to protect?
Are similar circumstances to those which were associated with the original incident of abuse likely to continue or exist or to arise again in the foreseeable future?
Does the cause of the injury or the identity of the perpetrator remain unknown, so that the level of risk cannot be accurately assessed?
Is there a need for a formal inter-agency protection plan? Such a plan may be indicated where:

- there are clearly identifiable objectives to provide a focus to planned and structured intervention;
- a formal written plan is necessary to emphasise the seriousness of the situation, particularly where legal proceedings are under active construction;
- meaningful cooperation from family members is unlikely without a formal written plan.

A protection plan will ensure a strong commitment to inter-agency collaboration and may provide priority access to resources that may not otherwise be available.
A protection plan ensures the primacy of the child's welfare over all other considerations.
A formal inter-agency protection plan will be subject to regular, independent monitoring and review (Hampson, 1997).

Despite the number of factors that should be considered in terms of planning, research indicates that, in practice, the focus of the initial conference is on assessing information and making a decision to register the child, with only nine minutes, on average, being devoted to planning post-registration interventions (Farmer and Owen, 1995). Planning post-registration interventions at the conference includes making recommendations to individuals and the agencies regarding ways in which they will work with other professionals and the family to ensure that the child will be protected from suffering significant harm. The tasks include the following:

- appointing a keyworker;
- identifying the professional membership of the core group;
- identifying family membership of the core group;
- establishing time scales;
- commissioning the assessment;
- outlining the child protection plan;

- clarifying the boundaries between the initial conference, core group and child protection review.

This is a significant number of tasks and, if they are completed quickly at the tail end of the conference, it is hardly surprising that the Department of Health, summarising the findings from their commissioned research studies, noted: 'Decisions about registration ... tend to receive undue salience and could be better balanced against plans to support the child and family in the months after the case conference' (DoH, 1995: 39).

One of the tasks for the initial child protection conference is to create a clear structure for post-registration practice. This should enable both practitioners and the family to understand exactly what is expected of them and what they can expect of others. If this is to happen, the following points should be considered at the initial conference.

## Appointment of a keyworker

If the keyworker is appointed at the initial conference, the child, family and other professionals have an immediate contact point. However, it is not always possible to appoint the keyworker because of workloads and staff shortages. In these situations, the name and contact number of the team manager should be provided to all those who will be engaged in post-registration activity. In many social services departments, the keyworker is automatically the social worker who undertook the investigation. This needs to be considered carefully, as Farmer and Owen (1995) found that, if the child and family were hostile and angry towards the investigating social worker, these negative feelings persisted if the worker continued to work with the family. In these situations a change of social worker often resulted in a more positive working relationship.

## Identifying the inter-agency membership of the core group

The core group should include the keyworker and professionals who will have direct contact with the family. All members of the core group should have an active role in the formulation, implementation, refinement and evaluation of the child protection plan. Attention should be paid to the size of the group. Too large a group can act against group function, as well as presenting too wide a range of interests (Brunel, 1988). Too small a group can concentrate too much power in relatively few hands (Hallett, 1995). These issues are explored in detail in Chapter 5.

The chairman of the initial conference should routinely identify the membership of the core group, by name if possible, but by designation if not. Gibbons *et al.* (1995) found that this is only happening in a small minority of cases. If the membership is not specified, the keyworker can be left 'holding the baby' (Hallett, 1995: 64) and feeling responsible for formulating and implementing the child protection plan.

A number of strategies are available to help manage the numbers included in the core group. Firstly, where more than one staff member from an agency is eligible to attend the core group – for example, school health adviser or health visitor – consideration should be given to including the most appropriate candidate on the understanding that they collect and disseminate information between each other outside the core group meeting. This would clearly require periodic review should circumstances change or the family request their inclusion, and it is essential that any such inclusions (or exclusions) are relayed to the Custodian of the Child Protection Register so that they can amend their records accordingly. Secondly, consideration should be given to identifying two separate core groups in particularly complex cases or where the needs of registered children differ significantly – for example, where there is a victim and an abuser and young people in the home or where some children in the family live at home whilst others live in substitute care. This is particularly helpful when there are large numbers of children in a family and there is a need to break down the planning into manageable parts. In considering this option, there is a need to balance overlapping membership and to ascertain whether key personnel are able to commit their time to separate groups. Thirdly, there may be transient core group members who can join the meetings only as and when they have something to contribute – for example, psychologists who report back on a commissioned assessment of a Schedule One offender and whose feedback is integral to the refinement of the plan. Finally, where core group members have completed their tasks and their role in the plan has significantly diminished, there should be sufficient flexibility to allow them to leave the group, but be available to attend the child protection review. In practice this rarely happens. Calder and Barratt (1997) found that only 19 per cent of core groups routinely review their membership.

Core group composition may change for a number of reasons – for example, staff leaving post or a child changing their address or school. This can be tackled through the core group and fully recorded in the plan unless this has been set out as a change of circumstances warranting reconvening the review. Firth (1995) found that the unrestricted membership of a group negatively influenced its work as members felt that they were contributing and achieving very little. Crossby (1992) found that membership can increase over time in cases where the concerns were escalating and this has the knock-on effect of intimidating the family. In other cases where the work is having some positive effect, the membership of the core group can diminish over time (Calder, 1996).

At the point of registration professionals should be clear about whether they can commit the necessary time to attend the core groups and about their role in the child protection plan. It is often difficult for core groups to operate effectively in the absence of key members, and this needs to be addressed. Some staff, such as school teachers, may find it difficult to secure supply cover and we sometimes have to accept that choices have to be made about their time – for example, whether to attend core groups or child protection reviews. In so doing, care has to be taken not to discourage collective responsibility.

## Identifying family membership in the core group

Local arrangements will determine whether parents and/or children are eligible to attend the conference and the core group meetings. Family participation is important as 75–80 per cent of children placed on the child protection register remain at home with at least one parent with no statutory order in force (DoH, 1995). Thoburn *et al.* (1995) found that, despite the fact that the majority of children remain at home, meaningful participation was apparent in only one-fifth of the cases they studied. Yet Farmer and Owen (1995) noted a correlation between the main parent being involved in the design and implementation of the plan and the child having a good or moderately good interim outcome. Plans formulated in the absence of parents tend to be idealistic and do not address the child and family's perception of need. Higginson (1990) reported three negative effects arising from parental absence from child protection decision making: not all the relevant information is available to the professionals who are making the decisions; the strengths of family members are nor exploited; and realistic plans are difficult to formulate or implement.

The way in which participation is facilitated at the conference is likely to influence the family's willingness to participate in the core group. If family members are patronised, ignored or intimidated by the conference, they may feel reluctant to attend the core group, fearing a repeat experience. Likewise, if the conference ignores specific needs, such as those associated with a severe hearing impairment or language difficulties, family members may feel unable to participate actively in further meetings.

In some situations there are very clear conflicts of interest between family members entitled to attend the core group, and wherever possible this should be resolved at the point of identifying the core group. Any procedures covering family attendance should specify whose right to attendance prevails between the parents themselves, the parents and the child's current carers (where different) and between the parents and the child. The general rule of thumb is that we should operate a policy of inclusion and this is based on a belief that we have everything to gain and nothing to lose by so doing (Calder, 1995b).

Inclusion should always be more than a means of helping the professionals do their job (Marsh, 1994).

Calder and Horwath (forthcoming) found a high level of ACPC commitment to parental participation in core groups: 69 per cent routinely invited them compared to only 3 per cent who would only do so if their involvement was needed. This is important since we know that parents can make a significant contribution to the protection of their children if they are provided with the right framework in which to work closely with professionals (Calder, 1990). There was a more varied response to the participation of children and young people at core groups: only 8 per cent always invited children and young people, 50 per cent did so occasionally, whilst 5 per cent never invited them. It seems rare for a child to be named as a member of a core group from the outset, although the core group should actively consider ways in which this could be achieved. Overall, we found that, whilst there was a move towards family inclusion in core groups, it has often not been thought through and is rarely backed by any guidance. Careful consideration should be given to identifying male, as well as female, parents in the core group, particularly where they have perpetrated the abuse in the first instance. Currently, many professionals focus on mothers as the parent, and this skews the assessment of future risk to the child. These issues are discussed further later in this chapter.

## Time scales

The child protection procedures should set out clearly the frequency with which core groups should meet, so as to discharge their delegated responsibilities. It is helpful if these are reinforced by the chairman of the initial conference in the recommendations. It is also useful if the date for the first core group meeting is agreed at the initial conference. Johnson (1991) noted that, where core groups do not meet immediately post-registration, there is a significant difficulty in arranging a time for the meeting which is acceptable and convenient to everyone. Different agencies have different patterns of work and some have regular commitments, such as classes or clinics, which make it very awkward to arrive at a mutually convenient time to meet. It is important that dates for meetings are not determined by professionals alone, as consideration also needs to be given to the needs of the carers and child. For example, in one situation a core group agreed to meet during the school day, which created problems for the young person who wished to attend but was due to sit GCSEs in a few months' time and did not want to miss school. Whilst regular meetings do create some problems for staff, there are very clear advantages in terms of clearer planning, allocation of responsibilities and the development of trust.

Horwath and Calder (1998) found that only 48 per cent of ACPCs had devised guidance regarding fixing a date for the first core group meeting. In the guidance examined, the core group was usually expected to meet within ten working days of the initial conference, although some guidance was very vague – for example, stating that the core group should 'meet as necessary' or, in one case, that the core group will decide upon 'appropriate liaison'. There was also wide variation in the guidance regarding the frequency of the meetings. Almost 25 per cent recommended meeting monthly while a significant number recommended more infrequent meetings. A balance needs to be drawn between meeting on a sufficiently regular basis to promote working together/ensuring that the plan is updated as circumstances change and ensuring that the plan is working effectively and placing too much emphasis on the meetings themselves. No ACPC in the study recommended that core groups should meet more frequently than monthly whilst 18 per cent recommended quarterly meetings, raising questions as to how the group maintains and monitors progress and works in partnership with the family.

The number of meetings taking place will depend on the complexity of the assessments being undertaken as well as the degree of risk involved in each individual case. In some cases, where weekly meetings are considered necessary, a careful evaluation of the level of risk and its management need critical review. Where a clear plan is in existence and the agencies and the family are effectively applying it, a less frequent core group may be considered, although they should always meet pre-review to collate the information as the basis of making recommendations on a continued registration. Calder (1996) found that, even where clear guidance has been issued for core groups, the frequency of meetings shows cause for concern. He found that core groups met as prescribed in 68 per cent of cases after registration, in 9 per cent of cases between the first and second review, with little evidence of continuing activity thereafter.

Issues can also arise regarding the time scale for circulating case conference minutes. Many workers rely heavily on the child protection conference minutes as the basis of any subsequent work, yet Firth (1995) found that a massive 60 per cent of core group members did not have any written information from the initial conference, leaving their capacity to operate effectively within the core group in question. Calder (1996) found that the average time scale for circulating minutes approached two months.

## The commissioned assessment

*Working Together* (DoH, 1991) recommends that a comprehensive assessment be completed in every case following the registration of a child. This assessment should include contributions from all relevant agencies to cover social, environmental, medical and developmental circumstances. The assessment should be planned, structured and explicit about the task of each professional.

In practice, several issues need immediate attention at the initial conference if these objectives are to be achieved. Firstly, the initial conference should set out explicitly the kind of assessment needed in each particular case. Calder (1996) found that the initial conference only specified the type of assessment required in 27 per cent of cases. Secondly, the expectation is that the core group will most likely 'do an orange book assessment' (DoH, 1988). This is not necessarily the most appropriate form of assessment. For example, the questions do not address many of the issues that need considering in terms of an assessment of sexual abuse, such as psychosexual histories. Ironically, as Katz (1997) has noted, assessment of risk to children who have been placed on the child protection register, enabling workers to formulate a clear child protection plan, is an area of assessment not specifically mentioned in the 'Orange Book'. Whilst good assessment remains the foundation of good child protection work, the simple commissioning of an assessment does not guarantee that an appropriate, tailored assessment takes place. Indeed, there remains widespread confusion about what constitutes a good assessment (Calder, 1997).

## Outlining the child protection plan

Our study of post-registration practice (Calder and Horwath, 1996; Horwath and Calder, 1998) found that there was great diversity in opinion regarding the role of the initial conference in devising the plan: 79 per cent of ACPCs noted that the outline of the plan was devised at the initial conference (several did reserve the right to go into more specific detail if this was warranted); 6 per cent stated that the core group inherited very little from the conference and consequently constructed both the broad outline and the specific child protection plan; and the remainder indicated that the plan was not formulated either at the conference or in the core group (in these cases it seems the keyworker and the keyworker's manager frequently formulated the plan). This begs the question about what is being implemented, by whom, and how it is being coordinated.

Where plans are outlined at the initial conference, planning is of a high standard, leading to 80 per cent of children being protected (Farmer and Owen, 1995). The outline plan should:

- identify risks and ways in which the child can be protected through an inter-agency child protection plan;

- establish short-term and longer-term aims and objectives that are clearly linked to risk reduction and promoting the child's welfare;
- consider monitoring devices that enable both workers and the family to evaluate the effectiveness of the plan;
- indicate the work that should be undertaken by the core group before attempting to implement the broad plan: for example, the assessment.
- explore how parents and children should be engaged in the planning process, particularly where they are absent from the initial conference (Calder, 1991).

## Clarifying the boundaries between the conference, core group and other meetings

The relationship between the conference and the core group needs to be made explicit and clear. Whilst the two forums should complement each other, the authority, aims and boundaries of the core group should be established by the initial conference. In this way the conference members provide the core group with a framework for operation. The core group members should remember that they are part of a sub-system and remain advisory and not executive in function. They must carry out the wishes of the larger group as indicated in the broad child protection plan. The core group cannot overturn recommendations from the conference, other than in emergency situations (Calder, 1990; 1991; 1995a). It should then go to child protection review as a major change of circumstances.

There have also been concerns over the degree of 'fuzziness' developing between the child protection review and the core group meeting, as this was leading to more responsibilities being placed with the core group and, by implication, with the keyworker (Summerhill and Frost, 1994: 13). Where core groups were functioning well, they noted a decline in review conferences.

There must be clarity over the status, role and names of different kinds of meeting, as any confusion over nomenclature and demarcation of responsibilities can be dangerous. It follows that a clarity of purpose follows on from a clarity over names and roles of meetings. Whilst we have to accept that different types of meeting may take place regarding a particular child, the goal must be that they are not occurring in isolation from one another.

Those areas that have formally adopted the core group in their child protection system should specify that these are *exclusive* planning forums for children on the child protection register. For those who have not adopted this model, then they need to offer guidance on where the planning will take place, when and who will be involved.

In some areas, core groups are not always convened for every child on the child protection register, and this is often a reflection of the degree of confusion and misunderstanding over the role, functioning and definitions of core groups (Summerhill and Frost, 1994: 12). There is sometimes confusion where no key-worker is allocated, and other meetings take place – for example, nursery or family centre reviews. Training courses have been helpful in uncovering notions of 'splinter', 'mini' and 'emergency' core group meetings, which compound the confusion. They also identified confusion when only some children in the family are registered, yet there is continued involvement with all the family.

As Giller *et al.* (1992: 76) found, the use of core groups to plan proactive action is far from being a uniform practice, and there was a shared responsibility between the core group and the planning meeting to formulate a plan, whilst the core group alone was responsible for its implementation. Crossby (1992: 21) found that the confusion did not end at the point of deregistration, in that some core groups continued to meet post-deregistration, albeit not as a 'proper core group', and she questioned whether this could be overcome by a procedural agreement for them to meet for a specified period post-deregistration (1992: 23).

Core groups will hopefully bring a common language to all meetings related to child protection to avoid confusion and duplication.

## From individual to collective responsibility?

Whilst the ultimate statutory responsibility for child protection rests with the social services department through the keyworker, recommendations from the initial conference can help mould a collective approach to planning and core group operation. It may be helpful to offer several models of collective responsibility which conferences and core groups can choose between, although this would clearly require prior approval from the ACPC and constituent agencies. Newton (1982) has offered the following three models of collective responsibility:

- **The identification model**. This holds the group and all its members responsible for the acts of individual members simply because of their identification as members of the group. Its roots lie in the idea of tribal responsibility in which the tribe as a whole holds itself accountable for the acts of any one of its members.
- **The participatory model**. This attributes to an individual the full responsibility for the acts or omissions of the group as a whole and all its members just because an individual is a participant in a situation at a particular time and place. When responsible action by an individual would have helped, the whole aggregate is held collectively responsible.

- **The authorisation model**. Here, the single act of authorisation on the part of the individual serves to signify membership in the collective. It bonds people to those who operate within the same rule-governed framework.

At present, post-registration work is not governed by any of these as it remains the decision of individuals and their agencies as to whether they accept their part in the plan and whether they are happy to implement it. Major problems currently emerge where members agree to take on tasks because they think they ought to and then do nothing about them. Others quickly become overwhelmed by their responsibility and default on their agreements.

## Summary

The initial conference can be compared to a group of individuals coming together to complete a jigsaw. All the individuals have pieces of the jigsaw, but it is only when the pieces are set out together that the whole picture emerges. Once a jigsaw is complete, there are a number of choices. Ideally, a box is found that is big enough to keep the jigsaw complete, but not so big that pieces begin to separate; but if no box is found or the box is too small, the jigsaw is dismantled. In the same way the members of a conference make a decision. They can design a box which keeps the picture complete: this would be the equivalent of identifying a core group made up of appropriate professionals who work together to develop and implement the clearly outlined child protection plan. Alternatively, the conference members can design a box that involves dismantling the jigsaw: this would be the equivalent of leaving decisions regarding the composition of the core group loose or undetermined, and providing little in terms of an outline child protection plan. Clearly, if the conference does not promote working together in the post-registration phase, through addressing the tasks outlined above, it is establishing a situation where the core group is established with no clear remit. Each individual clutches his or her pieces of the jigsaw rather than placing them in the box as part of the larger picture.

Mailick and Ashley (1989) have very clearly articulated the aim of working together in the post-registration phase. They argue that working together is based on a belief that it has the potential for achieving more than the sum of the collaborating parts operating individually. The central goal of working together is the achievement of some degree of consensus by a group of individuals about a plan of action and its execution. It usually includes an interpersonal process in which members of a group contribute, each from their own knowledge and skills, to the accomplishment of a task, yet are responsible as a group for the outcome. A process of cross-fertilisation of ideas is presumed to occur that encourages new perspectives and reformulation of difficult problems and solutions that exceed the boundaries of separate disciplines. The more generalised the task and the more the individual professional is dependent on the cooperation of others in its accomplishment, the greater their motivation will be for collaborative activity.

## The core group

The core group is the small group of professionals led by the designated keyworker, whose task is to translate the broad outline of a child protection plan sketched by the initial conference into a detailed, workable child protection plan. The work of the core group is to access and coordinate the different intervention strategies, trying to ensure that families are not overwhelmed or confused, and providing a central reference point to hear and provide feedback. Whilst the core group is responsible for formulating the plan, the actual implementation is carried out through the individuals who are party to it. They meet regularly as a group to review and revise the plan and collectively report back to the child protection review.

As outlined above, the core group is a sub-system of the child protection conference and primarily undertakes commissioned tasks. The initial conference sketches the picture and the core group colours it in. The initial conference strives to facilitate participation with parents, whilst the core group is the vehicle through which partnerships are forged. As a result of this, the core group represents an operational link between the child protection procedures and the child whose name is placed on the child protection register. The core group provides a framework within which services can be provided in a coordinated and corporate way, as well as providing a forum for mutual professional support.

It would be wrong to see the core group as an event. It is, rather, a process that continues throughout the period during which a child's name remains on the child protection register (adapted from Calder, 1995a and Calder, 1998). It has been described as the 'engine-room' of post-registration planning and the 'control-room' of inter-agency operations (Calder, 1998), as well as a 'catalyst for change' (Morrison, 1995). If the conference is said to be the formal expression of working together, then core groups epitomise working together in action. As the debate about rebalancing child protection and family support services continues, the core group does have considerable potential to act as a bridge between: protection and family support activities; problem identification and problem resolution processes; and formal and informal processes (Calder, 1998).

In this section we consider the tasks that the core group needs to complete, identify problems of working together to complete these tasks, and recommend a core group protocol to address the problems.

## The tasks of the core group

The core group is best framed as a 'task-orientated group' (Perlman and Whitworth, 1988) whose tasks rarely remain static. It has a number of tasks that it needs to complete. These include the following: engaging children and families through establishing a working and written agreement with the child and family; completing the comprehensive assessment; translating the outline child protection plan to a working plan, and implementing the plan; reporting to the child protection review; and reviewing the plan and membership of the core group. Each of these will be considered in detail.

### *Engaging children and families through establishing a working and written agreement with the child and family*

Research indicates that families are far more likely to become engaged in work during the post-registration phase if professionals begin working with the family immediately after the child's name is placed on the register (Farmer and Owen, 1995). The family are most likely to be actively engaged in the work when 'every effort should be made to ensure that they [children and parents] have a clear understanding of the objectives of the plan, that they accept it and are willing to work to it' (DoH, 1991: 32).

A written agreement has become a standard method for negotiating the content of the child protection plan with the family, yet our study revealed there was confusion in some ACPCs between a written agreement made with the family and the actual child protection plan (Calder and Horwath, 1996; Horwath and Calder, 1998). The agreement is the contract that is made with the family regarding the implementation of the plan. Its purpose is to translate the child protection plan into an action plan for the family. The Family Rights Group (FRG) and The National Foster Care Association (NFCA) have produced a written agreement for use with children and families. They suggest that the agreement is negotiated between parents, the keyworker and others who are working directly with the family. They also stress the importance of including the child in the negotiation of the agreement. The areas which should be considered within a written agreement are listed in Box 2.1.

**Box 2.1 Content of a Child Protection Agreement**

The reasons for registration, including details of the problems and behaviour that resulted in registration.
The aims and objectives of the work with the family with a time scale and indicators of ways in which progress will be measured.
The roles and responsibilities of core group members, their names and contact numbers.
Who will be working towards what objectives and with whom.
The frequency and purpose of contact with the child and family.
When and how progress will be monitored and reviewed.
Systems for managing disagreements and conflict.
Plans for protecting the child if the objectives are not achieved.

(Adapted from Child Protection Agreement, FRG and NFCA.)

## *Completing the comprehensive assessment*

One of the first major tasks for core group members is to ensure that a comprehensive assessment is made of the child and family's situation if this is deemed necessary by the initial child protection conference. The tools and methods for undertaking the assessment are considered in Chapter 3. In the present chapter we consider the roles and responsibilities of the core group in terms of managing the assessment process. The principal aims of a comprehensive assessment are as follows:

- to identify the factors leading to the concerns about the child's safety;
- to assess the needs of the child in terms of the impact of the abuse on their welfare;
- to reach an understanding of the child and family relationships, behaviour and support networks as they relate to the concerns about the child or children;
- to assess the motivation and capacity of family members to change, in order to protect the child or children.

Box 2.2 lists the elements which the comprehensive assessment should include. Pieces of this work, for example a psychological assessment, may be contracted out, and a report submitted to the core group for inclusion in the overall assessment.

**Box 2.2 Content of a Comprehensive Assessment**

A chronological history of all family members, detailing events relevant to the current concerns about the child.
A description of the family members' interrelationships and current behaviour patterns, both as reported by them and as observed by members of the core group.
Observed evidence of parent–child relationships obtained from family work, observations of contact visits and interactions with the family's professional network: for example, school, GP, health visitor, probation service.
An assessment of the child's physical, cognitive, emotional and social development.
An assessment of the risk that individual family members may represent to the child.
The wishes and feelings of individual family members, including the child, regarding the current situation.
An assessment of the family's ability to protect the child, including an assessment of the degree to which family members have demonstrated responsibility for their own behaviour and the ability to change.
An assessment of the further work/support networks needed to ensure that protection of the child or children is maintained.
An assessment of special needs and their impact on the child. For example, what impact, if any, do learning, physical disabilities or mental health problems have on parent skills?

## *Translating the outline child protection plan to a working plan and implementing the plan*

As described above, the initial conference should provide the core group with an outline plan. It is the task of the core group to translate that plan into a working document that specifically details the work to be undertaken by professionals and the family. Giller *et al.* (1992) found that 50 per cent of the plans in their sample lacked any clarity of expectation as regards the parties involved, thus enhancing the probability of misunderstandings, ambiguities and changing goal posts. More confusion will be created if, as Thoburn *et al.* (1995) found, only 43 per cent of parents contribute to the construction of the plan. An effective plan is one that attempts to establish a common understanding between professionals and the family, regarding what work needs to be done, why and by whom. It is likely to be achieved if the plan:

- sets out clearly the child's identified needs;
- contains objectives that are child-focused and are designed to protect the child and promote the child's welfare;
- has specific, achievable objectives that allow everyone to identify realistic strategies for achieving the objectives;
- specifies who is visiting the child, where, when and for what reason, rather than simply stating that 'the child will be seen when we visit the home';
- clearly identifies roles and responsibilities to both professionals and family members;
- is explicit and avoids administratively-oriented objectives, such as 'monitoring';
- contains the minimum number of areas that are necessary to protect the child;
- lays down clearly designed points at which a review of progress will be made and has an agreed mechanism for assessing any effected changes (see Morrison, 1995, ch. 8).

Plans should be negotiated with children and families in the first instance and only enforced where agreement cannot be reached and it is essential to protect the child. The child protection plan should be framed separately from any other plan, such as a child care plan for a child accommodated by the local authority. However, the plans must be consistent with one another. The protection plan should be constructed with the family in their first language and they should also receive a written copy in their first language. If the plan is being negotiated with carers with learning disabilities, consideration should be given to ways of negotiation that ensure that they understand exactly what the plan contains. This may involve consulting or working with specialist workers.

The plan should set out clearly any disagreements, how it can be changed and by whom, and information on complaints procedures as well as appeals against registration.

Whilst every child on the child protection register should have a written and detailed plan, Calder and Barratt (1997), in a sample of health visitors, teachers and social workers, found that only 78 per cent of health visitors and 50 per cent of social workers viewed the core group as *sometimes* formulating a plan, whilst a worrying 25 per cent of social workers felt the core group *never* attended to this task. Giller *et al.* (1992) found that 50 per cent of the plans in their sample lacked any clarity of expectation for the parties involved, thus enhancing the probability of misunderstandings, ambiguities and changing goalposts. The quality of plans and the parents' commitment to them is often directly linked to their involvement in their construction.

Thoburn *et al.* (1995) found that only 43 per cent of parents contributed to the plan. It is important that the core group adapts the plan over time, particularly embracing new information and changes of circumstances. Short-term reviews often act as a motivator to parents, as they have something to work towards. In doing so, the professionals have to guard against expecting too much, too soon, particularly as this can make the neat implementation of plans problematic.

## *Reporting to the child protection review*

The core group has a corporate responsibility to produce reports for the child protection review. The review requires clear, concise and collated information from the core group in order to endorse or reformulate any suggested longer-term child protection plan or to identify gaps. Some confusion can exist regarding corporate responsibility, as the keyworker is ultimately responsible for ensuring that a written assessment report is available for the review. The present writers' research indicated that it is consistently the social worker who is expected to prepare all subsequent reports to the child protection review. This sets no example of working together. We therefore advocate that a corporate report be produced by the core group which does the following:

1 It provides basic information:

- identities of the child/children,
- date of registration and category,
- legal status,
- placement details,
- names and addresses of other relevant family members,
- identities of core group members.

2 It provides an overview of work undertaken:

- identifies how often the core group has met, with dates,
- identifies frequency and purpose of contact with each child and parents/carers,
- identifies content of the child protection plan.

3 It evaluates and assesses work achieved:

- identifies whether the recommendations of the previous conferences have been acted on and if not, gives the reasons for this,
- identifies any significant changes or incidents which have taken place since the last conference,

- identifies any progress made and any difficulties encountered,
- identifies the family's views regarding the child protection plan,
- recommends a future course of action,
- identifies any proposed changes to the existing child protection plan and the reasons behind these,
- expresses a view about the need for continuing registration.

## *Reviewing the plan and the membership of the core group*

On the basis of the recommendations made by the child protection review, members of the core group may be required to change the child protection plan. The core group needs to consider the reasons why the review recommended certain courses of action and consider the ways in which these can be most effectively achieved. Our study indicated that core groups did not only review the plan as a result of recommendations made by the child protection review, but also made changes based on a change in family or professional circumstances. In many cases these were minor changes, such as altering the frequency of attendance at a family centre, but 10 per cent of the sample indicated that the core group could review registration itself (Calder and Horwath, 1996; Horwath and Calder, 1998). More worryingly, Calder and Barrett (1997) found that over half of the social workers believed that the core group always reviewed registration and only 16 per cent believed this task to be beyond their remit. The authors also found that nearly two-thirds of professionals believed that the core group reviewed the plan 'sometimes'. This has the knock-on effect that plans can remain unchanged even where the family circumstances change significantly; this is most critical when the original plan was unspecific, unclear and flawed. This is clearly the responsibility of the child protection review. It seems crucial that the core group is given clear guidance establishing boundaries regarding its ability to review and alter plans. The initial case conference should set out clearly what decisions should come back to review and be specific about the remit of the core group to alter plans (Calder, 1996).

As a result of alterations to plans it may be necessary to alter the composition of the core group. Review of core group membership should take the following factors into consideration:

1 Is the change in membership for the benefit of the child and family or the convenience of the professional?
2 If a discrete piece of work is being commissioned, such as a specialised assessment, should the person undertaking the work become a member of the core group for the duration of the piece of work, or could they liaise with the core group via the keyworker?

3 What impact will change in membership have on the group dynamics? Will the group become too big and disempower the family, or could the core group become so small that it is no longer an effective group?
4 Is the core group trying to meet too many different needs, in which case it might be more effective to have two core groups: for example, if there are a number of children in a family some of whom are at home whist others are being accommodated by the local authority? The needs of the children may be different, requiring different child protection plans.

## Managing the process through a core group protocol

The description of the tasks that need to be completed by core group members highlights what a complex area of practice post-registration work can be. Experience shows that workers are often committed to the tasks but the core group is ineffective because insufficient attention is paid to process issues. For example, if organisational details are not explicit, workers could be operating to different time scales. In other situations the core group may be unable to work together because of conflict between members. An effective core group requires not only commitment to the task but structure, organisation and clarity regarding the way in which its members will work together. Consideration needs to be given to the fact that the core group is a multi-disciplinary group; each member comes with different expectations, roles and responsibilities. In addition, within any multiprofessional group, there will be differences in terms of power, status professional values and ethics. Unless these differences are acknowledged and addressed, they are likely to interfere with the way in which the group works together. It is thus important that the professionals have an agreement between themselves to maximise the likelihood of a common philosophical and practical approach to the work. This is important as professionals often have different ideas about how best to protect a child.

Crossby (1992) found that many social workers were often having to open the first core group meeting by clarifying different understandings of the purpose of the meeting. As with any group, when members of a core group first come together they need an opportunity to establish some common ground. It could be argued that professionals should get together initially without the family, to gain a common understanding regarding the way in which they will work with each other and with the family, but this should never be used as an excuse or as an alternative to their subsequent inclusion (Calder, 1990) and they should always be informed of the meeting and outcome. The following are suggested areas for discussion and debate. They focus on gaining a common understanding of the task (what are we doing?)

and establishing an agreed way of managing the process (how shall we do it?).

1 The task:

- what needs to be achieved to protect the child?
- the focus of the plan,
- the content of the plan,
- the type of assessment required,
- work to be undertaken on a voluntary or statutory basis with the family,
- the level of partnership required between professionals,
- the level of partnership that is likely to be achieved with the family.

2 The process:

- how will the group work together to achieve the task?
- ways in which the group will work together to maintain a child focus,
- how the group will conduct its business,
- the specific roles and responsibilities of each professional involved with the family,
- the resources and services to be provided to the family,
- ways in which multi-agency communication will take place and information will be exchanged,
- systems for liaison with those who are not involved in core group meetings, but whose contact with the family has a bearing on the child protection plan,
- who will see the child, when and where?
- frequency of meetings,
- recording the contents of the meetings, including any agreements entered into between the agencies or between the agencies and the family,
- methods for evaluating the effectiveness and progress of the current child protection plan,
- ways in which the comprehensive assessment will be completed.

It can be very time consuming if this process has to be undertaken from scratch each time a core group is formed. Much time can be saved if each ACPC has a core group protocol which outlines ways in which the ACPC expects core group members to work together. Each core group would still need to discuss the implications of the protocol in terms of the particular group, but each member should be able to attend with some idea as to what the ACPC expects of them.

We believe that the following areas should be considered when developing a core group protocol: administration of the core group, agendas for core group meetings, establishing systems for managing conflict, and identifying criteria for exclusion of family members, and promoting young people's attendance. Each of these is considered in detail below:

## Administration of the core group

Whilst the keyworker is responsible for coordinating the activities of the core group, findings from our study indicated that it is presumed that the keyworker will manage the core group process, including chairing the meetings, minute taking, organising the venue, arranging transport for the family and organising any child care that is required (Calder and Horwath, 1996; Horwath and Calder, 1998). This has implications both for the keyworker, who can feel that they have been left 'holding the baby' (Hallett, 1995) and for other professionals who can feel marginalised. One way of promoting effective interagency practice is to share the administrative tasks amongst core group members. Such tasks might include arranging venues; minute taking and circulation of minutes; chairing of meetings; and transport and child care for the family.

Calder and Barratt (1997) found that social workers always convened core group meetings even when they were actually requested by others; 93 per cent always chaired the meeting; and 60 per cent took the minutes. This regularly left them unable to produce a working plan (achieved in only 10 per cent of the cases) and failing to circulate the plan to other core group members (in over half the sampled cases). Many social workers argue that such information reflects an uneven shouldering of responsibility, and this leaves the core group as a bureaucratic public relations exercise for interagency and professional–family relationships. Other agencies argue that this is often self-inflicted and grounded in an unwillingness to delegate and expose their practice to scrutiny.

## Agendas for core group meetings

The core group is a task-focused group; consequently, consideration should be paid to ways in which the process can be managed to ensure that the task is achieved. One way of doing this is by agreeing on a standard agenda that will be used for each core group meeting. There are several advantages to using an agenda for core group meetings: (1) it allows members to follow the process through clearly and methodically, (2) it facilitates an organised and structured meeting, (3) it provides a structure that is focused on the task – the protection of the child, (4) it provides a framework for the child and carers, and (5) members are less likely to interrupt and introduce their own agendas (adapted from Lewis *et al.* 1992: 11).

Boxes 2.3 and 2.4 present two specimen agendas: one for the initial meeting with the family and one that can be used for all subsequent meetings.

**Box 2.3 The Initial Core Group Meeting**

The following areas should be considered.

General introduction:
why each person is present,
purpose of the meeting.

Reasons for concern leading to registration:
professional and family perspectives considered.

Confidentiality:
boundaries of confidentiality should be outlined.

Assessment:
the type and purpose of the assessment should be made clear.

Child protection plan:
clarification regarding the objectives of the plan and the broad outline inherited from the initial case conference,
consideration of the ways in which the plan will be expanded and implemented,
breaking the child protection plan into clear areas of work, and assigning tasks to agencies or workers.

Roles of different core group members:
who will be responsible for the implementation of the child protection plan.

Review:
when the plan will be reviewed,
what are the deadlines for the work.

Outcomes:
what are the positive outcomes and the negative sanctions in this case,
how the effectiveness of the plan will be monitored.

Dissent:
Do any family or professional members disagree with the proposed plan?

Date, time and venue for the next meeting.

(Adapted from Calder, 1990.)

**Box 2.4 Subsequent Core Group Meetings**

Introductions and apologies.

Minutes of the last core group meeting.

Confidentiality restated.

Any changes in circumstances since the last meeting.

Action taken:
in respect of the recommendations of the last core group meeting.

Current situation and progress:
in respect of each child, covering health, education, social development.

Report of a child in care:
legal status, current situation, plans, views of the child/parents/carers.

The family:
feelings, support offered and accepted, relationships, home standards, willingness to work on a voluntary basis,
what changes in the family situation have taken place,
what still needs to be changed.

Is there a need to review core group composition, child protection plans?
Revised child protection plan – roles, tasks, responsibilities, contingencies.

Objections to the plan.

Date, time and venue of the next core group meeting.

(Adapted from Calder, 1990.)

## Establishing systems for managing conflict

We should not forget that conflict is both functional and diagnostic, and we should always examine, rather than try to eliminate, it (Charles and Stevenson, 1990: 99). The avoidance of conflict and the promotion of uniformity can limit our search for alternative viable explanations or solutions. Any group that works together over a period of time is likely to experience conflict at some stage. Firth (1995) found that conflict arose in some two-thirds of core group meetings she examined, and she questioned whether the remaining third would develop some conflict once some openness and honesty was established. She found that professional conflict arose over a number of issues, such as the focus of intervention and the varying perceptions of the child's and carers' needs. Mittler (1993) found that 39 per cent of professionals reported some level of conflict in meetings. Print and Baxter (in Chapter 5 of the present volume) consider reasons why this conflict may occur and identify ways in which it can be addressed within the core group arena. However, situations may arise where it is not possible to resolve the conflict amongst core group members. In these situations it can be helpful to have some agreed local procedures that set out the arrangements for resolving disagreements or conflict. Tameside ACPC utilise the following guidance for resolving disagreements:

> The complainant should discuss the nature of their disagreement with their line manager.
> That line manager should then approach the manager of the core group member with whom there is disagreement and attempt to find a satisfactory resolution by negotiation.
> In all cases of disagreement the line manager of the keyworker should be kept informed, and
> Where the disagreement remains unresolved, the matter must go back to review where it will be aired in an open and healthy way. The review will attempt to reach a consensus, but will properly record dissenting opinion if consensus cannot be reached.

## Identifying criteria for exclusion of family members

In our study of core group practice, we found that 71 per cent of ACPCs actively encouraged and supported parents' attendance and participation in core groups. Their contributions can be valuable (Calder and Horwath, 1996; Horwath and Calder, 1998). For example, IMPACT (1993) noted that 61 per cent of professionals found the information provided by parents enabled them to make a more detailed evaluation of risk. Although there is general recognition of the importance of working together with family members during the post-registration phase, there are certain situations where it becomes necessary to exclude family members from the core group. These exclusion criteria need to be considered carefully, as Mittler (1993) found exclusions create mistrust, anger and disillusionment, leading to an increased probability of re-abuse.

Few authorities in our study had developed clear criteria for making decisions regarding exclusion (Calder and Horwath, 1996; Horwath and Calder, 1998). It is left to each core group to determine when to exclude, with no clear framework on which to base its decision. Any exclusion criterion should be made explicit and should include guidance on whether it is appealable. It is important that professionals and the family have a common understanding of situations in which the criteria can apply. The decision to exclude should only be taken in exceptional circumstances and should only be taken either by the chair of the initial conference or a team manager. Calder (1991) has set out explicit criteria for family exclusion as follows:

- threats of violence to professionals;
- the need to have some discussion without the parents being present: for example, if information is being discussed that may be used in legal proceedings;
- the need to share and resolve any professional differences;
- parental refusal to cooperate with any plans to protect the child;
- instances where parental attendance would be detrimental to the child's welfare;
- instances where the meeting could not function with both parents present;
- instances where parental attendance would prejudice a full and proper consideration of the child's interests;
- cases where attendance may prejudice the parents' own legal position;
- cases where the parents may seriously disrupt the conduct of the meeting;
- situations where the child and/or non-abusing parent do not wish the abuser to attend;
- instances where the parent would be unable to cope adequately, perhaps owing to very low self-esteem;
- instances where the parent's attendance may inhibit the contribution of a participant and/or prejudice possible legal proceedings.

The exclusion of parents should not be considered permanent. Indeed, Calder (1990) has argued that parents should be excluded only for the purpose of planning for a more sensitive way to include them. The original exclusion must not be used as a mechanism for opting parents out of the process. Exclusions should be regularly reviewed with the aim of working towards including the family member when it seems appropriate. If family members are excluded, they should be informed of this, as well as the outcome of the meeting and the proposed child protection plan, in writing. Consideration should also be given to alternative ways in which they could contribute, such as by letter or tape, or via a worker representative.

## Promoting young people's attendance

> Listen to the children. People think children haven't got an opinion or a voice and they have. (NCH/Action for Children, 1994: 49).

This is the recommendation of a young person who was sexually abused. It reflects the philosophy behind the United Nations Convention on the Rights of the Child signed by the British government in 1991. Article 12 states that young people should have opportunities to express a view on matters concerning themselves. This is incorporated into the Children Act 1989 which has, as a fundamental principle, that the wishes and feelings of the child should be ascertained. It is reinforced in *Working Together*, which recommends that these principles underpin child protection practice and that workers should ensure that children participate in the process of investigation, assessment, planning and review (DoH, 1991).

However, despite legislation and guidance, children and young people are still not seen as individuals and given a voice (Davies *et al.*, 1996). This would seem to occur for a number of reasons. Professionals in our study presumed that only those over the age of 14 were old enough to participate (Calder and Horwath, 1996; forthcoming). In addition, they indicated that they did little proactively to encourage child participation (Calder and Horwath, forthcoming). Schofield and Thoburn (1996) found that workers tended to see children's participation as a problem to be overcome, rather than the basis of good practice. Eaton (1996) concludes that workers lack confidence in their ability to work with children and consequently pay lip service to the participation of children in the child protection process.

We found that very few ACPCs had given any consideration to ways of empowering young people to participate in the core group. The general view was that, if they were over 14 and wanted to attend, this would be 'allowed', but little thought had been given by any ACPC to facilitate proactively a child's participation. Unfortunately, this is very limiting, given the small number of young people over the age of 14 on the child protection register. We found that only 8 per cent of ACPCs routinely invited young people to the core group, 50 per cent did so occasionally, whilst 5 per cent *never* invited them. Furthermore, two-thirds of ACPCs had not considered facilitating the young person's attendance at the core group, although they would consider providing support if required. Only 55 per cent of young people were allowed to bring a supporter with them. Most ACPCs tend to rely on the initiative of the social worker or a direct request to attend from a young person.

In her sample, Firth (1995) found that children attended four out of 25 core group meetings, often by default – for example, when child care arrangements fell through or when the meeting was held in the family home. In cases where the child's attendance was unplanned it became disruptive, so care has to be taken against resistant parents using the child as a diversionary tactic. Mittler (1993) found that two-thirds of professionals felt that children should be excluded from some, or parts, of the meeting. However, those young people who did attend felt that their attendance had a positive effect on others, mainly their parents. Of those who expressed their views, 60 per cent did feel that they were listened to and agreed with the decisions made. Others continued to find difficulties expressing their views at the meeting, either through embarrassment, fear of upsetting their parents, fear of losing control and causing offence or fear of being overwhelmed by the adults.

We feel that the core group should consider ways of proactively engaging children and young people. After all, they are the focus of the plan and, whilst a distinction must be made between hearing their views and acting on them, they should be allowed a voice. Box 2.5 provides points to consider in terms of promoting participation.

**Box 2.5 Participation**

Do the young people themselves want to attend?
Are they of sufficient age and understanding to make sense of and contribute to the core group? (Calder and Horwath, 1996, found that those under ten were generally felt to be too young, those between 11 and 14 could attend after 'assessment', and those over 14 were presumed appropriate to attend.)
Are they willing and able to contribute?
Are there ways in which their participation could be enhanced, for example through the use of a supporter?
Is any potential emotional damage likely to occur?
If the young person does not wish to attend, are there other ways in which their views and opinions can be considered at the core group, for example by using tapes, letters or video?
What preparation and by whom is required to facilitate the young person's attendance?

It is only if professionals communicate with each other that they are able to work together effectively to protect a child. We hope a protocol that addresses the areas identified above will provide an effective basis for open communication. Preparatory work with young people has to attend to both practical and emotional preparation. Calder and Horwath (forthcoming) suggest that workers use the following checklists to deal with these tasks.

1 *Practical preparation*
Establish the following:
- Why the core group is meeting.
- Who will be present.

- What should happen, including the process, possible outcomes and the purpose of the child protection register.
- Where the meeting is to be held (allowing participants to view the venue in advance).
- Details concerning seating.
- How the information will be communicated (via reports and questions managed through the chair).
- What right of reply or general comment will be available.
- How participation of family members will be conducted by the chairperson during the meeting.
- The timing of the meeting and the possibility of any breaks.

2 *Emotional preparation*
- Give consideration to the age and understanding of the young person.
- Make sure that communication is clear, jargon-free and to the point.
- Make sure that explanations of the purpose endeavour to prevent the unexpected happening at the meeting.
- Take into account how the young people might respond – for example, by reassuring them that distress in such situations is natural.
- Clarify, at this point, whether they still want to attend!!

3 *The young person's participation*
- Help them to articulate their views, whether these be expressed orally, by means of drawings, audiotape, videotape or in writing (which you can read on their behalf).
- Don't coerce them to attend against their wishes. (Adapted from Taylor, 1996.)

## The child protection review

As outlined above, the core group has a responsibility to report to the child protection review. Concerns have been expressed over the blurring of remits between the child protection review and the core group (Summerhill and Frost, 1994). Mittler (1993) found confusion regarding the purpose of the two meetings. For example, there was a lack of clarity regarding the powers of each forum to alter the child protection plan or take responsibility for deregistration. *Working Together* is explicit about the role of the child protection review. The purpose is to 'Review the arrangements for the protection of the child, examine the current level of risk and ensure he or she continues to be adequately protected, consider whether the inter-agency co-ordination is functioning effectively and to review the plan' (DoH, 1991: 42).

We now elaborate on the purpose outlined above and translate this into tasks which each child protection review should attend to.

## Review arrangements for the protection of the child and examine current levels of risk

Members need to examine the plan, re-evaluate the risks to the child, ascertain the progress of the family and see if any further action needs to be taken to protect the child via registration (Giller *et al.* 1992). The review should ensure that the core group is focusing on the critical aspects of the plan and whether a different approach is required. The review should ensure that the core group has obtained quality information and then assessed and processed it in an appropriate way. The core group may have assessed risk, but the review needs to ensure that it is being managed effectively. Case management is clearly an explicit review function.

## Review the protection plan

The review is responsible for examining the plan. This should include assessing the quality of information received and ways in which it has been used within the assessment. Consideration should be given to aspects where the information itself or the way in which it has been processed is weak. The review needs to evaluate risk to the child, identifying any hazards. Consideration also needs to be given to family strengths and any change that has occurred and is likely to occur. The review has a role in recommending alternative approaches that could be used in working with the family.

However, Gibbons *et al.* (1995) found that the review was very rarely proactive and rescinded the original plan in only 8 per cent of cases and this reflects the reality that many plans are endorsed without critical review, thus accentuating any early weaknesses. Gibbons *et al.* also found that the degree of risk to the child was explored in only 64 per cent of cases, there was reference back to the original plan in 80 per cent of cases and in 50 per cent of cases they found some or considerable progress in implementing the plan.

## Ensure that inter-agency coordination is functioning effectively

The review has to combat any insularity and dominance by any one professional (Hallett, 1995), thus promoting continuing inter-agency coordination. It can also model shared responsibilities by going to a core group member other than the keyworker for information (Firth, 1995).

The review should ensure that the core group is clear regarding its delegated tasks and boundaries of responsibility and that prescribed time scales are followed. The review can delegate certain tasks to the core group, such as processing a return home, as long as this is explicit and agreed.

## Deregistration

Gibbons *et al.* (1995) found that reviews were not always held within six months of registration and this held up deregistration in nearly half the cases in her study. Infrequent reviewing can lead to the child protection register being a static list of names (Creighton, 1990). There should be a presumption of deregistration at each review unless there is a continuing need for an inter-agency child protection plan. Should registration continue, the review can ask the core group for a view on how long registration should last and for a timetable of action in resolving any child protection issues that remain outstanding. The review should also specify the objectives that still need to be achieved.

Although the review has been described as an 'expanded core group with an independent chair' (Hallett, 1995), it must aim to expose any deficiencies in the plan and reformulate it accordingly. Review is a time for reaffirming or revising goals, plans and tasks and, if necessary, negotiating a new plan. Members of the review must ensure that the goals are clearly stated, reasonable and appropriate and that the services on offer meet the family's needs. All cases should be reviewed regularly, even where a child protection plan exists and is working well.

## The advantages of core groups

- They can encourage and progress closer multidisciplinary working and early evaluation of problems – addressing professionally dangerous practice.
- They provide an excellent forum for promoting professional cooperation – ensuring that a multidisciplinary protection plan is frequently evaluated and refined, by offering a framework in which detailed negotiations can take place as to what is needed and can be done, in a practicable and realistic way.
- They provide a framework for collective inputs and a move away from doing or saying 'their own thing'.
- They bring a common language to all meetings related to child protection to eliminate or avoid duplication.
- They offer a more informal environment than the conference, thus increasing the contributions of all parties to the process. They offer a mechanism by which family and professionals can get to know each

other over time and develop relationships to overcome the initial confrontational approach that is inevitable at the investigative stage. They also reduce the possibility of manipulation by the family.

- They provide a framework of working towards a partnership that is effective, protective and empowering rather than paternalistic, but which nonetheless retains authority for 'decisive action' when families' actions endanger children.
- They streamline the child protection system, by selecting (collating) information which needs to be discussed in the conference forum. (**Note**: we should be concerned where information is shared for the first time at conferences.)
- They make effective use of time and resources across the board, positively streamlining the administrative functions in the ever expanding system (if a proforma is used). (Adapted from Calder, 1998.)

## Summary

Firth (1995) points out, that if the initial child protection conference is said to be the formal expression of working together, then core groups are working together in action. In this chapter we have utilised examples of innovative practice, procedures and practice guidance to provide a practice framework for post-registration practice, centring upon the core group. Consideration has been given to the role of the initial conference in setting the agenda for work with the child and their family when the child's name is placed on the child protection register. The tasks for the core group have been outlined and consideration has been given to the importance of process in terms of achieving these tasks. The authors advocate the use of a core group protocol to ensure clarity of task and process. The chapter concluded with a discussion regarding the role of the child protection review.

Recommendations have been made in this chapter regarding ways of developing existing post-registration practice guidance, on the basis that ACPCs who have developed policies have noted immediate benefits (Horwath and Calder, 1998), showing that core groups have much unharnessed potential. Crossby (1992) found that, where core groups are structured and organised properly, they are the most effective way of protecting the child, but, if they are not organised properly, people can be lulled into a false sense of security and children are left unprotected. This position has been reinforced by the Social Services Inspectorate which found that core group working was beginning to increase the influence of social workers in the multidisciplinary arena and that this, in turn, accelerated the coordination of tasks in this developing forum (SSI, 1993).

Core groups are clearly the embodiment of working to-gether, although they are a long way from modelling a corporate responsibility for a child's protection.

Firth (1995) identified the main ingredients of core group meetings: clarity of aims and purpose, clear plans, open communication, shared responsibility, understanding of, and respect for, one another and commitment. She also found that most people had a very clear idea of what made core groups effective. The main challenge for the future is how to translate this into practice. Indeed, Calder and Barratt (1997) found that the role and function of the core group still required further clarification and that shared responsibility is not filtering through to daily practice, with the social worker still bearing a greater share of the inter-agency responsibility for child protection. Social workers have expressed concern that the core group is a high-profile public relations exercise for inter-agency working, but one where they are faced with the anxieties of professionals rather than feedback on their identified part in the plan. Each ACPC area must follow a clear process if they are to redress any confusion and create an enabling environment for core group development (see Figure 2.1).

In the following chapters the authors consider professional practice issues within the post-registration stage.

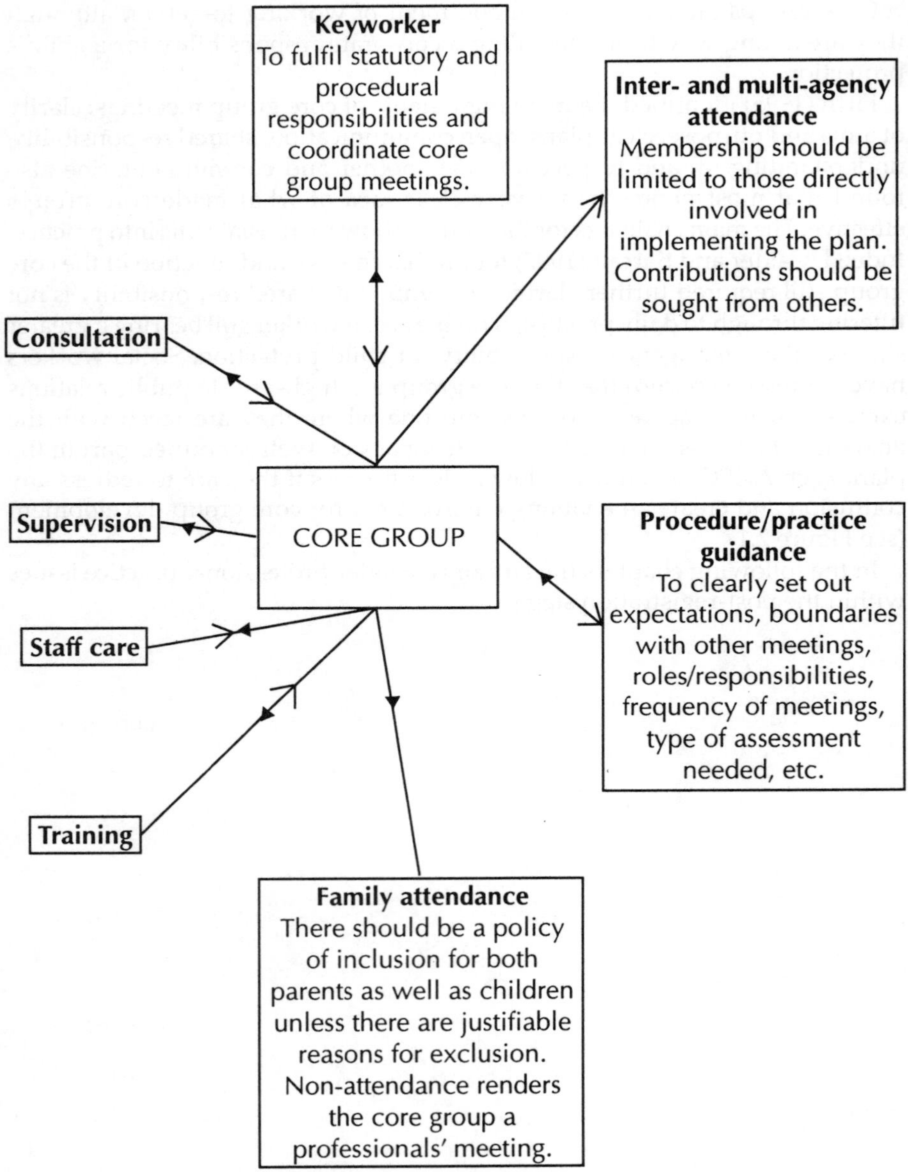


**Figure 2.1 The core group: creating an enabling environment**

# References


Adcock, M. (1995) 'Assessment', in K. Wilson and A. James (eds), *The Child Protection Handbook*, London: Bailliere Tindall.

Audit Commission (1994) 'Seen But Not Heard: Co-ordinating Community Child Health and Social Services for Children in Need', *Detailed Evidence and Guidelines for Managers and Practitioners*, London: HMSO.

Beckett, R.C. (1994) 'Assessment of Sex Offenders', in T. Morrison, M. Erooga and R.C. Beckett (eds), *Sexual Offending Against Children: Assessment and Treatment of Male Abusers*, London: Routledge.

Blyth, E. and Milner, J. (1990) 'The process of inter-agency work', in *Violence against Children Study Group 'Taking Child Abuse Seriously'*, London: Unwin Hyman.

Braye, S. and Preston-Shoot, M. (1992) 'Honourable Intentions: Written Agreements in Welfare Legislation', *Journal of Social Welfare and Family Law*, 6 November: 511–28.

Brunel Social Services Consortium (1988) 'The Professional Management of Child Abuse', unpublished draft report, Uxbridge: Brunel University.

Calder, M.C. (1990) 'Child Protection: Core Groups: Participation not Partnership', *Child Abuse Review*, **4** (2): 12–15.

Calder, M.C. (1991) 'Child Protection Core Groups: Beneficial or Bureaucratic?', *Child Abuse Review*, **5** (2): 26–9.

Calder, M.C. (1995a) 'Towards Good Practice in Child Protection', keynote presentation to a national conference, 'Core Group: Central to Child Protection – Myth or Reality?' Manchester Town Hall, 14 July.

Calder, M.C. (1995b) 'Child Protection: Balancing Paternalism and Partnership', *British Journal of Social Work*, **25** (6): 749–66.

Calder, M.C. (1996) 'Inter-Agency Working in Child Protection: A Review of Local Arrangements in Salford', *Report to ACPC*, March.

Calder, M.C. (1997) *Juveniles and Children who Sexually Abuse: A Guide to Risk Assessment*, Dorset: Russell House Publishing.

Calder, M.C. (1998) 'Understanding and Unlocking the Potential of Core Groups', keynote presentation to Wigan ACPC Development Day, Haigh Hall, 8 May.

Calder, M.C. and Barratt, M. (1997) 'Inter-agency Perspectives on Core Group Practice', *Children and Society*, **11** (4): 209–21.

Calder, M.C. and Horwath, J. (1996) 'National core group sample: analysis of questionnaire responses', unpublished manuscript, Salford ACPC/University of Sheffield.

Calder, M.C. and Horwath, J. (1998) *Working for Children on the Child Protection Register: an inter-agency guide*, Aldershot: Arena.

Calder, M.C. and Horwath, J. (forthcoming) *Passive Partnerships with Families: The Core of Post-Registration Practice?* (submitted for publication).

Charles, M. and Stevenson, O. (1990) *Multidisciplinarity is Different!*, Nottingham: University of Nottingham.

Creighton, S. (1990) *Child Abuse Trends in England and Wales 1988–1990*, London: NSPCC.

Crossby, K. (1992) 'Additional Mechanisms: A Study of Core Groups in Milton Keynes'. unpublished dissertation.

Davies, M., Gerber, P. and Wells, J. (1996) 'Partnership from the Child's Perspective', in D. Platt and D. Shemmings (eds), *Making Enquires into Alleged Child Abuse and Neglect: Partnership with Families*, Brighton: Pennant.

Department of Health (1988) *Protecting Children*, London: HMSO.

Department of Health (1991) *Working Together under the Children Act 1989: A Guide to Arrangements for Inter-agency Co-operation for the Protection of Children from Abuse*, London: HMSO.

Department of Health (1995) *Child Protection: Messages from Research*, London: HMSO.

Eaton, L. (1996) 'Minor Views', *Community Care*, 13–16 June: 22–3.

Farmer, E. and Owen, M. (1995) *Child Protection Practice: Private Risks and Public Remedies. Decision-making, Intervention and Outcome in Child Protection Work*, London: HMSO.
Firth, B. (1995) *Survey of Core Groups in the Rotherham Child Protection Committee Area*, Nottingham: School of Social Studies.
Gibbons, J., Conroy, S. and Bell, C. (1995) *Intervention and Outcome in Child Protection Work: a study of child protection practices in English local authorities*, London: HMSO.
Giller, H., Gormley, C. and Williams, P. (1992) *The Effectiveness of Child Protection Procedures: An Evaluation of Child Protection Procedures in Four ACPC Areas*, Knutsford: Social Information Systems Limited.
Hallett, C. (1995) *Inter-Agency Co-ordination in Child Protection*, London: HMSO.
Hampson, A. (1997) *Children Who Need Protection*, City of Salford Community and Social Services Child Care Manual.
Higginson, S. (1990) 'Distorted Evidence', *Community Care*, 17 May (817): 233–5.
Horwath, J. (1997) 'Child Protection Messages from Research: Issues for Inter-Agency Practice in the Late 1990s', *Northern Ireland Journal of Multi-disciplinary Child Care Practice*, **3** (4): 2–17.
Horwath, J. and Calder, M.C. (1998) 'Working Together to Protect Children on the Child Protection Register – Myth or Reality?', *British Journal of Social Work*, **28** (6): 879–95.
IMPACT (1993) *Parental Participation in Child Protection Conferences – An Independent Evaluation for the Rochdale Area Child Protection Committee*, Cheshire: IPMC.
Johnson, P. (1991) 'Core Groups in Child Protection', unpublished dissertation.
Katz, I. (1997) *Current Issues in Comprehensive Assessment*, London: NSPCC.
Lewis, A., Shemmings, D. and Thoburn, J. (1992) 'Participation in Practice – Involving Families in Child Protection', trainer's pack, Norwich: University of East Anglia.
Marsh, P. (1994) 'Family Partners: An Evaluation of Family Group Conferences in Child Welfare', in J. Tunnard (ed.), London: Family Rights Group: 17–24.
Mittler, H. (1993) 'The Participation of Children and Young People in Child Protection Core Group and Review Meetings: An Evaluation of Practice in a Northern Metropolitan Borough', unpublished MSc thesis, Manchester University.
Morrison, T. (1995), 'The Core Group: A Catalyst for Change', keynote presentation to the national conference 'Core Groups – Central to Child Protection: Myth or Reality?' Manchester Town Hall, 14 July.
NCH/Action for Children (1994) *Messages from Children: Children's Evaluations of the Professional Response to Child Sexual Abuse*, NCH Action For Children.
Newton, L.H. (1982) 'Collective Responsibility in Health Care', *Journal of Medicine and Philosophy*, **7** (1): 11–21.
Parker, R., Ward, H., Jackson, S., Aldgate, J. and Wedge, P. (1991) *Looking after Children: Assessing Outcomes in Child Care*, London: HMSO.
Perlman, M. and Whitworth, J.M. (1988) 'Group Process and Interprofessional Communication: The Human Aspects of Teamwork', in D.C. Bross, R.D. Knigman, M.R. Lennherr, D.A. Rosenberg and B.D. Summitt (eds), *The New Child Protection Team Handbook*, New York: Garland Publishers: 299–331.
Schofield, G. and Thoburn, J. (1996) *Child Protection: The Voice of the Child in Decision-making*, Institute for Public Policy Research.
SSI (1993) *Inspecting for Quality: Evaluating Performance in Child Protection. A Framework for the Inspection of Local Authority Social Services Practice and Systems*, London: HMSO.
Summerhill, J. and Frost, N. (1994) *The Operation of Core Groups in the Wakefield Child Protection Committee Area: An Evaluation*, Leeds: Department of Adult Continuing Education.
Taylor, M. (1996) 'Understanding and Improving the Participation of Young People at Child Protection Conferences', presentation to the 11th National Conference on child abuse and neglect, Dublin, August 1996.
Thoburn, J., Lewis, A. and Shemmings, D. (1995) *Paternalism or Partnership? Family Involvement in the Child Protection Process*, London: HMSO.

# 3 Assessment and planning

*Christine Samra-Tibbetts and Barry Raynes*

In this chapter, consideration is given to:

- the current guidance and expectations of government when undertaking comprehensive assessments;
- the limitations of the commonly prescribed documentation and materials;
- a framework for undertaking assessments within the core group, with a discussion of the six key stages and the provision of useful tools and techniques; and
- a framework for shifting our emphasis towards better utilisation of the information gathered.

## Introduction

What is a comprehensive assessment? When would you do one? Why and how? These are questions which currently elicit a wide range of responses from child care social workers, let alone from a multi-agency group of professionals. *Working Together* (DoH, 1991a) states: 'on registration of a child, the initial plan should include a comprehensive assessment. Its purpose is to acquire a full understanding of the child and family situation in order to provide a sound basis for decisions about future actions'. The SSI document, Evaluating Performance in Child Protection (SSI, 1993) reinforces this by setting the following standard:

a comprehensive assessment of the child and family's situation, which includes contributions from other agencies, is undertaken when a child's name is placed on the child protection register. This assessment informs the child protection plan. Assessment is a continuing activity throughout the child protection process.

Despite these expectations, Reconstruct, a training agency which has provided training on child care assessments since 1991, has found that workers are frequently unclear about what is meant by 'doing an assessment', or what the components of an assessment are and, because of this, are unlikely to clarify with their coworkers and the family and child with whom they are working the purpose and process of the assessment.

We find that assessment work is often carried out in an unstructured and unsystematic way and that workers tend to focus on gathering information, at the expense of testing and evaluating data, reaching decisions and producing solutions. Despite the requirement that assessment should be a multidisciplinary activity, it is clear from *Messages from Research* (DoH, 1995a) that post-registration assessments are carried out largely by social workers, working alone, or as part of a same agency group. Professionals, such as teachers and health visitors, may be expected to monitor the child and family, but are rarely seen to be part of a team that works together to evaluate all the information gathered and to reach decisions corporately about the needs of, and risks to, a child.

Perhaps these findings are not surprising. Until recently, there has been a paucity of useful written material on assessments and little attention has been given by social services departments and other agencies involved in post-registration assessments to ensure that their workers understand the task and have an agreed format, tools and techniques to assist them.

## Approaches to post-registration assessment

The nationally recognised format for comprehensive assessments is *Protecting Children: A Guide for Social Workers undertaking a Comprehensive Assessment*, commonly known as the 'Orange Book' (DoH, 1988). Published before the Children Act 1989, it represents principles and practice that are now outmoded. Writers, researchers and workers have all questioned the value of this guide, for a number of reasons.

### Insensitivity to difference

Much of the 'Orange Book' thinking is based on theories which have been questioned as being ethnocentric and outdated (such as those of Bowlby, Carter, Fahlberg, Sheridan and Winnicott). McBeath and Webb (1990) criticise the book for assessing families against the norms of middle-class, white families, and Phillips and Dutt (1990) argue that the impact of racism on the assessment process is not acknowledged. Similarly, there is little to assist workers assessing single parents, gay and lesbian couples or any other families where difference and discrimination are issues.

Socioeconomic issues are given little acknowledgement, so the impact of poverty, poor housing and unemployment are not well addressed by the assessment framework. In addition, complex issues for workers in assessing parents with mental health problems (Falkov, 1996), parents with learning disabilities (McGaw and Sturmey, 1994) and parents who misuse drugs and alcohol (Coleman and Cassell, 1995) need to be identified and workers provided with information about how to gain specialist materials and skills.

## Involvement of children and young people

The NSPCC booklet, *Current Issues in Comprehensive Assessment* (Katz, 1997) points out that the 'Orange Book' contains little about children's participation, focusing more or less exclusively on parents and their abilities. Of the 167 questions in the book, only five are meant to be asked of the child himself or herself. Many practitioners find this incongruous with later Department of Health guidance and this omission undermines the authority of the book. In response to the lack of child focus, a number of workers choose to use the headings provided by the welfare checklist in the Children Act as the basis for their assessment of the child, in order to ensure that the child's voice is heard. The issue of involving children and young people in the assessment is discussed further by Christie and Mittler in Chapter 6 of the present volume.

## Involvement of parents/carers

Because the 'Orange Book' preceded the Children Act 1989, the partnership principle was not included, whereas sections exist on the use of authority and control and dangerous families. This promotes an approach which assumes that practitioners need to have a high level of control over the families they are assessing. Workers do, at times, need to employ such an approach in order to protect children, but it is now recognised that the most effective way of enhancing a child's welfare and effecting change within the family is by establishing partnership with the parents. Again, Christie and Mittler expand on this point.

## The questionnaire format

The 'Orange Book' assessment format consists largely of a questionnaire: 167

questions to be asked of the family, linked with observations of the child. Many workers dislike this 'question and answer' approach, preferring to use genograms, ecomaps and other assessment tools and techniques to gather information from families, and then use the questions as a checklist, to ensure that all relevant areas have been addressed. We will consider some useful assessment tools and techniques later in this chapter.

Other practitioners, in our experience, adapt the questions they find inappropriate. The 'Orange Book' acknowledges that 'the more experienced may wish to modify and experiment with the format', but contradicts this by going on to say that 'the formulation and phraseology have been carefully devised to try to avoid putting leading questions or suggesting there is a right or wrong answer. Changes and supplementary questions should, therefore, be considered with care'. However, we suggest that many of the questions are inappropriate and leading – for example, '72c. When you were a child were you ever sexually abused?' – and that workers, experienced or not, should always ask themselves why they need to ask a question and, if it is relevant, how it should best be presented. Quite clearly, each individual case requires very careful individual selection of the questions needing to be answered, rather than a blanket approach being assumed.

### Lack of a detailed framework for evaluating the information gathered

While many pages of the 'Orange Book' are devoted to information gathering, the complex task of evaluating the assessment as a basis for planning is given one and a half pages plus a planning table. It has already been noted that many practitioners fail to give sufficient time to this stage of the assessment process, and it is suggested that any framework needs to provide workers with detailed tools and techniques for this. These concerns have resulted in many agencies and individual practitioners adapting the guide or developing their own formats.

The Department of Health has, for some time, acknowledged that adaptations do need to be made and we understand that the 'Orange Book' is currently being revised, although it is as yet unclear what type of framework this may provide and when it will be available.

## New initiatives

Recently, there have been a number of initiatives which have led to a refocusing on assessment work. The concerns raised by *Messages from Research* about the high numbers of families drawn into the child protection process where the child is found not to be suffering significant harm has led many authorities to question the assessment process. This has resulted in ACPCs developing more rigorous formats which address both need and risk. Some have followed the Association of Directors of Social Services (ADSS) recommendation quoted in *Children still in Need* (Harper, 1996) to explore 'a single, robust assessment and care management framework for all expressions of concern for children and families' and developed a general format which can be used for all child care assessments. Others have taken a lead from the 'Looking After Children' (LAC) materials (Parker *et al.*, 1991) and required workers to consider the seven developmental dimensions identified in these materials to assess children living in the community. (We discuss the LAC materials in a little more detail later in the chapter.)

## A framework for undertaking assessments within a core group

In response to the lack of appropriate assessment materials, Reconstruct developed a framework, supported by tools and techniques, to assist workers in developing assessment skills. It does not provide a format as such, because many agencies either have developed their own or expect workers to use an appropriately adapted version of the 'Orange Book'. Rather, this framework focuses on the process that the core group of professionals need to follow in order to work together effectively with the child and family. It draws on the Social Services Inspectorate's standards and criteria for assessment work (SSI, 1993), on recent research, and on the care management model utilised in adult services (DoH, 1991b). It enables workers to address both need and risk, to gather and evaluate evidence, to make decisions, develop care plans and offer a coordinated and needs-led response.

The process for all child care assessments drawing on the care management model is given in Figure 3.1. When applying this to comprehensive assessments, the cause for concern – the immediate risk to the child – will have been clarified by the section 47 investigation and the initial child protection conference. The initial child protection conference will then develop a broad plan to assess the functioning of the family, the longer-term levels of risk/need and the potential for change. This is set out in detail in Chapter 2 of the present volume. The initial case conference should outline the assessment tasks and identify the core group of professionals who are to be involved. These workers are then responsible for gathering and evaluating information, reaching conclusions about the level of harm and the child's needs, suggesting possible solutions and devising the child protection plan. The child protection

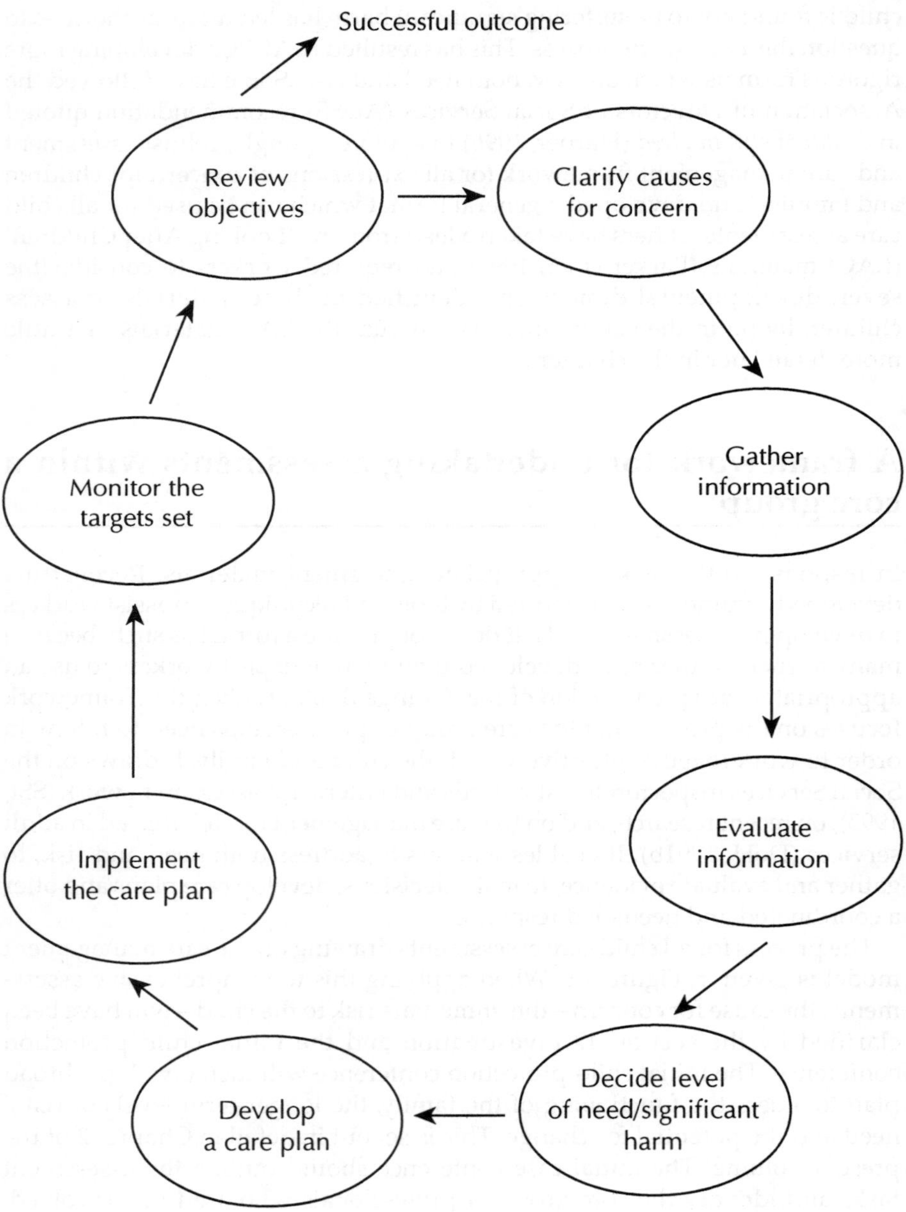


**Figure 3.1 The process of child care assessments**

review should independently evaluate the core groups findings, take a final decision on the way forward, outline further plans where necessary, and give directions on the implementation, monitoring and reviewing of the child protection plan. Assessment is frequently a continuous, circular process. Implementing and monitoring the plan may raise further concerns which require evaluation and action. These later stages of implementing the plan, monitoring the targets set and reviewing objectives are generally not well addressed by the child care services. Further debate is required, but space dictates that we focus on the earlier stages of the process.

Figure 3.2 outlines the six stages that the core group will need to address in order to produce evidence and recommendations for the initial child protection conference, child protection review or court, and it is these stages that are discussed in detail in this chapter.

## Planning stage

Where a group of professionals, particularly those who do not regularly work together, are jointly to undertake an assessment, they need to agree, not just how they will assess the family, but also how they will work together effectively. In our experience, workers tend to concentrate on the tasks they need to undertake in respect of the child and the family, but spend little time considering how they will maximise the group's combined skills and knowledge, and support and complement one another's work. In addition, consideration should be given to developing strategies for resolving difficulties and differences of opinion. It may well be legitimate to meet initially as a 'professionals only' group to do this. Parents must be consulted and informed about decisions taken in 'professionals only' meetings (unless this would jeopardise the welfare of the child), but many of the discussions which the core group needs to have, such as on what assessment model is to be used or strategies for resolving differences of opinion between professionals, are not discussions which many parents should, or often want, to be involved in.

The issues which need to be covered in order to facilitate an effective interprofessional assessment are as discussed below.

### The type of assessment required

The initial child protection conference should give directions to the core group regarding the areas to be addressed in an assessment, as well as the type of assessment needed (Calder, 1996). In practice, core groups may only receive very general directions or simply be requested to 'do a comprehensive assessment', and so need to agree in detail what areas require assessment. The core

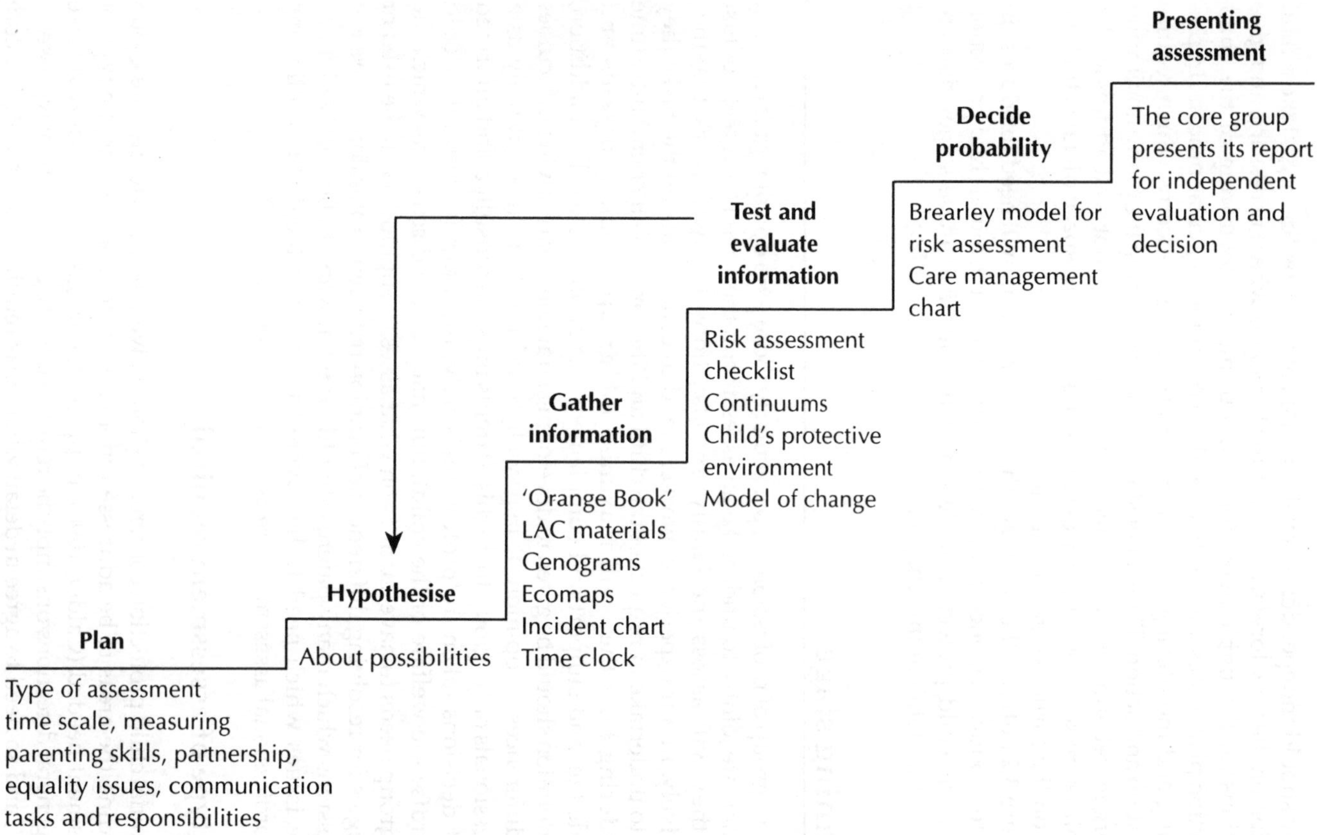


**Figure 3.2 A framework for undertaking assessments within a core group**

group should identify which assessment model will best meet the specific assessment needs of the individual family and children. Group members will also need to clarify what is meant by an assessment. To a teacher, the request for an assessment of a child may have a very different meaning from what the social worker expects. Many professionals may not know the 'Orange Book' and will need clarification if it is to be used. If alternative materials are to be used, these should be discussed, and copies of this material should be circulated to each core group member to ensure consistency of approach, work and subsequent evaluation.

## The time scale

Time scales for assessments will vary according to the complexity of each case. Everyone involved, including the family, should be clear about how long the assessment will take and what is expected of them at different stages. This is important for the following reasons:

1. decisions about the child should not be unnecessarily delayed;
2. the family will feel more empowered if they have a clear understanding of the time parameters and when decisions are likely to be taken;
3. professionals contributing to the assessment need to be clear about how long they have for information gathering, when and where to provide information and when and how this will be evaluated.

The 'Orange Book' indicates that an assessment should take around 35 hours to complete, but this is idealistic when it does not allow for the engagement of the family, the inter-agency network or the complexity of many cases.

## Measuring parenting skills

It is important that the family and the professionals involved in an assessment know what indicators will be used to evaluate the family; that is, what is a reasonable level of parenting for the children in this particular family? There will not always be a consistent view within the core group. Agreement will need to be reached on what is a 'good enough' level of parenting so that the family can understand what is expected of them, what they will have to do to meet those targets, and what are likely to be the thresholds for deregistration or, in some cases, legal action.

In cases where these issues have not been discussed and some level of consensus has not been reached, core groups can become split and unable to function, assessments can be flawed and decision making impaired. If dissension remains within the group, supervisory input or an early return to conference will be required (see Chapter 9). The process of discussing this issue will, in itself, be helpful to the group in planning their intervention with the family.

## Partnership

Another area where core groups require a consistent approach is the level of partnership which can be safely achieved with the family. Research by Thoburn *et al.* (1995) states:

> It is important to note that in the early stages of child protection work, there are few cases where it is possible to involve parents fully as partners, many where serious obstacles will be encountered because of the nature of the case, and a small number where even to attempt to involve a family member would be inappropriate.

However, they concluded:

> whilst failure to work in partnership can sometimes be attributed to aspects of the case itself or characteristics of family members, differences between cases where family members were informed, involved and consulted and those where they were not were almost always attributable to either agency policy and procedures or the social work practice, or both together.

The investigative stage of child protection intervention is often stressful for parents and professionals who may view parents' initial anger and/or resistance to intervention as immutable. But parents' reactions to intervention can change. Research by Farmer and Owen (1995) showed that, while 70 per cent of parents were unhappy with the treatment they received up to the initial child protection conference, 70 per cent of these became more sympathetic to professional concern and came to regard the enquiry as having been beneficial. Thus there is a ladder of partnership, and families will be on a different 'step of the ladder' at different times and with different professionals. These steps can be described as follows:

- full partnership
- participation
- involvement
- consultation
- keeping fully informed
- no partnership.

At the beginning of an assessment, core group workers will need to consider how best to engage the family, and what level of partnership can be achieved to promote partnership during assessment. There will always be cases where the family refuse to engage, and a small number where to attempt to involve a family actively could put a child further at risk. But strategies should be developed to engage every family as productively as possible. Core groups need to:

- ensure that the family understand the purpose, function and time scale of the assessment;
- give clear information about the reason for the assessment and what may need to change;
- discuss with the family how to make the assessment appropriate to their particular lifestyle and needs;
- inform families of their rights and what action they can take if they do not receive a satisfactory service;
- prepare families for meetings;
- enable families to contribute to meetings and receive feedback – even when they do not attend;
- keep meetings small and informal – they should be facilitated and recorded, not chaired and minuted;
- avoid professional jargon and produce records and written agreements in user-friendly language;
- recognise that not all families want or are able to be involved in the same way, and that the family that does not attend meetings is not necessarily less committed.

Core group professionals will also need regularly and jointly to assess how effectively they are working in partnership, whether they are all working at a similar level and what is the highest level of partnership they can achieve without jeopardising the welfare of the child. Christie and Mittler develop these issues in Chapter 6 of the present volume.

## Equality issues

In order to empower families, it is important to take an approach which assesses both strengths and weaknesses. MacDonald (1991) provides a useful tool for working with the strengths of black families which we have adapted for work with all families, particularly those that have experienced discrimination. This is shown in Table 3.1.

## Tasks and responsibilities

The initial child protection conference should broadly outline the areas of responsibility for the workers. The core group will need to consider this in

**Table 3.1 Working with the strengths of families**

*Aims*

To enable participants to recognise the strengths of families.
To examine critically the effects of the 'weakness' model of social work practice.
To analyse critically the response of social work agencies to families where there is difference and may be discrimination.
To work towards a model of empowerment in social work practice.

*Weaknesses*

| | |
|---|---|
| 1 Pathological assumption | families labelled as aggressive, abusive |
| 2 Cultural stereotypes | drug user = bad parent<br>learning disabled = inadequate parent |
| 3 Blaming the victim | single parent = inability to cope<br>return to work = uncaring parent |
| 4 Professional superiority | we know best |
| 5 Knowledge base of social work | institutional care = inadequate parents<br>nuclear family model best |
| 6 Power relationship | inherent imbalance between parent and professionals |
| 7 Cultural superiority | black parents cannot cope because there are a large number of black children in care |
| 8 Racism, sexism, ablism heterosexualism, ageism etc. | pervades the whole process |
| 9 Social work action | worst – removal of child |

| | |
|---|---|
| *Strengths* | |
| 1 Recognition of life experience | surviving care as a single parent |
| 2 Understanding of discrimination | learned hard way about being disabled, the experience of being black, gay or lesbian within this society |
| 3 Sensitivity to cultural pride | hearing impaired parents' right to use own language (sign language) |
| 4 Positive self-image | use of pictures, play material and so on depicting different life styles. |
| 5 Knowledge of family/support system | holistic approach |
| 6 Role model | children in care can parent well, get jobs, survive |
| 7 Redress power imbalance | work in partnership with parents, break down 'them and us' divisions |
| 8 Work against discrimination | stop stereotyping, use positive images, accept different norms and different, not inferior, acknowledge worker's power base |
| 9 Social work action | anti-discriminatory practice promotion of welfare needs of child |

*Source*: Adapted from the model produced in MacDonald (1991).

greater detail, to ensure that workers are able to carry out the tasks, do not duplicate work and work in a complementary way. Families also need to be set tasks and a written agreement (see Chapter 2 of the present volume for guidance) and/or responsibility chart (see Table 3.2) should be drawn up to record who is accountable for undertaking the various tasks. These have been very useful in relaying information to child protection reviews alongside more detailed and structured written reports. Calder explores this issue further in Chapter 7. Both authors agree that a good assessment will address issues of equality, including the following:

- Do family members need particular resources – for example, accessible venues, loop systems, child care facilities?
- How will the race and gender of the workers impact on the assessment? Can family members be better engaged by using certain workers? Will consideration be given to race and gender when tasks are allocated to core group professionals?
- Is the assessment focusing on women – can men who are significant to the children be engaged?
- Are there issues which require specialist input to assess certain aspects of the family – for example, parents with mental health problems and learning disability?
- Does any member of the family have a first language which is not English. If so, can the assessment be carried out in that language? If not, it is likely that the assessment will provide an inaccurate picture, thereby putting service users at a disadvantage and children at risk.
- If there are no workers who can undertake the assessment in the appropriate language an interpreter must be used. Check out that the interpreter has the same first language as the family/service user and is acceptable to the family. Make sure that the same interpreter can be used throughout the assessment and involve them in all planning meetings so that they understand the tasks and processes involved.

## Communication

Most communication between professionals, when they are not actually in the core group meeting, is usually channelled, verbally or in writing, through the keyworker. Of course, concerns about further harm must always be relayed direct to the keyworker, or, in his or her absence, to a previously agreed person. The problem is that, if the keyworker is the central focus, all information is passed through that one person, and the dynamic outlined in Figure 3.3 occurs. Keyworkers thus control information and take decisions, resulting in other professionals feeling they merely provide the information.

**Table 3.2 Tasks and responsibilities chart**

| Tasks | Parent | Social worker | Teacher | Family centre worker | Health visitor | Police |
|---|---|---|---|---|---|---|
| Monitor child's sleeping arrangements | | | | | monthly | |
| Work on appropriate methods of disciplining | weekly | | | weekly | | |
| Check child has not been left alone | | at random | | | | at random |
| Monitor hygiene | | when visiting | daily; inform social worker of concerns | | monthly; inform social worker of concerns | |
| Work on parenting skills | with health visitor and family centre | | | weekly | monthly | |
| Monitor height and weight | | | | | monthly; inform social worker of concerns | |
| Monitor nursery school attendance | | | daily; inform social worker of unauthorised absences | | | |

Keyworkers can feel overloaded, while other professionals feel marginalised. It can also be a dangerous dynamic, because, as Reder *et al.* (1993) identify, when the pivotal worker is absent, inter-agency communication is more likely to break down.

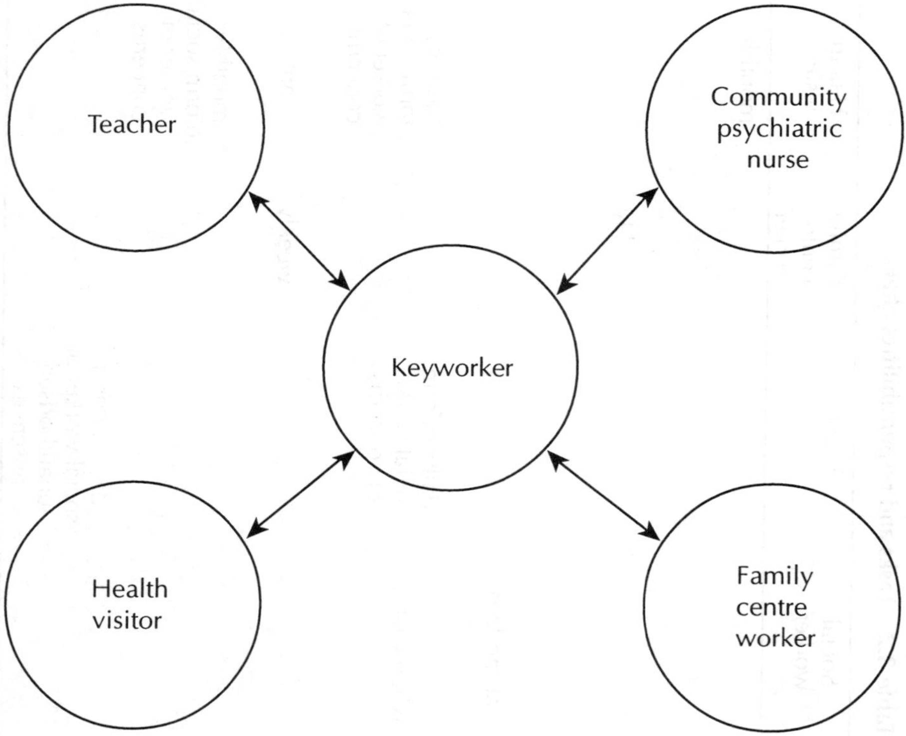


**Figure 3.3 Core group communications dynamic**

Core groups need to have rules about how they communicate. Could sub-groups take responsibility for completing parts of an assessment, and feed back their overall findings to the keyworker? What responsibility does every member of the core group have for ensuring that action will be taken to protect a child? These are issues which could be included in the core group protocol, agreed between professionals at the start of their work (see Chapter 2 of the present volume for a detailed discussion of a protocol).

To summarise this section, planning is essential to a good assessment, and should address the process of working together as well as the task of assessing the family.

## Hypothesising stage

Child protection investigations are carried out to a tight time scale and focus on immediate risk. Workers at the post-registration stage often remain narrowly focused on proving or disproving whether the immediate risk still exists and fail to consider the broader picture. The core group should consider all the possibilities regarding the harm that the child could be suffering, both within their family and in the wider community. Each hypothesis should be addressed and only discounted when there is clear evidence to support doing so.

While this stage has been placed at the beginning of the assessment process in Figure 3.1, it is important to recognise that this process should be repeated when any new evidence comes to light, which may challenge previously held views.

The following case scenario illustrates the importance of hypothesising.

> Sylvia is a young woman with four children under the age of seven, their ages are one, three, four and six. The six-year old, Amanda, has a learning disability and receives respite care.
>
> Yesterday, at bath time, a member of staff at the respite care unit noticed a red mark which looked like a hand imprint at the top of Amanda's leg. When asked about it, Amanda said that 'mummy smacked her'. Sylvia had previously phoned the unit to say that Amanda had a nappy rash which had left a mark at the top of her legs.

Various hypotheses could be made about this case:

- Sylvia has smacked and injured Amanda and regularly does so because she dislikes and does not want to care for this child.
- Sylvia has smacked and injured Amanda and is likely to do this again because she is under considerable stress.
- Sylvia has smacked and injured Amanda because she is under stress, but is unlikely to do this again if she receives support.
- Sylvia has smacked and injured Amanda, but has never done so before and is unlikely to do so again.
- Another adult within the family has smacked and injured Amanda.
- Another adult within the community, for instance in a school or a respite care unit, has smacked and injured Amanda.
- Another child has injured Amanda.
- Amanda is being sexually abused and the mark has resulted from her being forcibly held down.
- The red mark has been caused by an accidental injury or rough handling.

- The red mark is the result of a self-injury.
- The red mark is nappy rash.
- Amanda calls a range of people 'mummy'.

All of these, or a combination of some of them, are possible. The reason why Amanda stated that her mother had smacked her, if this was not the case, would need further assessment. But whatever has happened, this family is likely to be under considerable stress, and deserves a service which considers all possibilities and provides an appropriate and holistic response to its needs.

## Information gathering stage

Information for the assessment should be gathered from all adults who are significant to the child, plus, of course, from the child himself or herself. The core group will need to be clear about their reasons for approaching people beyond the immediate family. These could include members of the extended family, people who are not relatives but act as carers, such as child minders or friends, workers in voluntary community organisations and other professionals. They can all provide valuable information, but parents need to be aware that they are being asked to contribute and issues of confidentiality will need to be addressed.

There are a range of tools available to assist workers in gathering information, and these are outlined below. Many of the tools can be used equally well with adults and children, but will need to be adapted to meet particular needs, such as the age and understanding of the child or the abilities of parents with learning disabilities. Babies and young children, or children with severe learning disabilities who have limited or no language skills, can be more difficult to assess, but detailed observation using specialist workers such as nursery nurses can provide invaluable information.

### The Orange Book

The components of an assessment outlined in the 'Orange Book' are listed below and provide a useful checklist of areas to address when gathering information.

#### *The causes for concern*

Type of abuse; marital or family conflict/violence; physical, behavioural or emotional problems exhibited by the child; parents' perceptions of the problems and feasibility for change.

### *The child*

Parents' perception; routine and care; early and subsequent history; physical and emotional development; child's perceptions; professionals' perceptions.

### *Family composition*

Family tree; names and ages of all family members; births, marriages, separations, divorces, deaths; details of occupation; places of residence; important life events; relationships/alliances; main carer(s); legal status of child and contact with parents.

### *Individual profile of parents/carers*

Experiences as a child: parenting received, positive relationships, mistreatment, disruptions and other major events; current relationships with birth family/friends/others; health; disabilities; personality/mental disorders; personal strengths; ability to cope with stress/anxiety/frustration; self image; use/effect of alcohol/drugs/substances; religious/cultural beliefs; employment/education and interests.

### *Family relationships and interactions*

History and quality of relationships: stability, commitment, openness, affection, support, communication, ability to resolve conflict; physical or emotional mistreatment between carers; plans to have more children; how parent/carers relate to the children and how siblings relate to each other.

### *Networks*

Relationships and role of extended family, neighbours and friends in supporting or undermining the parent/carer(s); significant persons with whom contact has been lost; religious/community/social organisations offering support.

### *Finance*

Sources of income; any financial difficulties/ability to manage and effects on family; allocation of money within family, any incomes not being claimed.

### *Physical conditions*

Suitability of the family's accommodation (size, facilities and so on); how it meets family's needs; responsibilities for household tasks; any plans to move. The issues covered in each component will not all be appropriate to use with every family, and there may be areas that this format does not address. It is recommended that, because many of the actual questions in the 'Orange Book' are insensitive, workers should give very careful thought to whether the questions are necessary and how they should be asked.

## The 'looking after children' materials

The section on assessing the child in the 'Orange Book' is based on theoretical models that are now seen as somewhat dated and ethnocentric. Some authorities are recommending to staff that when they assess children they make reference to the Department of Health *Looking After Children* materials (Parker *et al.*, 1991). These materials have been developed for children who are being looked after by the local authority in residential or foster care and are used to assess their progress, monitor the quality of the care they receive and make plans for their future. Seven developmental dimensions are identified: (1) health, (2) education, (3) identity, (4) family and social relationships, (5) social presentation, (6) emotional and behavioural development, and (7) self-care skills.

These dimensions are the framework of the assessment formats – the Assessment and Action Records (AARs). These have been produced for six separate age groups up to 18 years, to ensure that the questions asked are age-appropriate and that the issues address developmental changes and needs. Obviously, many of the issues in these records are not relevant to children living in the community, but workers could use the dimensions as general headings and refer to the age-appropriate AAR for providing ideas for the assessment. This would provide an informed and consistent approach to assessing children. Refer to Parker *et al.* (1991) for a more detailed discussion of the issue.

## Genograms

The use of genograms (or family trees) for all post-registration assessments is common in many agencies. Some suggested symbols and structure are given in Figure 3.4. Genograms are particularly good for working with families to clarify complex relationships, to indicate gaps in knowledge and to make visible intergenerational and life cycle issues. They can be used to gather information and to work therapeutically.

As genograms can be powerful in raising painful and suppressed memories, it is important to explain to the family what they are, and what issues they are likely to raise, before undertaking this task. Some of the symbols used can

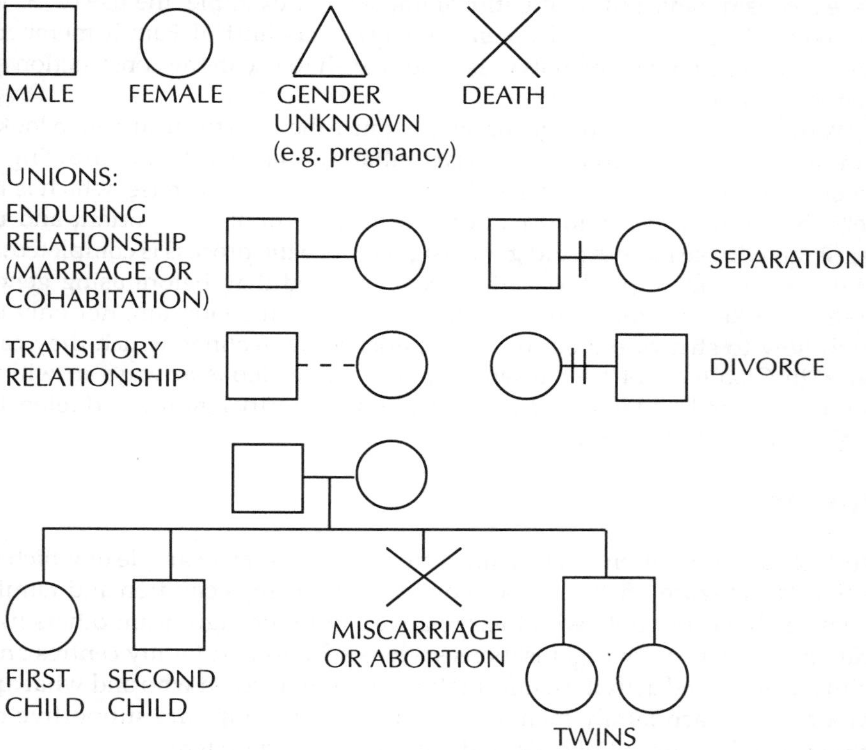


*Dotted lines should be drawn around the people who currently live in the same house*

A genogram or family tree covering three or more generations may be compiled using these symbols. Social workers who have not drawn a genogram before should practise doing so with colleagues beforehand. In order to compile a genogram, the worker needs a large sheet of paper, pen or pencils (various colours if possible) and a table at which to work. In addition to parents and children, other relatives can be involved. More than one session may be needed if the exercise is used to discuss the family's history in detail and to enter significant dates and other information. Working on a genogram also provides the social worker with an opportunity to observe family relationships: for example, how open family members are with each other, how well they respond to each other's needs, how flexible they are and how much they know about each other.

**Figure 3.4 Genogram or family tree**

*Source*: DOH (1988).

have a considerable but unintentional impact. For example, the use of 'X' to symbolise the death of a family member may be very hurtful. Family members should be asked what symbols they would wish to use in the construction of their own genogram.

Workers sometimes avoid genograms because they feel the result often looks a mess, or the family structure is so large that they have difficulty drawing it on one sheet of paper. This misses the main point of the exercise, which is to help the family provide information which they think is important and to assist them to see patterns and gain insights. Once the process is completed, a neat version can be produced. It is recommended that, before using genograms, workers should draw and discuss their own genogram, not only to learn how to structure them but to experience the feelings which they can raise. In Chapter 7 of the present volume, Calder looks at ways in which genograms can be adapted for use with ethnic minority families and refers to useful articles on this topic.

## Ecomaps

Additional information can be gained from ecomaps, an example of which is included as Figure 3.5. These focus on the relationships children and family members have, not only with their relatives, but with significant others like friends and pets, with organisations such as schools and family centres and with pastimes and activities. Information can be gained on who and what are important to each family member, whether relationships are supportive or stressful and the extent of child and family's support systems.

Ecomaps should not be seen as a static record of the child or family's ecosystem. Family relationships change: children may feel hostile towards a parent one week and have resolved the conflict the following week. Therefore ecomaps should be undertaken on a number of occasions to map any changes. It is preferable, particularly when working with children, not to draw ecomaps on paper but to use moveable objects to represent their ecosystem. Play people can be used, or cardboard circles on which can be drawn happy, sad and angry faces. The child can then choose the appropriate play person or face to represent themselves and the people or things they are identifying as significant, and be able to move them around to indicate what their feelings are and how they can change.

This type of approach is empowering as it gives children and families greater control over the information-giving process, it can provide information that a structured question-and-answer session would not elicit, and may help families to gain insights and to assess their own situations. There is also a range of material by Dunst *et al.* (1988) for collecting information on family needs, supports and resources.

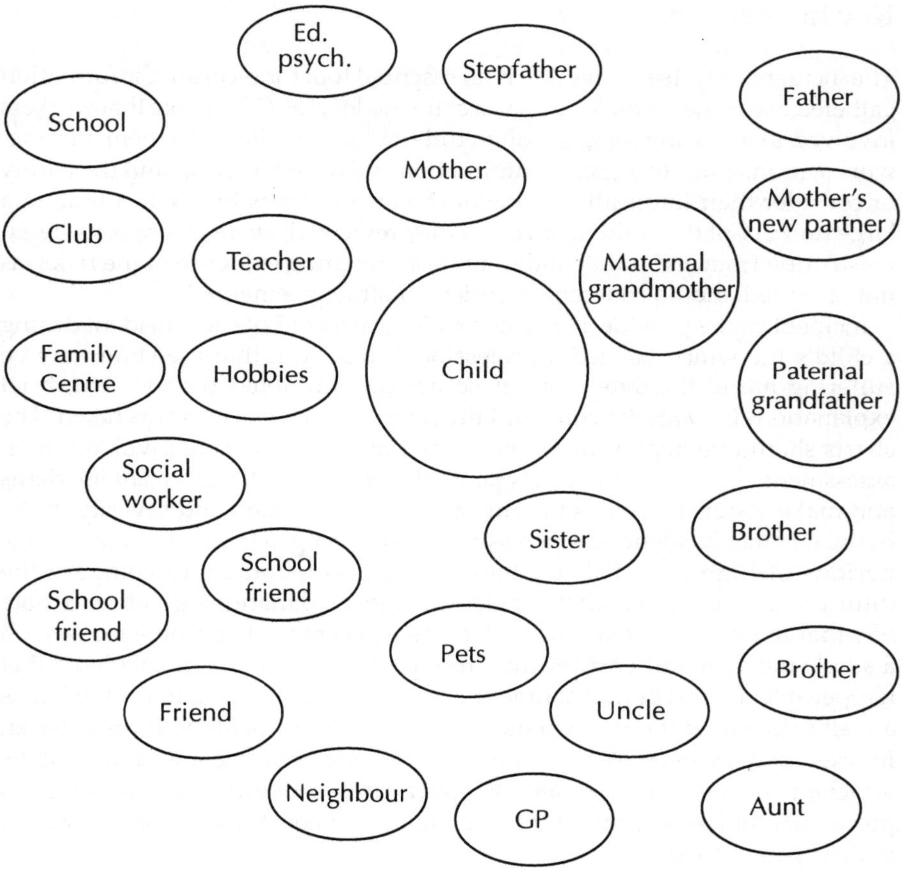


*Place individual family members or the child or family in centre circle.*
*Identify important people, organisations or pastimes and draw circles as needed.*
*Draw lines between circles where connections exist.*
*Use different types of lines to indicate the nature of the link or the relationship:*

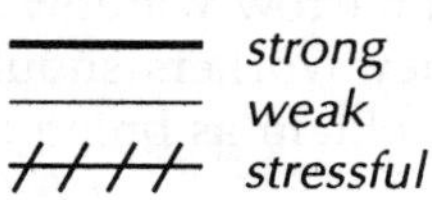


*When working with children, use movable objects.*

**Figure 3.5 Ecomap**

*Source*: DoH (1988).

## Key incident chart

The incident chart (see Table 3.3) is an essential tool for recording information gathered about the possible harm to a child. Reder *et al.* (1993) note that workers involved in assessing families 'often did not have available to them a framework within which to organise information and observations about the family or consider their implications'. Reder *et al.* were struck by the fact that, in a large number of the child death cases they reviewed, events were considered in isolation from each other and so the accumulating evidence of the risk was not observed and no coherent overview or strategy emerged.

Incident charts provide a brief, chronological record of each incident during a child's life which has led a professional to believe that the child may be suffering harm: the date when it occurred, who noted the incident, brief explanations by both the child and the carer, and what action was taken. The charts should be kept at the front of the files of all workers involved in an assessment and provide an easily accessible record of all significant incidents and make visible patterns of harm, such as the duration and severity of the harm, whether incidents are increasing or decreasing in frequency and specific periods of high risk. This enables core group members to compare the information they have about incidents and explanations given and note whether there are inconsistencies. It helps workers not to become focused on a single incident, but ensures that multiples of similar single incidents that happen over a short period of time and are observed by different professionals are all recorded and not erroneously seen as a single incident. It provides an index, based on dates, to help workers locate the fuller records, and it can be attached to the final assessment report, thus providing the initial child protection conference, child protection review or court with information that is clearly formatted.

## The time clock

Professionals need to be clear about when the child is at risk, because families face different stresses at different times of the day. There is a danger that observations of the way a family functions may cover a narrow window of time. In order to combat this, the team of multi-agency workers should organise their assessment sessions at different times to obtain as broad an overview as possible.

Using clock faces (see Figure 3.6), workers should record with the family what happens throughout the 24-hour day. When this work is undertaken with young children or parents with learning disabilities, symbols rather than numbers can be used to indicate the time of day. Families may function very differently at weekends, so this must also be assessed.

**Table 3.3 Incident chart**

| Date | Incident/ injury | Notified by | Explanations given by carer | by child | by other | Advice given | Action taken |
|---|---|---|---|---|---|---|---|

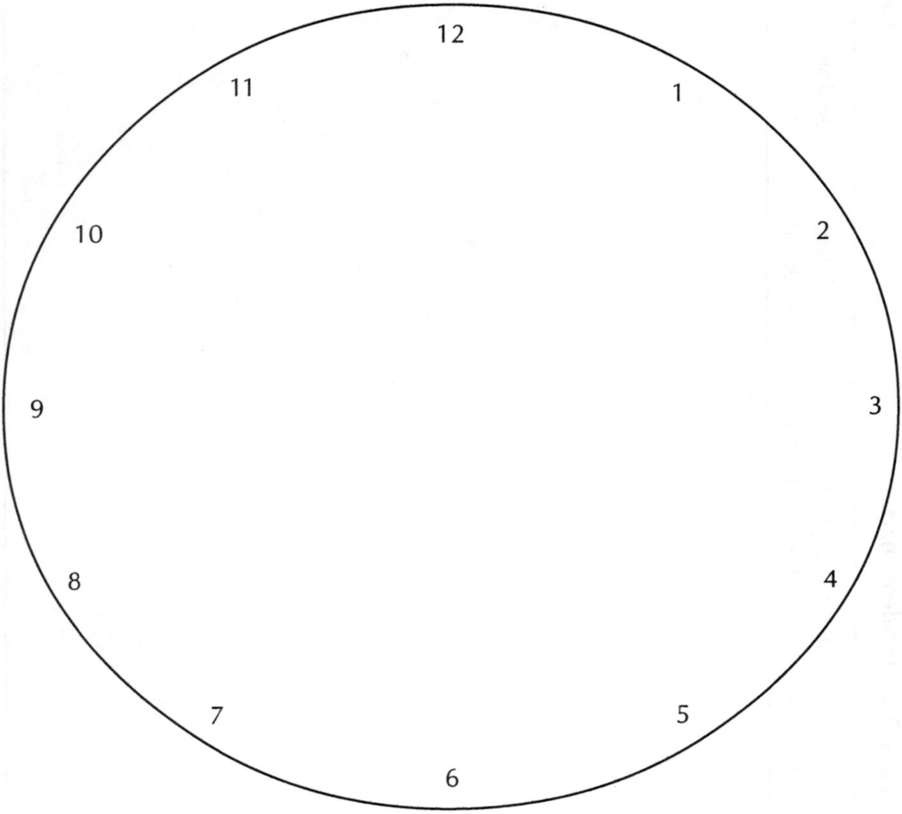


**Figure 3.6 The time clock**

This tool is also valuable in assisting workers at the service planning stage to identify the key times to provide resources.

We have listed the key tools for information gathering, but there are many other creative ways of helping children and carers share information and insights about themselves and their families.

## Testing and evaluating stage

The testing and evaluating stage of an assessment is particularly important, but is often given limited attention. Workers frequently use most of the time allotted to the assessment to gather information and produce a report which details this, but fail to evaluate the information or draw conclusions. Alternatively, they may leave this stage to the very end of the process, often reaching conclusions and making decisions as they are producing the report.

Although post-registration assessment work is a multi-agency task, it is often the keyworker who is left to evaluate the information, and consequently members of the core group from non-social work agencies are not involved in this process. This is not good practice as inconsistencies, different interpretations of evidence gathered and differences of opinion may only come to light as the report is being presented to a child protection review or court.

Parents also need to be involved in this process. Arranging core group sessions to test and evaluate the findings jointly will ensure that parents are given a forum in which to understand, discuss and contribute to the conclusions that are being reached before the report is produced. A number of tools which may be useful in this phase of the assessment work are discussed below.

## The risk assessment checklist

Those involved in evaluating information will need tools to assist them. The risk assessment checklist (see Table 3.4) can be used by individuals in their assessment work and as a basis for joint discussion within the core group. The checklist asks a series of questions which will help workers to consider the type and level of harm a child may be suffering, the possible effects of that harm, the likely outcomes of intervention, the safety factors in the child's environment and the potential for change within the family.

Associated with the checklist are a range of tools, some of which have already been covered at the information gathering stage. Tools like the incident chart will help to answer very clearly questions such as 'Are the injuries/incidents acute/cumulative/episodic?' and 'What is the severity and duration of the harm?' Genograms and ecomaps can assist discussions on 'What does the child mean to the family?' and 'What are the strengths and weaknesses of the family?' Further tools associated with the checklist are outlined in the following sections.

## Continuums

Some questions in the checklist, such as 'Did the injuries/incidents result from spontaneous actions, neglect or intent?', can be difficult to answer. Workers may feel that they have insufficient evidence or there are differences of opinion. Families may have made a statement which workers are not sure whether to believe or not. The continuum is a tool to assist discussions about

**Table 3.4 Risk assessment checklist**

- Does/could the suspected harm meet the definitions of abuse in the child protection procedures?
- Are there cultural, linguistic or disability issues which could effect the level of risk to the child?
- Are the injuries/incidents acute/cumulative/episodic?
- What is the severity and duration of the harm?
- When and how is the child at risk?
- Did the injuries/incidents result from spontaneous actions, neglect or intent?
- What are the parents'/carers' attitudes and response to your concerns?
- How willing are they to cooperate?
- Is their explanation consistent with the injuries/incidents? (Is there need for a medical?)
- What does the child mean to the family? What role does the child play?
- What are the effects on the child's development? What may be the long-term effects?
- What is the child's reaction to and perception of the harm?
- What are the child's needs, wishes and feelings regarding intervention and likely outcomes?
- What may be the effects of intervention?
- Are the injuries/incidents likely to recur?
- What are the protective factors?
- What are the strengths and weaknesses of the family?
- What is the potential for change within the family?
- How safe is the child?
  - What are the possibilities?
  - What are the probabilities?
  - How imminent is the likely risk?
  - How grave are the likely consequences?
- Can the level of risk that has been identified be safely and satisfactorily reduced by the voluntary provision of services? If so, intervention and services outside the formal child protection process should be the preferred option.

such issues: simply draw a horizontal line to represent the continuum; as an example, anxiety about whether an injury could have resulted from poor supervision or from intent.

Poor supervision ———————————————————— Intent

Each professional places a cross on the line to indicate where their 'gut feelings' tell them they are between the two extremes. This will clarify whether all the professionals hold a similar opinion, one worker is seeing the case differently or the group is completely split. The professionals can then discuss why they may disbelieve the family, hold different views or feel anxious when there appears to be little evidence of risk. Further work to obtain more information about the areas where there is high anxiety or dissension may be required. Professionals may wish to use this tool with or without parents present, but should always share their final conclusions with the family.

## The child's protective environment

One of the most critical issues to assess is the safety of a child, and a framework developed by Margaret Boushel (1994) (see Figure 3.7) provides an excellent assessment tool. This framework has the child at the centre of an ecosystem, surrounded by their immediate family, then the extended family, the local community and finally, agencies from state and society. Four key factors are identified for assessment:

1. the value accorded to the child;
2. the value and status accorded to the child's mother and other key carers;
3. social interconnectedness – whether or not the child and family can make use of the protective safety nets; and
4. the protective safety nets – the formal and informal sources of protection.

Professionals need to consider each of these in relation to the different sections of the ecosystem. In the quadrant which examines the value accorded to the child, consideration should be given to the extent to which a child is valued and feels valued within his or her immediate family, the extended family, the local community, school and so on, plus how the state values the child in terms of making resources available for their welfare. The quadrant which focuses on how women and other carers are valued raises issues identified in research by Farmer and Owen (1995): that, if carers' welfare needs are not adequately addressed by family, community and state, this will have implications for the welfare and protection of their children.

Social interconnectedness refers to the way the networks operate that link the child with the different parts of his or her ecosystem. A child may be poorly parented at home, but if they are easily able to gain good support from relatives, peers, youth leaders, school and so on they will fare better than a child who is similarly poorly parented but has little or no access to support networks. The protective safety net relates to the way individuals in the child's ecosystem would use the networks operating between them

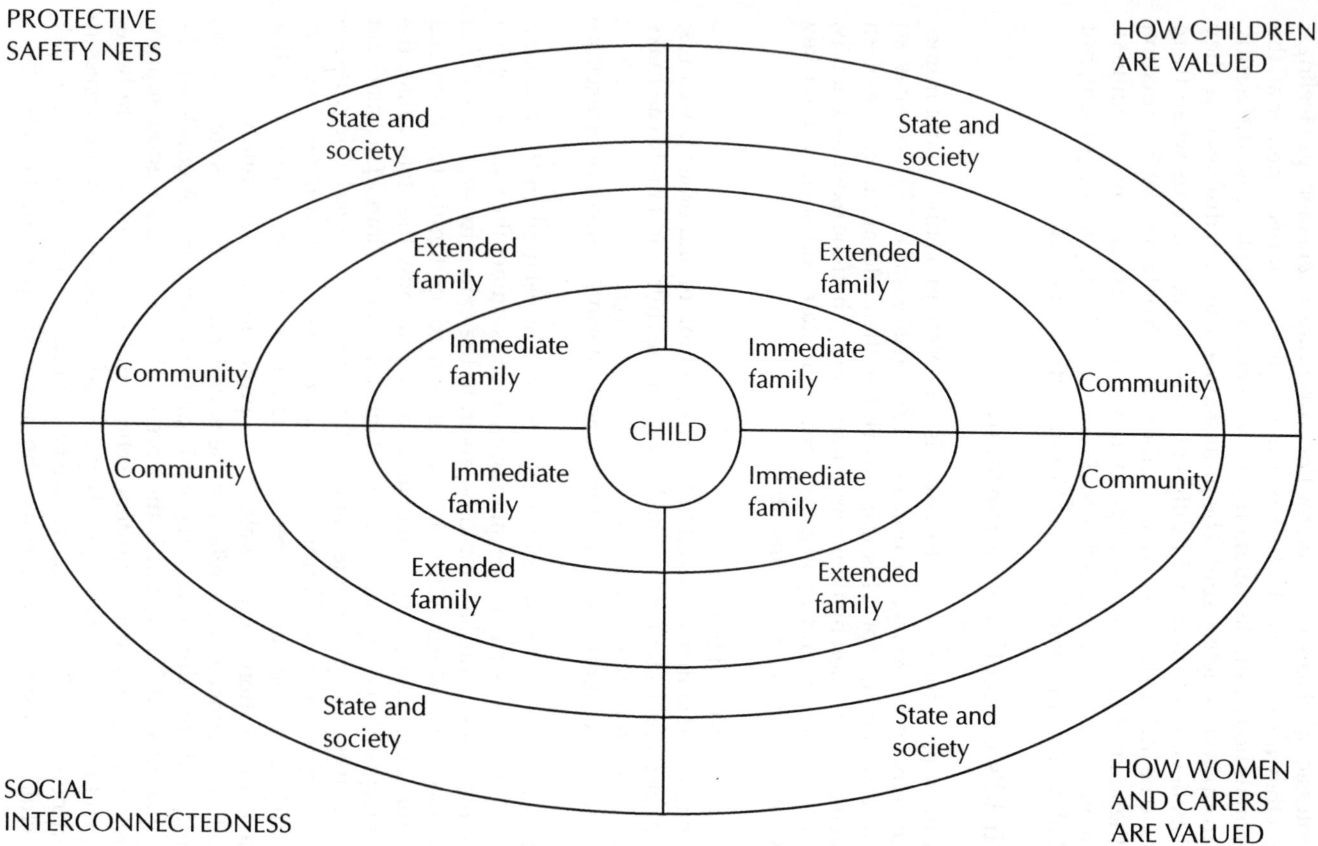


**Figure 3.7 The child's protective environment (Boushel, 1994). Reproduced by permission.**

to take action and alert the appropriate agencies to protect the child from harm.

Shading in each of the 16 sections of Figure 3.7 (dark shading for strong, no shading for non-existent) causes a pattern to emerge. This can show the level of support which exists within the child's protective environment, where the strengths and weaknesses are, whether there are gaps in the worker's knowledge, and the areas where further work should be undertaken.

### Model of change

The final tool in this section looks at the potential for change within the family, and is based on a model originated by Prochaska and DiClemente. Tony Morrison outlines the use of this model fully in Chapter 8 of the present book. For the purposes of the present chapter, assessments tend to focus on the action stage when families are receiving a high level of support which enables them to function more effectively. But the assessment must also consider the maintenance and relapse stages. Families need to have strategies for maintaining new behaviour when they have less support and may meet resistance from friends who may not want them to change.

The model also accepts that relapse is a normal and incremental part of the change process – that is, two steps forward and one back – and that any assessment needs to identify what strategies the family and their informal support networks may have to deal with future lapses. Where families have shown that they have developed and successfully used relapse prevention plans, it is likely that the outcome for the child will be more positive.

## Deciding the probable level of need or harm

Once the core group has evaluated the information it should be able to order its evidence and reach conclusions about the risks and what solutions there may be for meeting needs. This discussion should take place before the report is produced. The following tools assist this part of the process.

### A model for risk assessment

This tool is a set of questions produced by Paul Brearley (1982) (see Table 3.5) for analysing the evidence regarding risk to a child. By considering the possible dangers and then dividing the hazards (the things that might cause the danger to occur) into two types – predisposing and situational – workers and the family are helped to examine the processes which may lead to a child being harmed and actions which could cause or prevent situations from becoming dangerous. This model also focuses on strengths in family and community networks which can be used to reduce risk and also gaps in information – what the professionals have not been able to find out during the assessment.

**Table 3.5 A model for risk assessment**

For each stage of the analysis, try to answer the question WHY?

1 List the dangers in this case
A 'danger' is something you want to avoid, so what possible events would you fear in these circumstances? Rank these dangers in order of their significance. Consider not only the 'effect' of the danger if it occurs but the 'chance' of it happening.

2 List the hazards in the case
A 'hazard', in this context, is something which might result in a danger being realised – something that helps to bring about the circumstances you want to avoid.

3 Divide the list of hazards into two: (a) predisposing hazards, (b) situational hazards
A 'predisposing hazard' makes the danger more likely. It is something that creates vulnerability, though it may need to be activated by something else, perhaps a situational hazard.
A 'situational hazard' is something that happens and which has an immediate effect directly related to the danger.

4 List what you consider to be the strengths in this case
Strengths are those factors whose effects counteract the danger and make it less likely to become a reality.

5 Identify the additional information which you believe to be necessary
Evaluating the information you already have may indicate that there are some important gaps in your knowledge, gaps which should be filled before a final assessment.

6 Indicate the decisions you feel should be taken

*Source*: Brearley (1982).

## Care planning chart

This chart enables the development of thinking from assessment of need to care plan. The nature of the concern is identified and listed in the left hand column. The needs and possible solutions are then drawn in the second column. It is important to be creative – for example, a service-led response to a child with speech delay is likely to be referral to speech therapy whereas, as Table 3.6 shows, there are a range of solutions which could meet this child's needs. Creative, flexible solutions which draw on both formal and informal resources can be cost-effective and are often more empowering for the child and family. Once the resources have been identified and listed in the third column, thought needs to be given to the targets and monitoring arrangements. These should reflect the desired outcomes – for example, improvement in the child's speech – and not the process – for example, whether or not the child attended speech therapy.

# Presenting assessments for independent evaluation and decision

The assessment report should summarise the findings of the assessment and make recommendations to an independent body, that is, the child protection review or court, for a final evaluation and decision. Ideally, the report should be produced jointly, with core group professionals writing up the sections of the assessment they have been responsible for.

Reports should not be a lengthy record of all the information gathered, but an evaluation of the key information and how this has led to the recommendations made. It is useful to use materials, such as genograms or incident charts, as appendices to any report, as they have the advantage of saving writing effort whilst offering a powerful visual picture for professionals and others. All reports should address the following areas.

- Reason for the assessment:
  - how the assessment was undertaken,
  - professionals involved,
  - level of contact with child and family,
  - assessment plan and/or written agreement.
- Assessment of the child:
  - health,
  - education,

**Table 3.6 Care planning chart**

| Nature of concern/risk | Needs | Possible solutions | Possible resources | Targets and monitoring arrangements |
|---|---|---|---|---|
| Language delay which could result in child's health/development being significantly impaired | to improve child's language | through language development programmes | speech therapy | reports on outcome of language development programme |
| | | | family centre, direct work with child/parents | discussion with, and observation of, parents |
| | to help mother to stimulate and talk to her child | by addressing her depression and providing her with parenting knowledge and skills | mental health services<br>parenting classes<br>parent's support group | liaison with medical health services |
| | to provide play opportunities | with other children, with other adults | playgroup<br>parent and toddler group<br>play workers to visit the child at home | observation visits of child in play provision and at home |
| | to engage the child in conversation with adults | encourage adults in the child's informal support network to spend more time with the child | s.17 money to enable contact with extended family | discussion with extended family |
| | to check the possibility of physical problems leading to language delay | medical checks regarding possible physical problems, disability | GP<br>audiologist<br>education psychologist | feedback on medical examinations and treatment |

- identity,
- family and social relationships,
- social presentation,
- emotional and behavioural development,
- self care skills,
- wishes and feelings of the child.

• Assessment of the family:

- family composition,
- individual profile of parents/carers,
- family relationships and interactions,
- networks,
- finance,
- physical conditions,
- wishes and feelings of parents/carers.

• Equalities issue:

- race, religion, language and culture,
- disability,
- gender and sexuality,
- impact of core group members' identity on the assessment process.

• Factors/circumstances which decrease/increase the risk of harm/significant harm:

- in the immediate family,
- in the extended family,
- within the community,
- within state and society.

• Potential for change:

- the strengths and weaknesses in the family,
- willingness to cooperate,
- ability to sustain change.

• Information gaps:

- areas that the assessment, for whatever reason, has failed to address.

• Assessment of level of harm/significant harm:

- sexual abuse,
- physical abuse,
- emotional abuse,
- neglect,

  - child beyond control,
  - parents/carers unable to care for child,
  - child's health/development likely to be impaired/significantly impaired,
  - child is a danger to others,
  - child harming or neglecting self.
- Care plan recommendations:
  - family and community,
  - registration,
  - legal orders,
  - support networks,
  - section 17 services,
  - monitoring/review process.
- Disagreements with the risk/need assessment:
  - by the family,
  - within the core group,
  - by others.

## Conclusion

Undertaking a comprehensive assessment within a core group is a complex task which requires an approach that (1) shares responsibility within the group, (2) involves and empowers the child and the family, (3) is sensitive to difference, (4) is structured and systematic, (5) plans process as well as task, (6) follows the six stages of planning, hypothesising, gathering and evaluating information, deciding probability and presenting the assessment for an independent evaluation.

It is hoped that, if core group professionals work together using the frameworks and tools outlined in this chapter, they will produce assessments which:

- reflect the views of all those involved in the assessment,
- summarise and evaluate information gathered,
- present evidence that is well ordered and accessible,
- address both need and risk,
- provide solutions,
- make recommendations which are not resource led, use both informal and formal support, and can be met within available resources,
- enable the initial child protection conference, child protection review or court to reach an informed decision and make appropriate plans.

## References

Boushel, M. (1994) *Child Protection Assessments – Assessing Needs of Individual Children*, School for Policy Studies: University of Bristol.
Brearley, P. (1982) *Risk and Social Work*, London: Routledge.
Calder, M.C. (1996) 'Inter-agency Arrangements for Post-registration Practice', Report to Salford ACPC.
Coleman, R. and Cassell, D. (1995) 'Parents who Misuse Drugs and Alcohol' in P. Reder and C. Lucey (eds) *Assessment of Parenting: Psychiatric and Psychological Contributions*, London and New York: Routledge.
Department of Health (1988) *Protecting Children: A Guide for Social Workers undertaking a Comprehensive Assessment*, London: HMSO.
Department of Health (1991a) *Working Together Under the Children Act 1989: A Guide to Arrangements for Inter-agency Co-operation for the Protection of Children from Abuse*, London: HMSO.
Department of Health (1991b) *Care Management and Assessment: practice guide*, London: HMSO.
Department of Health (1995a) *Child Protection: Messages from Research*, London: HMSO.
Department of Health (1995b) *Looking After Children Forms*, London: HMSO.
Dunst, C.J., Trivette, C.M. and Deal, A.G. (eds) (1988) *Supporting and Strengthening Families*, Cambridge, Mass.: Brookline Books.
Falkov, A. (1996) *Fatal Child Abuse and Parental Psychiatric Disorder: An analysis of 100 ACPC Case Reviews*, London: HMSO.
Farmer, E. and Owen, M. (1995) *Child Protection Practice: Private Risks and Public Remedies*, London: HMSO.
Harper, N. (1996) *Children Still in Need: Refocusing Child Protection in the Context of Children in Need*, London: NCH/Action for Children.
Katz, I. (1997) *Current Issues in Comprehensive Assessment*, London: NSPCC.
MacDonald, S. (1991) *All Equal Under the Act*, London: Race Equality Unit, NISW.
McBeath, G. and Webb, S. (1990) 'Child Protection Language as Professional Ideology in Social Work', *Social Work and Social Sciences Review*, **2** (2): 122–45.
McGaw, S. and Sturmey, P. (1994) 'Assessing Parents with Learning Disabilities', *Child Abuse Review*, **3**: 36–51.
Parker, R.,Ward, H., Jackson, S., Aldgate, J. and Wedge, P. (1991) *Looking after Children: Assessing Outcomes in Child Care*, London: HMSO.
Phillips, M. and Dutt, R. (1990) *Towards a Black Perspective in Child Protection*, London: Race Equality Unit, NISW.
Prochaska, J.O. and DiClemente, C.C. (1982) 'Transtheoretical Therapy: Toward a More Integrative Model of Change', *Psychotherapy: Theory, Research and Practice*, **19**: 276–88.
Reder, P., Duncan, S. and Gray, M. (1993) *Beyond Blame: Child Abuse Tragedies Revisited*, London and New York: Routledge.
Social Services Inspectorate (1993) *Inspecting for Quality: Evaluating Performance in Child Protection*, London: HMSO.
Thoburn, J., Lewis, A. and Shemmings, D. (1995) *Paternalism or Partnership? Family Involvement in the Child Protection Process*, London: HMSO.

# 4 The role of the keyworker

*Barbara Firth*

Within this chapter consideration is given to:

- definitions of the role of keyworker;
- tensions within the role;
- components of the role;
- the keyworker and the family;
- some aids to effectiveness; and
- a summary of the knowledge, skills and qualities required by the role.

'Keyworker' is the term used to describe and delineate a primary role in the post-conference phase of the child protection process. *Working Together* (DoH, 1991) describes the task of the keyworker as threefold: (1) to fulfil the statutory responsibilities of his or her agency, (2) to act as lead worker for the inter-agency work, and (3) to ensure that parents and children are fully engaged in the implementation of the child protection plan.

At an initial child protection conference, if a decision is made to register a child, it is then that a named keyworker is appointed along with a core group of professionals to carry out the inter-agency work. *Working Together* talks about the need for a written child protection plan and states:

> Once the plan has been agreed, it will be the responsibility of individual agencies to implement the parts of the plan relating to them and to communicate with the keyworker and others as necessary. The keyworker will have the responsibility for pulling together and co-ordinating the contributions of different agencies. (DoH, 1991: 32)

*Working Together* is unequivocal in stating that it is not appropriate for anyone other than a social worker from either social services or the NSPCC to be a keyworker because the role derives from that of the lead agency in child protection. In this context, 'lead agency' refers to the agency with statutory powers, which is social service departments. They take the lead role in managing individual cases as well as carrying responsibility for managing key parts of the child protection system. It is important to note that *Working Together* stresses that the keyworker is not necessarily the person with the most face-to-face contact with the family or the one who plays the most active role in the provision of treatment and service delivery.

What all of this suggests, then, is that the role is very much a matter of coordination without takeover, of ensuring that work is progressing in the form of assessment and intervention strategies, while generating shared ownership of and responsibility for that work with children and families. This chapter will explore some of the tensions inherent in the role of the keyworker, examine the different facets of the role and suggest some aids to effectiveness.

## Definitions of the role

*Working Together* specifies that one of the tasks of the Area Child Protection Committee (ACPC) is to produce local procedural handbooks which should be concerned mainly with inter-agency procedures in child protection practice, rather than with the details of professional practice. Sanders *et al.* (1996), in their study of a comparison of local procedural handbooks, found that they said little about the post-conference territory and the provision of treatment and after-care. Their main focus was on the process of investigation. Horwath and Calder (1998) also noted a lack of guidance regarding post-registration practice. For example, there was little clarification of the coordinating role of the keyworker.

When procedural guidance does refer to the tasks of the keyworker, a picture is created of a role which is pivotal to the post-conference process. In other words, it is a role on which everything else depends, this includes coordination and the convening of the core group, the keyworker as link with the family and the keyworker as social worker. Casson and Manning (1997) state that, as coordinator,

> the key social worker is responsible for co-ordinating the activities of those engaged in delivering services to meet the requirements of the child protection plan. They may commission services from the private or voluntary sector as appropriate and may request input from staff of the statutory agencies. The written agreement is

> signed by all of those participating in the plan including the family. They must be informed if:
>
> the written agreement has not been met;
> there is a change in the circumstances of the child or family; or
> there is an increased risk to the safety of the child or young person. (Casson and Manning, 1997: 164)

Coordinating the activity of the core group comes high on the list of keyworker tasks. To do this effectively requires that keyworkers have an awareness of what tasks are assigned to each professional as part of the child protection plan, the intended and actual impact of the individual professional interventions, and how these are contributing to the plan as a whole. Therefore the keyworker has to act as a focal point, liaising with the core group, collating and disseminating information and noting and communicating any significant changes in a situation. At the same time he or she must ensure that the practice tasks required by the child protection process in the form of assessment, planning, monitoring and review are progressing appropriately.

## Keyworker as coordinator and convenor of the core group

Keyworkers are also often required to manage the process by convening core group meetings, usually in accordance with an agreed frequency and format, which may include a pro forma for minutes and formal contact with the child protection system as and when necessary, as described in Chapter 2 of the present volume. There would seem to be an expectation that core group meetings are formal, are chaired and recorded and that parents (and sometimes children) are present. In some ACPC procedures the conduct of these meetings is a shared responsibility, with the task of chairing and taking minutes rotating amongst the professionals in the core group. In other ACPCs there are arrangements for another person, usually the keyworker's supervisor, to come in specifically to chair the meeting. However, such practice is not universal and some keyworkers find themselves trying to chair, take minutes and be a participating professional in such events (Calder and Barratt, 1997).

## Keyworker as link with the family

The keyworker is also expected to ensure that parents and children are clear about the process, the causes for concern and the roles and remits of everyone involved. This can either be done by the keyworker directly or allocated to another professional within the core group.

### Keyworker as social worker

It must not be forgotten that the keyworker is a social worker and as such must carry out the social work task. This could include anything from coordinating, participating in and writing the comprehensive assessment to being involved in direct therapeutic work with a child, commissioning services or preparing for court hearings if care proceedings are being considered.

The keyworker as link with the family and the keyworker as social worker are explored in detail later in the chapter.

## Tensions within the role

In reality there is much confusion and lack of clarity about the nature and extent of the role, with social workers often feeling overwhelmed by all that is expected of them. Far from having a sense of shared responsibility in this post-conference territory, they experience it as having to do most of the work themselves and some would even describe it as everything being 'dumped at their door', for them to take action on. A study of core groups in one local authority area revealed that, with the introduction of a formalised system for the conduct of core groups, the feeling of responsibility had intensified for some keyworkers. As one described it:

> As the social worker I always feel that I have to take the lead role and accept all responsibility for the core group, such as chairing, minute taking and the distribution of minutes. Plus I always feel that the tasks of the assessment land on my back and it is extremely difficult to get other members to accept responsibility. I am unsure what priority and importance is attached to core group by other professionals – in my opinion it seems to be low. (Firth, 1995: 15)

It would seem that having a lead role has, for some keyworkers, become synonymous with doing most of the work. This is mirrored in Hallett's (1995) findings that inter-agency collaboration is much more highly developed in the initial stages of the child protection process than it is in the post-conference phase. She found that, in 40 per cent of the cases in the sample, there was no mention in the child protection plan of other agencies besides the social services department. Similarly, Farmer and Owen (1995) found that, in 30 per cent of registered cases in their study, the only recommended intervention was social work contact. Hallett found that in current intervention the social services department played a dominant and sometimes, it appeared, almost exclusive role with little 'hands-on' collaborative work.

The dominance of social services and the social worker in the role of keyworker is perhaps exacerbated by the feeling amongst other professionals, such as health visitors and teachers, that child protection is only a small part of an expanding workload. One head teacher in a survey of core group practice highlighted this dilemma: 'In the present climate it is becoming increasingly difficult for me, personally, to maintain the quality time previously allocated to child protection issues. There are so many pulls on that time. I am sure other professionals are in the same predicament' (Firth, 1995: 16).

If other professionals feel the constraints of time take them away from child protection work, it is easy to see how keyworkers might take on more responsibility and therefore become increasingly dominant in post-conference work. The fear is that this could develop to the point where other professionals feel a loss of expertise, with a consequent decline in collaborative working.

Given the tensions inherent in the role of keyworker, the complexity of the professional task in implementing a child protection plan and the organisational constraints experienced by everyone in the inter-agency network, it is not surprising that many social workers find it difficult to coordinate inter-agency contributions and promote shared responsibility in terms of planning, assessment and intervention. This can be illustrated by considering how the task of chairing and taking minutes of a core group meeting is negotiated (Firth, 1995). Whilst many procedure manuals suggest this is something that can be shared among the group, more often than not it is the keyworker who does both. In the early stages of the life of a core group there may be some attempt to make this a shared task, but barriers such as feelings of lack of skills in chairing, or knowledge of core group processes, or lack of facilities for the typing and distribution of minutes, prevent this. The social worker, therefore, takes on the task. After a time the question ceases to be asked and the assumption prevails that it is indeed the keyworker's job to steer and record the meeting.

This assumption of total responsibility by the keyworker for the post-conference process may mean a consequent confusion between being the lead agency and being the agency that does everything. A recent evaluation of the functioning of core groups in one local authority (Collin, 1997) sought the views of health visitors about their perceptions of post-conference work and the role of the keyworker. They described a number of difficulties they had experienced around the convening and running of core group meetings and the roles and responsibilities of the professionals involved. Some of these are listed below.

1 Meetings being cancelled at the last minute, or arranged at very short notice, making attendance difficult.

2 Meetings starting late and being poorly managed by the keyworker, with no clear agenda and structure.
3 The keyworker having unrealistic expectations of the health visiting service.
4 Keyworkers not addressing important aspects of the child protection plan and making decisions to change it without consulting other core group members.
5 A feeling that core group members are not being listened to or taken seriously by the keyworker.
6 Issues being raised insensitively by the keyworker at the meeting when they have not been discussed with the parents beforehand.
7 No communication amongst the professionals between meetings.

This list of difficulties conveys a picture of single agency predominance at odds with the concept of working together. It would seem to suggest a lack of understanding of the role of the keyworker by everyone in the scenario, not least the keyworkers themselves.

## Components of the role

Expectations of the keyworker are indeed varied and extensive and it is not surprising that they can feel overwhelmed (Robinson, 1996), especially as the majority of child protection social workers have a keyworker role in more than one core group. However the remit is expressed, it does seem to have three main components which are to do with process, statutory obligations and practice. Each of these will be considered in detail.

### Keyworker as facilitator of process

The core group is a diverse collection of professionals who come together and engage in a crucial and intricate piece of work, within the complex framework that is the child protection system. They may not know one another, may never have worked together before and yet, immediately after the initial child protection conference, have to find a way of becoming an effective working unit. With time at a premium and much to be done, there is little space for attending to group processes and the impetus is to move straight into the task. The challenge for the keyworker is to assume the lead role but also to help to generate shared responsibility and a distribution of tasks amongst the core group members.

How is the keyworker to achieve this? If we look for a moment at group processes, Heron (1989) refers to three modes:

1 *The hierarchical mode.* Here, a facilitator directs the process and does things for the group. This includes deciding on objectives and the agenda, interpreting actions, managing group feelings and providing structures. In other words, in this mode, the facilitator takes full responsibility and is in charge of all major decision taking.
2 *The co-operative mode.* Here, the facilitator shares power with the group and enables the group to become more self-directing. Aims and objectives are worked out together through negotiation and, although the facilitator's views are influential, they are not final but are merely one amongst many. The key tasks of the facilitator in this cooperative mode are those of guide and enabler.
3 *The autonomous mode.* Here, the facilitator respects the total autonomy of the group, giving them the freedom to find their own way. It is the group which evolves the programme, with the facilitator creating the space for them to do this. The key words here are unprompted, self-directed practice.

It would seem that some of the problems cited earlier (Collin, 1997) arise from keyworkers operating in a hierarchical mode, when shared responsibility is best generated by moving into a cooperative and perhaps autonomous mode.

This same study found that, when this happens, a much more positive picture emerges of the value in meeting other professionals to share information, to clarify roles and responsibilities, to deepen understanding of one another's roles and to plan and evaluate work with the child and the family (Collin, 1997). The professionals were clear that core group meetings needed to be structured and purposeful, but that they were not the 'end of the story'. It was essential that communication between the professionals continued throughout this period of post-conference work and that this could be achieved by means of regular telephone calls, face-to-face contact, letters and so on. It is the keyworker, in the lead role, who can perhaps be expected to coordinate this activity. There was acknowledgement that conflict can arise amongst core group members and that an early professionals' meeting was a helpful way of trying to resolve difficulties. If such difficulties persisted, access to independent professional advice could be more effective than expecting the keyworker to resolve the issue.

That shared responsibility is possible and can achieve much is illustrated by a health visitor who said:

> The children in this family have recently been removed from the Child Protection Register. It has been a pleasure to witness the improvement in this family's emotional health as they have worked through very serious issues. Mum is experiencing a new-found sense of esteem and well-being which she transmits to

the children. The core group have worked well together to achieve their aims. (Firth, 1995: 18)

## Keyworker as representative of a statutory organisation

As representative of and accountable to social services, the lead agency in the child protection system, the keyworker must work within the procedures, frameworks and value base established by that organisation. This includes abiding by the priorities set by the department, complying with prescribed recording practices and operating with the resources available. There is potential here for conflict if the resources required by a child protection plan developed by a core group are not seen as a priority or made available by the lead agency. This can further complicate a keyworker's efforts to generate collaborative working and shared responsibility.

In addition, as representatives of a statutory organisation, keyworkers also have to engage with legal systems and court proceedings. Courts can request a comprehensive assessment of a child and family to be undertaken in a time frame of their specification. As the person having prime responsibility for ensuring that this happens, it is the keyworker who is under pressure to work to a deadline. This can be yet another source of potential conflict and may lead to the keyworker moving away from collaboration and cooperation into a hierarchical mode as the social worker, in turn, places pressure on other professionals to complete the assessment within the specified time frame.

## Keyworker as social work practitioner

Often overlooked in the detailing of procedures is the fact that keyworkers are social workers and as such have to engage in professional practice with the child and family. Essentially, alongside others in the scenario, they can be seen as change agents making informed assessments of families, using specialist resources and employing a variety of intervention techniques to promote the safety and well-being of children. However, Cooper *et al.* (1995) argue that the rise of managerialism over the last decade has had the effect of deprofessionalising the social work task. Managerialism concerns itself with the detail of policy, practice, beliefs and values in an organisation. In child protection, as a consequence, less time is spent on exercising professional discretion and more and more on following managerial guidelines, completing checklists and searching for legally admissible evidence. There is no doubt that the development of child protection systems has concentrated an inordinate amount of energy on investigations, with forensic considerations outweighing those of welfare and leading to what Corby (1987) describes as therapeutic paralysis in the post-conference phase.

The advent, to a greater or lesser degree, of the purchaser–provider split within social service organisations has also had an impact on the social work task. Some departments are following a care management model of commissioning and purchasing services from other agencies, following assessment, whereas others are still charged with both assessment and 'hands-on' intervention by the social workers themselves.

Gibbons *et al.* (1995), examining the operation of the child protection system, identified some common elements of good social work practice which resulted in the situations studied showing a reasonably good outcome after six months:

1 The initial child protection conference needed to make a clear plan that was capable of being fulfilled, taking into account the history and current problems.
2 A social worker needed to be allocated as soon as the child was placed on the register and parents and children needed to be involved from the beginning in the carrying out of the plan. Farmer and Owen (1995) found that, when there was serious friction during the investigative stage between a family and the social worker, a change of worker post-initial child protection conference was found to be the key to a better relationship and a fresh start.
3 The social worker needed to build personal relationships of trust and respect with all the key parties involved in the situation.
4 The social worker needed to mobilise appropriate practical and specialist help at an early stage in order to relieve the severe stress that affected so many of the families.
5 The members of the conference, the social worker and the agency sometimes needed courage to confront dangerous adults and take decisive protective action. (Farmer and Owen also found that, although physical injuries were inflicted in equal numbers by father figures and lone mothers, social work focused almost exclusively on mothers either as the perpetrator or as the protector of the child).

Gibbons *et al.* concluded that the qualities and skills contained in these five elements seemed:

> more important than technical social work methods, which were rarely used, and also more important than comprehensive assessments in the form recommended by the Department of Health (1988), which were more often undertaken. All too often these seemed to become an end in themselves, never feeding back into the child protection plan nor actually influencing what was done.

So, in order to manage the role of keyworker, these three elements of process, agency representation and professional practice need to be recognised and attended to. What makes the role of keyworker uncomfortable at times is that these three aspects can conflict, with, for instance, the requirements of the agency being at odds with the way the social work task is perceived by families and by the social worker themselves. The keyworker must therefore constantly strive for both balance and integration of these component parts.

## The keyworker and the family

The keyworker is charged with the responsibility for ensuring that a child and family move through the child protection process and that the core group of professionals work together to effect this. Furthermore, this work with families must be based on the concept of parental responsibility and working in partnership with parents and other family members or carers, a principle emanating from the regulations and guidance accompanying the Children Act 1989. The Department of Health (1995) identifies four reasons why partnership should be aspired to.

1 A more cooperative working relationship is likely to lead to a more effective service in safeguarding the child's welfare.
2 Family members have unique knowledge about their difficulties but also their strengths.
3 Family members have rights as citizens to hear what is said about them and to have a say when important decisions are made about them.
4 Being involved in this way may help parents and children to feel less powerless and to function more competently.

How then is the keyworker to achieve partnership in order to achieve the aims of the child protection plan? Charles (1990) described the development of a multidisciplinary learning environment which could be equally applicable to the development of an effective partnership with parents and families. (See Figure 4.1.) The first prerequisite is safety: if people feel safe then they are more inclined to be open and honest. Only when safety and openness are present can trust begin to build. When people trust one another, they are more likely to challenge appropriately, and with challenge comes movement and development and change.

Within the context of working with families, the keyworker needs to think about how to create safety and what factors ought to be addressed. If the professionals are clear about the causes for concern and communicate these clearly and honestly, if the family understand why they are in the child protection system, what this entails and what will be expected of them, as well as being clear about the process and the place and role of others within it, then they may begin to feel 'safe'. This, in turn, may help them to work alongside the core group and to concentrate on the issues of concern in their lives.

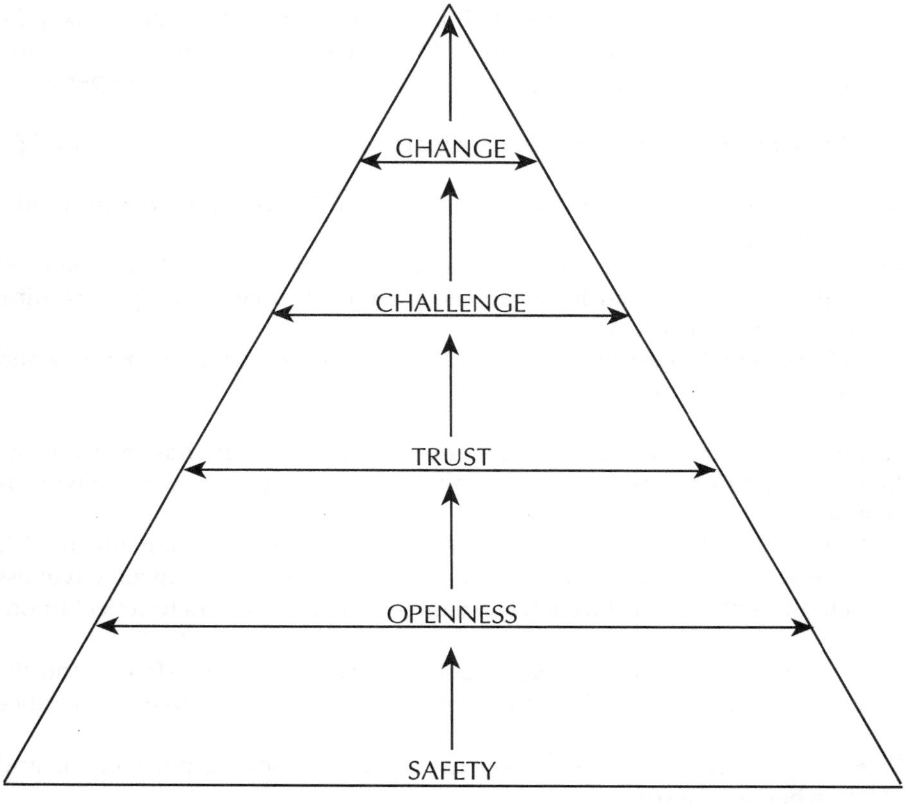


**Figure 4.1 The multi-disciplinary learning environment**

*Source*: Charles (1990). Reproduced by permission.

Implicit in all of this is that the keyworker must also fully understand the causes for concern and the aims of the child protection plan. If the keyworker was not the investigating social worker then the keyworker must both understand and trust the previous assessments so that they can 'own' them. Careful attention therefore needs to be paid to the handover which often coincides with the end of the conference. Unfortunately, given the volume of work, this can often be a neglected area with keyworkers left struggling to make sense of what has gone before.

As well as the development of effective working relationships with the family, there are also different dimensions that need attending to. Heron (1989) identifies six, each of which has a question to be addressed.

1 *The planning dimension*: how shall the core group and the family acquire their objectives and programme in the form of the child protection plan?
2 *The meaning dimension*: how shall meaning be found in the experiences and actions of family members?
3 *The confronting dimension*: what is it that must be confronted and how might this be done?
4 *The feeling dimension*: how shall the feelings and emotions within the family be managed?
5 *The structuring dimension*: what methods of intervention should be used with this family and how can the family's and core group's learning experiences be structured?
6 *The valuing dimension*: how can a climate of personal value, integrity and respect be created?

It is the keyworker as a prime worker in the situation who has to take some responsibility for considering these questions as the progress of the work is reviewed.

How can the keyworker assess whether or not they are being effective? If we look to Heron again he suggests some criteria for measuring effectiveness which it might be useful for keyworkers and their managers to reflect upon:

- *authority* – a keyworker has what he describes as 'distress-free' authority, which has more to do with professional assertiveness than dominance and takeover;
- *confrontation* – the keyworker is able to confront supportively as and when necessary;
- *orientation* – the keyworker is able to provide some clear conceptual orientation as a context for the work in progress;
- *care* – the keyworker presents as caring, empathetic, warm and genuine;
- *range of methods* – the keyworker has a repertoire of techniques for working alongside the child, the family and the professionals;
- *respect for persons* – the keyworker can, in practice, respect the individuals within the family and their right to choose when to change and grow; this respect must, of course, also extend to all other members of the core group;
- *flexibility of style* – when working with the family, the keyworker can move between different modes as appropriate so that the group dynamic can flourish.

## Aids to effectiveness

What might help a keyworker towards effectiveness in the role? Perhaps the most obvious is the need for good and regular supervision, an opportunity for the individual to step back from practice and reflect on role, task and process. In other words, supervision sessions need to provide the keyworker with the chance to think about how the core group is working together; the plans for work with a child and family; the roles and contributions of other professionals; the nature and quality of the social work intervention in the situation and how the whole process is being facilitated. In order to do this, supervision does truly need to fulfil its three main functions, which are normative, formative and restorative. Too often the pressure on operational managers and practitioners means that supervision agendas are dominated by business and organisational matters. Supervision for keyworkers is considered in detail in Chapter 9.

Linked to the importance of supervision within a keyworker's life is the necessity for their training and developmental needs to be considered. This goes beyond the building of a knowledge base about child protection. Keyworkers would also need the opportunity to develop real skills in the generation of shared responsibility and collaborative working within the core group, as well as knowledge and skills in the use of intervention techniques with children and families. In the current climate of financial constraints, imaginative approaches have to be found to help people gain these skills; coworking might be one way.

Finally, all the professionals engaged in the task of formulating and implementing child protection plans would be greatly helped if they had more opportunity to meet outside the child protection process. Too often the child protection conference and the ensuing core group represent the first time that some professionals have sat alongside professionals from other agencies. The pressing nature of the task means there is little time to explore perceptions or to begin to generate the questions to ask of one another. Other forums where this could legitimately happen would be of enormous benefit to the inter-agency network. Inter-agency training is perhaps the most obvious meeting ground and those who are engaged in promoting and assessing it know it can be a powerful vehicle for positive change. In addition to training sessions, there are the possibilities of other contact, both formal and informal, such as local lunch-time meetings or short seminars that can provide opportunities for progressing the dialogues and debates among the network of professionals engaged in child protection.

If a keyworker, then, has access to these three things it could go some way towards making the role both manageable for the individual and effective within the child protection process.

## What does the role require?

The role of the keyworker as described above is twofold: firstly, one of coordinating activity, reconciling and using the different value bases represented in the core group in order to achieve collaborative working; secondly, of engaging the family in all of this whilst at the same time being the 'face' of social services. What, therefore, does the social worker need in order to be effective? This would seem to require knowledge and skills on many different levels.

### Knowledge

Keyworkers need to understand and be able to work within their own agency procedures as well as inter-agency policies and protocols. On a wider level, they also need to understand the legal and statutory framework within which they must operate and the nature of the child protection system. If they are to be more than administrators, their knowledge base must encompass aspects of professional practice such as the effects of abuse on children and families, the nature of different family systems and the range of appropriate intervention techniques that promote change and protection.

To avoid duplication and to draw up realistic plans, keyworkers must have a good working knowledge of the roles of other professionals, together with all available resources and how to gain access to them effectively (Calder and Barratt, 1997: 209–21). Finally, their practice needs to be demonstrably implemented within a framework of anti-discriminatory and empathetic principles. This includes respecting the contribution of both the family and other professionals to the current work. Only then will they truly be able to engage the cooperation of families within the child protection process and offer support, as well as assessing and monitoring the risk for the child.

### Skills

Alongside a sound knowledge base lies a set of skills integral to the role of the keyworker. These include skills in forming relationships, in working with families as a group, as well as therapeutic work with individuals, both adults and children. These are the abilities associated with the social work task, but there are also a set of skills that are connected with the core group process. These include organisational skills, communication and presentation skills and skills in delegation, negotiation and liaison. Being a representative of a statutory organisation requires the keyworker to be competent in record keeping and report writing and, with the volume of work that is the reality for most keyworkers, a sound grasp of the principles of time management and setting priorities would seem to be essential.

It is not enough merely to list prerequisite skills and knowledge, as they need to be filtered through a particular set of attitudes, values and qualities if they are to be experienced by other professionals and families as having a positive impact on a situation. These qualities include having a commitment to, and a belief in, the possibility of change and improvement in individual and family circumstances and having a confident and properly assertive professional presence.

## Conclusion

The role of the keyworker is indeed a complex one that demands attention to and integration of the three major components of process, practice and statutory obligations. There is no doubt that this will often prove to be a rather tricky balancing act, as the keyworker strives to meet the challenge of undertaking a lead role in the post-conference arena whilst helping to generate shared 'ownership' of the work with children and families within the interprofessional network.

The area, then, that the keyworker needs to think about is the promotion of shared responsibility within the core group so that the role is truly one of coordination. This will be greatly facilitated if the keyworker has a real understanding of the roles and remits of all involved and operates in a cooperative way, where aims and objectives are arrived at through a process of negotiation. Alongside working closely and cooperatively with other professionals, the keyworker must build effective working relationships with the family in order to achieve the aims of the child protection plan. Finally, keyworkers need time for review and reflection on their knowledge, skills and qualities and the opportunity to learn from their experiences through the medium of such things as supervision and training and development programmes.

## References

Calder, M. and Barratt, M. (1997) 'Inter-Agency Perspectives on Core Group Practice', *Children & Society*, **11** (4).

Casson, S.F. and Manning, B. (1997) *Total Quality in Child Protection: A Manager's Guide*, Dorset: Russell House Publishing.

Charles, M. with Stevenson, O. (1990) 'Multi-disciplinary is Different. Part 1: The Process of Learning and Training', University of Nottingham.

Collin, A. (1997) 'A Survey of Core Groups in Buckinghamshire County Council', unpublished management project.

Cooper, A., Hetherington, R., Baistow, K., Pitts, J. and Spriggs, A. (1995) *Positive Child Protection: A View from Abroad*, Dorset: Russell House Publishing.

Corby, B. (1987) *Working with Child Abuse*, Milton Keynes: Open University Press.

Department of Health (1988) *Protecting Children: A Guide for Social Workers undertaking a Comprehensive Assessment*, London: HMSO.

Department of Health (1991) *Working Together under the Children Act 1989: A Guide to Arrangements for Inter-agency Co-operation for the Protection of Children from Abuse*, London: HMSO.

Department of Health (1995) *The Challenge of Partnership in Child Protection: Practice Guide*, London: HMSO.

Farmer, E. and Owen, M. (1995) *Child Protection Practice: Private Risks and Public Remedies – Decision Making, Intervention and Outcome in Child Protection Work*, London: HMSO.

Firth, B. (1995) *Survey of Core Groups in the Rotherham Child Protection Committee Area*, Nottingham: School of Social Studies..

Gibbons, J., Conroy, S. and Bell, C. (1995) *Operating the Child Protection System*, London: HMSO.

Hallett, C. (1995) *Interagency Co-ordination in Child Protection*, London: HMSO.

Heron, J. (1989) *The Facilitator's Handbook*, London: Kogan Page.

Horwath, J. and Calder, M.C. (1998) 'Working Together to Protect Children on the Child Protection Register: Myth or Reality?', *British Journal of Social Work*, **28**, 6: 879–95.

Robinson, J. (1996) 'Social Workers – Investigators or Enablers?', in D. Batty and D. Cullen (eds), *Child Protection: The Therapeutic Option*, London: BAAF.

Sanders, B., Jackson, S. and Thomas, N.A. (1996) 'Comparison of Child Protection Local Procedures Handbooks', *In Practice*, **8** (3).

# 5 Groupwork processes and the impact on working together in core groups

*Elaine Baxter and Bobbie Print*

In this chapter, consideration is given to:

- some of the identified problems facing core groups, including how they may fail or get stuck;
- the core group as a task-centred group;
- the stages of group development and group processes, and the application of such issues to the core group forum; and
- some proposals to counter problems or process issues that may arise.

## Introduction

Previous chapters have detailed the evolution of central government guidance (Chapter 1), identified some of the problems associated with core group working (Chapters 2 and 4) and introduced briefly the concepts of core group dynamics. This chapter will consider in more detail some of the lessons from research about how groups operate and look at some of the problems associated with working in core multi-agency groups. Practical suggestions are given to address some of the difficulties that can arise.

The principle of multi-agency working through child protection conferences is well established amongst agencies which have a child protection remit. However, it was only in the mid-1970s that it began to be recognised that there was a need for better coordination of other aspects of child protection work between the disciplines involved. Since then there has been a considerable amount of research regarding the implementation and functioning of child protection conferences and register mechanisms. Some of the child abuse enquiries, following the death of children who were the subjects of child protection interventions from workers, have highlighted difficulties which are pertinent to inter-agency working. For example, the Department of Health (1991a) study of inquiry reports highlighted the need for workers to make a plan for intervention to which all agencies adhered without deviation. In the case of Doreen Aston, and indeed many others, it was emphasised that minutes of meetings should accurately record which individual worker was responsible for what action.

Subsequent central government guidance advocated more structure surrounding the processes which followed on from an initial child protection conference and led to the establishment of multi-agency core groups, initially as a forum for parental participation in planning for children at risk (DHSS, 1988) and more recently as a vehicle for inter-agency communication and planning (DoH, 1991b).

## Working together in core groups: lessons from research

In common with other child protection sub systems, the development of multi-agency working via core groups has not been without its problems. Some of the potential and actual difficulties that occur were relatively easy to foresee. For example, the different perspectives on human behaviour held by different professionals can raise conflicts. The police carry out their responsibilities within a justice framework which assumes that individuals are responsible for their behaviour and that they execute a significant level of conscious choice in the actions they take. Health workers and social workers adopt a more deterministic approach to understanding human behaviour, which places more emphasis on the background causes and external influences affecting behaviour.

These different perspectives can be further reinforced through the use of jargon and technical language which may be unfamiliar to anyone outside that professional group or may be open to quite different interpretations. Different workers from different agencies use professional terminology; for example, the police may refer to 'Schedule One' offenders to refer to those who have a conviction of offences against children, or health staff may use terms such as 'osteogenesis imperfecta' (brittle bones).

Local agency rivalries, alliances, individual relationships and established communication patterns can affect and seriously interfere with responses to individual children. Recent research (Hallett, 1995) showed that workers considered it easier to establish effective inter-agency methods where they remained in their job for a considerable period of time. Therefore the mobility of staff within any agency may affect the level of inter-agency cooperation achieved. This is particularly true where child protection is based on the multidisciplinary relationships between individuals rather than relationships between organisations. Early research into multi-agency cooperation in child protection cases also found that inter-agency collaboration was often slow in developing. Indeed, Blyth and Milner observed that: 'given the opportunity, professionals would probably work better alone' (Blyth and Milner, 1990: 195). This compounds the difficulties of front-line workers working together to protect children. If the personal and organisational relationships do not exist, any response is a lottery for recipient families.

Hallett (1995) found that, where children were on the child protection register, core groups had been established in only a small number of cases. They were relatively informal processes, without clear guidelines governing who should chair them, parental attendance, frequency of meetings or clarity regarding the extent of their decision-making powers. Hallett found that inter-agency cooperation: 'was much more highly developed up to and including the initial conference than it was thereafter' (ibid.: 275). However, Birchall and Hallett (1995) argued strongly in favour of inter-agency work, showing that there had been some shift of attitude since the earlier research of Blyth and Milner. Both Birchall and Hallett acknowledged that part of this shift in perception may be a consequence of changes in the working culture, with inter-agency child protection becoming the accepted way of working.

One of the common themes to emerge from research studies into inter-agency collaboration in child protection has been that of professional agencies' perspectives on how work is shared and who carries responsibility for tasks. The studies of Farmer and Owen (1995) and Hallett (1995) identified considerable variation in the quality of the child protection plans made at initial child protection conferences. Social workers were consistently responsible for a high proportion of the planned protective intervention. As the local authority social worker is usually the keyworker for the family, this has led to situations where the child protection planning mechanism is viewed by others as yet another 'social services meeting' (Calder and Barratt, 1997). This can mitigate against other agencies recognising the importance of their direct input or involvement. In some areas this has led to social workers assuming that other workers are not prepared, post investigation, to take on child protection work, and other agencies have perceived that social workers believed they should retain all knowledge and expertise in this work (Calder and Barratt, 1997; Firth, 1995).

Recent research studies suggest that some progress has been made in moving the situation forward. This means that multi-agency plans are not vested so heavily in the resources and skills of social workers in isolation.

Hallett (1995) asked respondents to rate the contribution of other agencies in multi-agency working in terms of essential, important or not important. Each professional group was asked to comment only on the other professions, not their own. When the two categories of essential and important were brought together, it was found that six professions had scores of more than 90 per cent; that is, were seen as very important. These were social workers (98 per cent), police (96 per cent), teachers (95 per cent), paediatricians (94 per cent) and general practitioners (90 per cent). Such high expectations, however, do not directly correlate with actual attendance at core group meetings. Hallett, like other researchers (Farmer and Owen, 1995), found that paediatricians and general practitioners were frequently absent from the child protection forum. When asked to consider how well each profession performed its role, most respondents believed that social workers did very well. Given the frequent and widespread criticism of the social work profession in the press (Franklin and Parton, 1991), this may indicate that other professionals do have some insight into the difficulties that their social work colleagues face.

At times there is role confusion between different agencies. Perhaps not surprisingly, given their lead role, defined and supported by statute, the social worker's role was seen to be very clear by more than 66 per cent of respondents. The professions whose roles were most unclear were teachers and general practitioners, where 32 per cent and 34 per cent, respectively, of respondents thought the roles of these professionals were unclear. However, all respondents were inclined towards the view that the understanding of different roles and perceptions increased with the passage of time and as more experience of working together was gained. Although there was some lack of clarity about the role of teachers, they were still seen as having a valuable contribution to make by other professions. Social workers and health visitors were considered the most positive to work alongside, perhaps because of the close contact with family members their work entails (Hallett, 1995).

The roles of social workers and health visitors were seen by many to have some overlap, again perhaps because they are the two professions which characteristically have most face-to-face contact with families. That such role confusion does exist reinforces the need for a written protocol regarding the tasks and responsibilities of different core group members. As Calder and Horwath noted in Chapter 2, such a protocol has the potential to reduce the duplication of tasks and, similarly, other tasks are not overlooked or assumed to be someone else's responsibility. Once the core group goes on to meet, not all the anticipated problems have always been resolved. Horwath and Calder (1998) found that, although in 83 per cent of cases the decisions of core groups were recorded, in only 60 per cent were there full minutes of the meeting available in written form. The failure to record collectively the agreements and points of dispute in the meeting can lead to a variety of interpretations of the actions required, by whom and what outcome is planned. This suggests that there is considerable scope for refining and improving core group practice and policy in many areas of the country.

Calder and Barratt (1997) conducted some small scale research on core group practice which elicited the views of health visitors, teachers and social workers on their respective roles within the core group itself. They found a high degree of consensus between the groups, suggesting a real understanding of their own and each other's roles. The differences tended to emerge as workers moved beyond child protection considerations to what they might ideally want their colleagues to do. For example, teachers and social workers wanted health visitors to promote children's health and development via enhancing parenting skills and suggesting to parents remedies for identified problems; teachers and health visitors expected social workers to represent and support children as well as meeting the objectives of the child protection plan; social workers and health visitors expected teachers to offer less than the teachers themselves were prepared to contribute. The authors concluded that core group roles and responsibilities should be grounded in what can be delivered rather than idealised hopes and aspirations.

## The core group as a task-centred group

Whilst there may be a number of reasons why difficulties arise in multi-disciplinary core group working, including a lack of resources, policies and procedures, experience and research, Hallett and Birchall (1992) and Stevenson (1995) suggest that problems in carrying out a child protection plan often arise from the process of working together rather than the content of the work being undertaken. One example of this can be seen in cases where a core group member is undertaking work with an abuser within the family. It is not uncommon for the core group to regard the individual worker engaged in this work with an element of suspicion and mistrust, which often reflects their own attitudes towards the abuser. In these circumstances the group member may be left feeling devalued, angry and uncertain, with consequent damage to inter-agency relationships.

It is important for workers involved in this area of work to recognise that initial child protection conferences and core groups are in essence dynamically no different from most other task centred groups and are subject to the same strengths and pitfalls that are inherent in the processes of all such groups. To illustrate some of the difficulties that can occur, we can use the analogy of a football team. The team members play the same game but each has a specialist role within the team. The roles are highly interdependent and if one member of the team refuses to receive passes, or to send passes to another, the team does not perform effectively. The team is unlikely to meet its objectives unless the entire team understands and agrees the strategy to be adopted. If players believe they can achieve more playing as individuals, they may well sabotage the work of the team. Similarly, if they see the game purely as an opportunity to show off their skills, irrespective of whether they are an appropriate part of the team's strategy, they may sacrifice the overall objectives of the team.

Such behaviours can highlight some of the reasons why core groups fail or get stuck. Other reasons include some of the features identified by Calder (1995) as characteristics of newly formed core groups:

- local inter-agency rivalries or conflicts that influence individual attitudes or the behaviour of core group members;
- the absence of a universally agreed child centred philosophy;
- a lack of clarity regarding key tasks or time scales;
- no clear understanding of others' agency and individual roles;
- some of the child's needs being ignored;
- some members being antagonistic towards the group's objectives;
- some members guarding their resources – particularly information;
- the needs of the child being adapted to fit the skills of the core group;
- a hierarchy of importance established amongst core group members that leads to some members' contributions being devalued;
- cliques forming within the group, leaving some individuals isolated; and
- dissension and dissatisfaction with group leadership.

In order to avoid the problems outlined above becoming the basis for core group working, it is essential that attention is paid to the functioning and processes involved in task-focused groups. Whilst group dynamics are often complex and idiosyncratic, they are governed by a number of generalisations and are open to the influence of particular strategies and skills.

## Stages of group development and group processes

Brown (1992) and Tuckman (1965) suggest that groups generally progress through a number of stages: forming, storming, norming, performing and mourning. Garland *et al.* (1965) also suggest a pre-group stage. The model of group decision making outlined by Douglas (1976) can be used in conjunction with stages of group development to highlight some of the tasks that each stage includes: see Figure 5.1. We will now explore each of these stages in detail. Whilst we will address these sequentially, this is not to suggest that all

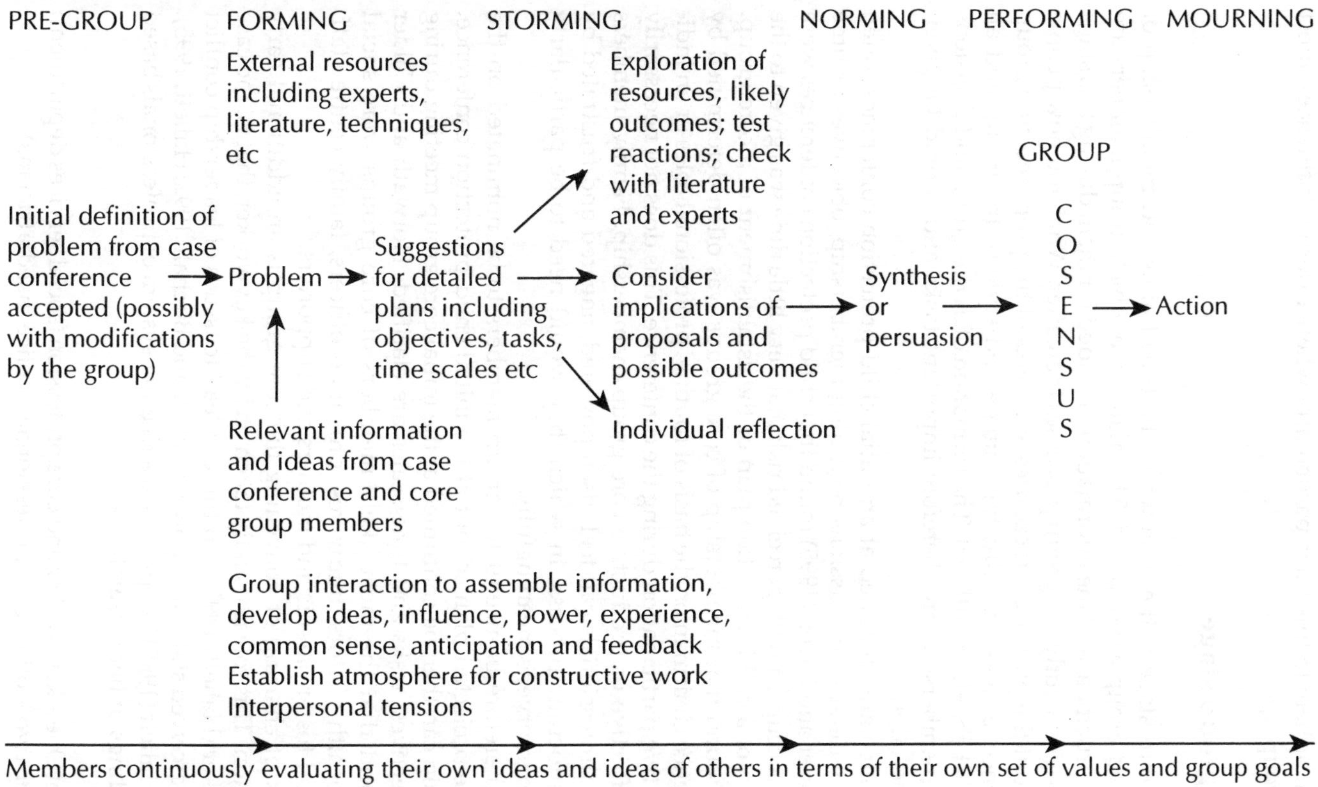


**Figure 5.1 A model of decision making by a professional work group**

*Source*: Adapted from Douglas (1976).

groups will adhere to this flow, particularly where external influences affect the core group.

## The pre-group stage

The pre-group stage is the time when the broad aims and membership of the proposed group are outlined. The manner in which group members are invited to participate and the information provided for them during this stage will affect significantly the group processes thereafter. What and how people are told about the purpose, procedures and tasks of the proposed core group will influence, at least initially, the climate and style of the group and an individual's behaviour within it. The formation of a core group and decisions regarding membership are therefore important tasks and should be given due consideration.

Core groups are identified at an initial child protection conference, often without any detailed discussions regarding membership, objectives or time scales. Farmer and Owen (1995) found that child protection conferences were often so preoccupied with perceived risk that very little time was given to the formulation of a child protection plan or the establishment of a core group. They also found that membership of core groups was often determined by the conference chairman on the basis of routine, professional roles or an individual's active participation during the conference. This does not necessarily result in effective or productive core group membership. Family members and many professionals can feel disempowered, angered and frustrated by such an autocratic process, in which they would need to be particularly assertive to intervene meaningfully.

It may therefore be useful for group members to be nominated on the basis of the projected plan set out at the initial child protection conference. Membership can then be confirmed at the initial core group meeting during which objectives, tasks and time scales are clarified. Horwath and Calder (1998) found that the most likely members of core groups were social workers, health visitors, midwives, probation officers, family centre staff, teachers and foster parents and mothers and supporters.

The task of chairing or convening the core group is an additional early consideration. This role is usually taken on by the keyworker, that is, the case social worker (Hallett, 1995) and this can lead to issues of leadership conflict based on perceived status and power (Hallett and Birchall, 1992; Hallett, 1995). Christine Hallett (1995) has proposed a five-tier system of professionals based on the findings of her research:

- Level One – key worker and core profession (social services department)
- Level Two – other core professionals (police, paediatricians)

- Level Three – front-line professionals (health visitors, teachers and general practitioners)
- Level Four – peripheral contact professionals (education welfare officers and school nurses)
- Level Five – case-specific professionals (lawyers, psychologists, psychiatrists).

The core group has to bring together this range of professionals with different backgrounds, training and status and facilitate inter-agency partnerships. This hierarchy also demonstrates just how many professionals may be involved in any given case. Jones and others (1987) pointed to 42 professionals that could be involved in a single case.

It is therefore important that there is group consensus regarding the person identified as the convenor of the core group and the responsibilities and powers this entails. It may be, in a majority of cases, that the group will agree to the social worker taking on this role, but if the social worker, for example, lacks confidence in the role or there is another group member who is more skilled and able to act as convenor, this might be considered.

## The forming stage

The forming stage is the period covering initial meetings. Most research and literature to date describes the core group as comprising professional staff. This now needs to be extended to consider the inclusion of parents, supporters and, occasionally, children in the group. It must be remembered, however, that family members at this stage are often feeling overwhelmed by the impact of the child protection process on their family and will need considerable support to enable them to participate, or even attend the initial meetings.

The Social Services Inspectorate (1995) recommend that, in order to prepare family members' participation in conferences, they should be engaged in a pre-conference meeting with the chairman. This suggestion is equally applicable to families engaging in core groups. Recommendations are as follows:

- to clarify the purpose and objectives of the core group;
- to check that families have the necessary information about the core group process;
- to discuss any special needs arising from disability, race, language, religion or culture which should be accommodated by the core group;
- to provide a brief description of the way the core group will be conducted;

- to discuss and clarify with the family the role of any supporter who may accompany them, and to meet the supporter;
- to clarify any exclusions and the reasons for these;
- to discuss the boundaries of confidentiality;
- to agree a possible timescale for core group meetings which takes account of any constraints on the family, for example collecting children from school.

The forming phase is usually characterised by polite, tense and restless behaviour whilst individual group members get to know each other, share information and attempt to understand how the group will behave and what their role will be. Group members will often engage in 'small talk' and social rituals, such as introductions, whilst they are establishing their status, seeking alliances, testing out whether their expectations will be met and how they compare to others.

Problems that can arise at the forming stage include the following:

1 Stereotyping, which can arise out of perceptions concerning status, gender, race, age and so on. An example was the assumption by workers in the Tyra Henry case that Tyra's grandmother was an all-coping black mother figure (London Borough of Lambeth, 1987).
2 The forming of cliques, based on prior relationships, similar expressed opinions and so on. For example, a health visitor and social worker who have previously worked well together always may look to support one another's views in the belief that this will lead to a replication of their good experience.
3 Mistrust, based on present or previous individual or agency relationships; for example, where agencies are in dispute about provision of resources, workers may offer opinions that reflect their agency's standpoint rather than the best option for the family.
4 Lack of confidence, individually or as a group. Groups or members without experience are less likely to risk decision making and may spend a disproportionate time contemplating alternative courses of action, their disadvantages and merits.
5 Confusion regarding tasks, roles, resources and responsibilities: for example, unless clarified, the task of monitoring a child can mean anything from catching sight of a child to frequent health checks and/or interviews with the child.

From the outset, attention to anti-oppressive processes is an essential task for all group members if the group is to function in an effective and meaningful manner. The work of all those engaged in the child protection system is directed at preventing the oppression (abuse) of children. A core group which mirrors or colludes with oppressive practices within or outside the group only serves as a model for abusive behaviour and is more likely to reinforce such attitudes and behaviour, rather than diminish them.

The core group is a powerful forum which has a significant role in determining the future for the children and families with whom it works. Parents, understandably, often feel vulnerable in these groups and power can easily be misused to punish parents or to set them up to fail. Again the need for shared understanding is emphasised by the researchers. Cleaver and Freeman (1995) found that, if there is no common understanding of purpose, each group member may attend the meeting with a different agenda, and confusion and conflict arises as people have different expectations of each other and themselves. Thoburn *et al.* (1995) found that workers and families had to strive to reach some common understanding on central issues if the potential for partnership and, ultimately, outcomes was to be enhanced. These central issues included agreement about the extent and culpability of the abuse; the alleged abuser not living within the home; the parents requesting help; no threats being made towards social workers; and a history of violent behaviour.

Thoburn *et al.* also found that family members stressed the importance of being respected and recognised as individuals. They could understand that the workers had a job to do, but they objected strongly to workers, in whatever profession, who did not appear to listen, did not show warmth or who only did things by the book.

There are a number of ways in which core group members can attempt to operate in an anti-oppressive manner. For example, consideration must be given to the language used in the core group. The use of interpreters, (explored in detail in Chapter 7 of the present volume) may be necessary, although language is not always verbal and, where appropriate, equal consideration should be given to the use of sign language interpreters. Horwath and Calder (1998) also found it was important to attend to the micro-level detail, such as the setting and timing of meetings and the use of supporters. They found that such considerations are all too frequently left to the families to raise, rather than being an integral part of the process. Group dynamics can be affected by a continued overlooking of partnership and anti-oppressive practice – with both workers and families – such as focusing on issues which detract from the principal tasks of planning, engagement and review.

Jargon can be a very powerful mechanism to assert authority and disempower families within a core group. Discussing issues and sharing information in a clear way at a pace that all group members can manage is essential. As MacDonald (1991) identified, our evaluation and response to others is:

> as much a product of our own views and experiences as it is of the information we gather. Part of the skill we need to employ is to recognise this and understand its influence on perceptions and decision making. In addition our identity and behaviour affects the way in which clients and other workers perceive us; this will define some of the information they give us or the way in which they behave with us. (MacDonald, 1991)

Oppression is not restricted to the worker–parent dynamic, however. Core group members who are black, young, elderly, female, disabled, working class, or members of different ethnic or religious groups, can also be negatively stereotyped, marginalised, undervalued or undermined. It should be the shared responsibility of all group members to challenge any inappropriate statements, behaviours or attitudes. In the initial stages of the core group, however, when many group members are anxious, wishing to conform and to be accepted by the group, it may require the group convenor to ensure that issues of anti-oppressive practice are addressed by the group. This demands that the convenor be skilled in recognising and responding to oppressive behaviour or statements and in challenging these in a sensitive and positive manner. As Calder and Horwath suggested in Chapter 2, a core group protocol might embrace anti-discriminatory practice issues to ensure 'ownership' among the core group members of the way to conduct themselves individually and collectively in the group.

Another role for the group convenor at this stage is to carefully observe the group interactions whilst helping members get acquainted. Individuals often give significant clues during the formal and informal introductory processes about their needs, hopes, expectations, resistances and abilities. Some may keep their distance from others, some may speak without listening, some may confront others in order to try and establish some status. The group convenor can facilitate the group's progress through this stage by allowing time at the start of meetings for informal interaction amongst the members, perhaps with refreshments, before focusing the group on the purpose for which they are there. The combination of social interaction and purposeful discussion can help to develop the group's cohesion and enhance its problem solving ability.

Feelings of mistrust and a lack of confidence in the group can be minimised if group members spend time sharing information, developing a consensus on a child-centred perspective, clarifying aims and objectives, recognising skills and deficits and agreeing the most effective methods of achieving aims.

The group should confirm that they have a common philosophical approach to the work to be undertaken. The adoption of a child centred philosophy is essential, but its implications and meaning have to be fully understood and agreed. Problems may arise when there is little or no agreement and, in these circumstances, differences should be openly discussed and resolved wherever possible. Failure to achieve any degree of consensus would suggest that the group has fundamental problems and should seek help in an attempt to resolve the difficulties (see those solutions suggested in Chapters 2 and 9). The possible conflict, delay and anxiety that these situations can give rise to can be very much reduced by the core group agreeing at commencement a mechanism for seeking help if necessary, for example from an identified consultant.

Identification and recognition of the group members' skills, resources, roles and limitations (for example, time) is also an important task at the commencement of a core group. Hallett (1995), in her research on inter-agency coordination in child protection, found that significant problems arose regarding tasks, priorities and role confusion between workers, which resulted in unrealistic or incompatible suggestions about who should or would undertake certain tasks.

Group members should be afforded equal respect for their skills and contributions. Those who know the child best, for example parents, foster carers and residential workers, often have the least professional qualifications. Their views and the information they provide should be afforded the same weight as those whose professional status might otherwise result in their views taking precedence. The establishment of mutual respect in the group is important, as individuals are more likely to reach a consensus with those whom they regard positively than with those whom they dislike and disregard. The use of a group agreement between core group members, which is discussed later in this chapter, can help to promote such collaborative behaviours.

Individual members should be encouraged to be clear about the commitment they give to undertake work. A plan of work can easily be sabotaged by members who agree to take on tasks because they think they ought to and then fail to meet their commitments.

The overall aim at this stage is to develop a clear understanding and agreement of objectives, tasks, roles and time scales. Whilst group consensus is desired, swift agreement can often be a sign that a group is approaching its goals uncritically, perhaps in the hope of a speedy solution or because members are afraid to deal with disagreement or face new ideas. Unquestioning consensus can, in many circumstances, be as dangerous as conflict. Dingwall *et al.* (1983), in research into child protection conferences, found that decisions and suggestions were generally made by high-status or powerful group members. An adequate idea or plan was quickly adopted by other group members and direct pressure to conform was placed on those who were assertive enough to dissent. The perceived pressure on multidisciplinary groups to work together in unison and maintain the idea that practitioners 'know what to do' acts as powerful inhibitor to individuals questioning decisions, presenting new ideas or dissenting from the consensus. As Calder and Horwath pointed out in Chapter 2, conflict is healthy if it is carefully managed, as it often opens up several possible avenues to achieve a desired outcome. In this way there are choices for the core group and family involved.

Groups proceed best when as many opinions and suggestions as possible are made and examined. As Barbara Firth identified in Chapter 4, in order for this to occur group members must feel confident to make suggestions without fear of being ignored, personally challenged or criticised. Sufficient time must be also be given for discussion, with breaks to relieve tension and prevent participants becoming impatient or bored.

## The storming stage

The storming stage of a group's development can be a turbulent period during which individuals may have become disenchanted with each other, resentful of the demands made of them and less optimistic about outcomes. Whilst some groups will enjoy a strong feeling of integration and appear to move swiftly through to the 'norming' stage, others will undoubtedly recognise that the honeymoon is over and will face conflict, anger, withdrawal and apparent disintegration. Even if the group does not demonstrate extreme negative behaviours, it may not enjoy a strong 'team spirit'. Some members, for example, may feel very uncomfortable when disagreements and negative views are expressed. Others may be confused or uncomfortable with their role, while some may consider the objectives to be unrealistic. Groups can easily become stuck at this stage and, while some or all of the group's tasks may be completed subsequently, group members may be left feeling dissatisfied, angry or dispirited. Berne (1963) suggests that, when problems occur at this stage, it is essential that time is given to addressing the processes involved, even when this means delaying the completion of tasks. Problems that can occur during this stage include the following:

- scapegoating of group member(s) (frequently family members or group convenors);
- competitive behaviour or attempts to dominate;
- rejection of original agreements, aims and tasks;
- hidden agendas surfacing (agency or individual);
- attempts by cliques to wield power, such as family versus professional cliques or other sub-groups within the group; and
- previously active members withdrawing, remaining silent or becoming inactive.

Each group member brings into the group his or her own beliefs, biases, hopes and fears. These may result in some members holding hidden agendas or feeling a sense of conflict with all or some of the other group members. Whilst conflicts and disagreements between organisations, individuals, families or workers are to be expected, the way in which they are managed within the group is crucial to the group's future functioning.

This stage of a group's existence requires positive, sensitive and careful management by the group convenor. There is a strong need for structure and clear agendas for meetings in order that the group remains focused and to avoid becoming sidetracked or enmeshed in irrelevant issues. If, however, the group becomes so dysfunctional that it cannot operate effectively then Hartford (1971) suggests the convenor may need to consider one or more of the following strategies: (1) to help the group members refocus their attention by reflecting on the group, themselves and their expectations, (2) to bring conflict to the surface to attempt to find a resolution by confronting the issues, (3) to engage the group in reviewing its membership, and (4) to assist the group in renegotiating objectives, tasks, roles and time scales.

Kakabadse *et al.* (1988) recommended the following approaches to improve collaboration and understanding amongst groups of people:

- the use of reflective listening to improve the understanding of problems and build trust between individuals;
- employing assertion skills, which can have a powerful impact on people and help maintain their commitment to the work;
- avoiding dominating, threatening or aggressive behaviours and making judgements only on the basis of fact to reduce communication blocks;
- issues rather than interpersonal tensions should be emphasised, which involves gathering facts, breaking larger issues into smaller workable units and confronting each problem separately; and
- careful appraisal of the agreed actions and an assessment of the consequences of those actions to deter individuals or groups from needless disputes in the future.

Groups which experience significant problems during the storming stage and manage to reach resolution can go on to achieve higher levels of integration, cooperation and satisfaction than some groups who sail through this stage without disturbance.

## The norming stage

This stage is depicted by the development of a group culture and routine. Group members tend to refer to 'we' and often seek and offer each other support and approval. Relationships stabilise and defences are lowered so that group members become more cohesive, trusting, open and task-focused. As described in the forming stage, a 'cosy' atmosphere or complete lack of disagreement in the group can be a dangerous symptom and disagreement or suggestions should be consistently and actively explored. If conflict does arise, its value in allowing alternative suggestions should therefore be recognised. By the 'norming' stage, however, it is usually dealt with as a shared problem rather than a head-to-head battle. The task of the convenor is generally to enable the group leadership to be shared and to encourage all members to participate in decision making. Whilst this stage is often problem-free, it is important that a core group remains focused on its objectives and tasks and that members are not tempted to rest in this comfortable stage.

## The performing stage

The performing stage is the period of task-focused activity conducted by a self-sufficient group. Problems that arise are often resolved within the group, with members offering high levels of energy and positive attitudes. Creative solutions can often emerge, since group members are now willing to explore new suggestions collectively. Ideas developed by the group may often result in more positive outcomes than the original suggestions individuals may have made.

It is important to review regularly the functioning and membership of the core group throughout this stage so as to ensure that all members have clear, identified tasks. During the progress of the child protection plan it may be appropriate for the membership of the core group to change so that those who have completed tasks can leave the group and others who have skills required at later stages can be included. Changes in group membership, however, may involve the group in revisiting previous stages in the group's development.

The core group remains accountable to the child protection review, who retain the responsibility for critically analysing the plan, the outcomes attained to date and the anticipated future risks and continuation of registration. Where the core group has operated well as a group and presented unanimously agreed recommendations to the child protection review, there is the potential for major conflict and emotional hurt if these recommendations are overturned (Calder, 1990). Indeed, the core group could mourn if it does not feel its work has been accepted. Alternatively, where they are accepted, they have to deal with deregistration and the disbanding of the core group, which can be particularly difficult if the group feels that there is still work to be done over and above the threshold criteria for deregistration.

### The mourning stage

The prospects of the group ending, whether planned or not, can induce anxiety in its members. The need to pay attention to separation is no less significant if it involves a group rather than individuals. This can be most acute for families who have experienced a sense of belonging in the core group, and the ending can resurrect other painful experiences for them, thus escalating their sense of anxiety and loss. This requires careful management. It is important to clarify from the outset that the core group is a time-limited exercise which will continue for the duration of registration and no longer. Within the group's life, this needs to be periodically restated, so as to remind members and try to ensure that they do not become overly dependent on the support that the group can offer.

Parental reluctance towards deregistration is not uncommon and, where parents have found the process enabling and supportive, can lead to difficulties in disengaging. Parents may argue that the group is still needed and may become aggressive or withdrawn towards the other members who they believe are deserting or rejecting them. Such feelings may also affect the professional members of a core group, particularly where they have enjoyed a sense of achievement and satisfaction in their role. In such circumstances it may be that a professional is keen for the group to continue and they may therefore suggest further tasks to complete in order to prolong the life of the group.

In either of the above circumstances, it may be helpful to recall the original goals of the child protection plan and compare these with the tasks that have been completed and the outcomes accomplished by the group, as well as clarifying the nature and purpose of any future contacts (Vernelle, 1994).

## Other factors influencing group dynamics

### Emotional aspects

Child protection core groups are not merely task-centred groups, but have as their focus the emotive subject of child abuse and child protection. The emotional aspects of the work cannot be diminished or ignored and are likely to be a significant factor in the development and progress of a core group, regardless of how 'professional' its ethos and style. It is not uncommon, for example, for members of core groups working closely and intensively with family members to begin to mirror the problems, attitudes, fears and hopes of the individual or family with whom they are working. It is possible, during the implementation of a child protection plan, for workers to begin to form positive, perhaps empathic, relationships with individual members of a family and the feelings, wishes and rationalisations of the family member will become known to the professional. When the worker then reflects these thoughts and feelings to the core group they may overidentify with them and regard them as more important than those of other family members. In this way conflict within the family can be mirrored within the core group team. The line manager has a role in resolving such inter-agency danger (see Chapter 9 for further details).

## Failure to confront

Problems can also arise when workers fail to confront difficult issues in the family (Dale *et al.*, 1986). The core group may avoid issues with each other for fear of having to then raise them with the family. Thus the core group can mirror a family which minimises or ignores difficult and sensitive issues. Morrison (1993) identified such problems as components of a 'professional accommodation syndrome' and suggested that workers may be affected by each component. Groups that do not resolve each issue as it arises, inevitably move on to the next stage of the syndrome, which includes:

> Secrecy: Many staff do not want to speak about the impact on them of the work they do because they feel the agency or colleagues covertly restricts permission to do so.
>
> Helplessness: Staff who feel helpless are ashamed of themselves because they experience the agency as despising helplessness in them as adults and professionals who should 'cope'. Myths exist that they should behave rationally and logically.
>
> Entrapment and Accommodation: Staff are trapped in a paradox whereby telling the truth about their feelings is seen as unprofessional and maintaining the lie is seen as 'coping'. The accommodation is made by then deciding that the fault lies with them for feeling as they do and that this would not happen if they were a better professional or person. The solution appears to lie in suppressing their feelings and working harder.
>
> Delayed or unconvincing disclosure: Eventually disclosure of the distress may be triggered by conflict, training, or talking to a colleague. Where conflict triggers disclosure, this may be in the form of unpredictable behaviour such as aggression, resignation or sickness. If this behaviour is not understood, the underlying distress will remain undetected e.g.: 'She should never have been a social worker anyway' or 'It's because she's a woman.'
>
> Retraction: The delayed or confusing nature of the disclosure followed by disbelief, insensitivity or avoidance on the part of the agency, then leaves the worker

psychologically and professionally abandoned, fearing that she/he will now be written off as incompetent. In the face of this threat to their whole career the only solution appears to be retraction on the part of the worker e.g.: 'I'm fine now, it was nothing to do with work.' Secrecy resumes.

These examples highlight the importance of identifying and processing issues in core groups and yet attention to such issues is often suppressed, with remarks such as 'Let's just get on with the job.' This can happen when members are uncomfortable with any self examination or when they fail to recognise the impact that disruptive processes can have on group members and the outcome of their work.

Such resistance may be contained at the outset if group members are helped to recognise that core groups can benefit from attention to task and process. When sufficient time is given to both these aspects of core group functioning it is likely to result in a more cohesive and productive group, who can agree and enact decisions rather than repeatedly discussing and shelving them. The production of a group agreement can involve the members in identifying the mechanisms the group will employ to monitor process and the action to be taken if difficulties arise.

## Practical considerations for the core group

In the light of research findings and what is known about group processes and dynamics, it is important that we try and consider these matters in the practical application of core group working. Some issues come easily to mind when considering factors which may impede successful core group working.

### Venue

The first such issue is the venue for core group meetings. Social services' offices are often venues which parents as well as other workers do not feel comfortable attending and can reinforce the concept that social services have ownership of core groups. It may be possible to hold meetings in a community-based facility which does not carry with it the same level of stigma for parents. Care needs to be given to which facility is used, as meetings in schools, for example, can reinforce a family's feeling of failure if they are asked to explain their attendance at that venue by other school users (Calder, 1991). Similarly, for workers, a more neutral venue can help ensure that core group meetings do not become just another 'social workers' meeting'. Horwath and Calder (1998) suggested that consideration is given to whether the meetings can be held within the parents' home as a way of bridging the gap between parents and workers, although consideration also has to be given to the potential sources of disruption from the task in hand.

## Size

The size of the core group is an important consideration. Extensive research into groups has led to the accepted view that the dynamics of large groups (ten or more members) can be very complex (Argyle, 1972) and hierarchies and sub groups begin to form (Argyle, 1983). In core groups, a way of limiting membership is to require each member of a core group to have a task or tasks within the child protection plan. This should include family members so that there is equal status for each member of the core group. This avoids core group numbers being swelled by those whose role is purely to 'monitor' the child or the family situation. Information gained from those undertaking monitoring tasks can be fed into meetings via written reports or direct liaison with an identified core group member. Whilst there is no absolute majority size for a core group, it should not exceed half a dozen people if it is to be functional, informal and practical. Calder and Horwath, in Chapter 2 of the present volume, also suggested the possibility of more than one core group if numbers become too large: for example, one for each child with differing needs.

## Evaluation

Continuing evaluation of the child protection plan and the progress of the core group in meeting its defined objectives and outcomes is an essential task for any core group and should be an integral task in meetings. Without consistent evaluation, the core group is not in a position to adjust plans when necessary, to recognise when its work is complete or to make recommendations to review conferences. Calder and Barratt (1997) found that only one-third of staff felt it 'always' reviewed the protection plan, whilst 59 per cent felt it happened 'sometimes'. This suggests that there is a failure to reformulate the plan to reflect new information or changing circumstances, particularly leaving children in situations of actual or potential harm.

Even in those circumstances where a core group has worked well and true multi-agency collaboration has taken place, the collective achievement can be dissipated at the child protection review if each member of the core group presents an individual report. Multi-agency collaboration would be more effectively reflected by a single report compiled by the core group, which could incorporate individual views if the group had not reached a complete consensus. If minutes of each core group meeting have been recorded, assessing the progress achieved and the tasks still outstanding, they can form the basis of the report, with recommendations for future action at the conclusion of the report. In this way duplication of information could be avoided and a clear overall picture presented to the child protection conference. Alternatively, a format for a collective report is suggested by Calder and Horwath in Chapter 2.

## Establishing a framework

As previously indicated, the use of a written protocol between core group members can be a useful management tool. An agreement should include details of how the core group will operate, who will undertake which tasks, on what, and in what time scale. Although producing detailed agreements can be time consuming, they can be very helpful in ensuring that everyone is clear about what needs to be done and can be used to measure progress.

Issues to be covered in an agreement between core group members include the following.

1 Frequency of meetings: it is often advantageous to book meetings for three months at a time, rather than from one meeting to the next, as diaries are often difficult to coordinate in the shorter term.
2 Who to contact if members are unable to attend meetings, and a commitment that in such circumstances members will forward a written report if possible.
3 The appointment of a person who will take on the role of organising and confirming the venue.
4 The establishment of a system for taking the minutes, perhaps using a preformatted form which simply needs details to be inserted. It may be appropriate to rotate the role of minute taker.
5 The procedure to be followed if one member needs to call an earlier core group meeting.
6 A commitment by members to undertake allocated tasks within agreed time scales.
7 The appointment of a chairman for each meeting to ensure that the agenda is adhered to and that the meetings run to time. Many child protection procedures require the local authority social worker to be both the keyworker for the case and the chairman of the core group. This often proves to be less than ideal and detracts from the concept of core groups as a multi-agency rather than a social services forum. Social work training does not often provide social workers with the necessary skills for

effective leadership and the chairing of meetings. There may be other group members with greater skills and resources who are able to take on the role.

8 A set of principles governing how the group will function. These may include rules about listening, challenging, language and so on.
9 Strategies for resolving any difficulties which may occur. For example, the use of an external consultant may be beneficial although, to maintain the multi-agency structure of core groups, consultants should be individuals with a working knowledge of child protection issues, from across the range of child protection agencies. They may, for example, be a member of the Area Child Protection Committee.

## Summary

Multi-agency core groups are increasingly being recognised as a mechanism with significant positive potential for effective multi-agency work in the child protection system. A cohesive core group can draw on a range of ideas, skills and resources in a focused and efficient manner in order to engage and support families and carry forward a child protection plan. Problems of duplication of work, role confusion and inter-agency miscommunications are minimised and the families worked with can benefit from a clear understanding of expectations of them and how they may meet them.

Effective core groups are, however, almost always the product of skilled management and effort rather than luck. All too often it is assumed that identifying group members and providing them with a set of goals is sufficient to enable the group to operate successfully. If we wish to realise the potential benefits that core groups have to offer, recognition must be given by Area Child Protection Committees and the agencies that are involved to the resources, training and support that core group workers will need.

## References

Argyle, M. (1972) 'The Nature of Social Relationships II', in *Social Relationships*, Milton Keynes: Open University Press.

Argyle, M. (1983) *The Psychology of Interpersonal Behaviour*, Harmondsworth: Penguin Books.

Berne, E. (1963) *The Structure and Dynamics of Organisations and Groups*, Philadelphia: J.B. Lippincott.

Birchall, E. (1992) *Report to the Department of Health: Working Together in Child Protection: Report of Phase Two: A Survey of the Experience and Perceptions of Six Key Professions*, Stirling: University of Stirling.

Birchall, E. and Hallett, C. (1995) *Working Together in Child Protection*, London: HMSO.
Blyth, E. and Milner, J. (1990) 'The Process of Inter-agency Work', in *Violence Against Children Study Group, Taking Child Abuse Seriously*, London: Unwin Hyman.
Brown, A. (1992) *Groupwork*, 3rd edn, Aldershot: Arena.
Calder, M.C. (1990) 'Core Group or Network? A Chance to Comment', *Child Abuse Review*, **4** (3): 16.
Calder, M.C. (1991) 'Child Protection Core Groups: Beneficial or Bureaucratic?', *Child Abuse Review*, **5** (2): 26–9.
Calder, M.C. (1995) 'Towards Good Practice in Child Protection', keynote presentation to the National Conference, 'Core group: central to child protection – myth or reality?', Manchester Town Hall, 14 July.
Calder, M.C. and Barratt, M. (1997) 'Inter-agency Perspectives on Core Group Practice', *Children and Society*, **11** (4): 209–21.
Cleaver, H. and Freeman, P. (1995) *Parental Perspectives in Cases of Suspected Child Abuse*, London: HMSO.
Dale, P., Davies, M., Morrison, T. and Waters, J. (1986) *Dangerous Families*, London: Tavistock.
Department of Health (1991a) *Child Abuse: A study of Inquiry Reports 1980–1989*, London: HMSO.
Department of Health (1991b) *Working Together under the Children Act 1989*, London: HMSO.
Department of Health and Social Security (1973) *A Report from the Working Party on Collaboration between the NHS and Local Government in its Activities to the End of 1972*, London: HMSO.
Department of Health and Social Security (1974) *Report of the Committee of Inquiry into the Care and Supervision Provided in Relation to Maria Colwell*, London: HMSO.
Department of Health and Social Security (1988) *Working Together: A Guide to Arrangements for Inter-agency Co-operation for the Protection of Children from Abuse*, London: HMSO.
Dingwall, R., Eekelaar, J. and Murray, T. (1983) *The Protection of Children: State intervention and family life*, Oxford: Blackwell.
Douglas, T. (1976) *Groupwork Practice*, London: Tavistock.
Farmer, E. and Owen, M. (1993) 'Decision Making, Intervention and Outcome', in *Child Protection Work: Draft Report to the Department of Health*, Bristol: Department of Social Policy, University of Bristol.
Farmer, E. and Owen, M. (1995) *Child Protection Practice: Private Risks and Public Remedies – Decision Making, Intervention and Outcome in Child Protection Work*, London: HMSO.
Firth, B. (1995) *Survey of Core Groups in the Rotherham Child Protection Committee Area*, Nottingham: School of Social Studies.
Franklin, B. and Parton, N. (eds) (1991) *Social Work, the Media and Public Relations*, London: Routledge.
Garland, J., Jones, H. and Kolodny, M. (1965) 'A Model for Stages in the Development of Social Work Groups', in S. Bernstein (ed.), *Explorations of Group Work*, Boston: Boston University.
Hallett, C. (1995) *Inter-Agency Co-ordination in Child Protection*, London: HMSO.
Hallett, C. and Birchall, E. (1992) *Co-ordination in Child Protection*, Edinburgh: HMSO.
Hartford, M.E. (1971) *Groups in Social Work*, New York: Columbia University Press.
Heron, J. (1989), *The Facilitator's Handbook*, London: Longmans.

Horwath, J. and Calder, M.C. (1998) 'Working Together to Protect Children on the Child Protection Register: Myth or Reality?', *British Journal of Social Work,* **28** (6): 879–95.
Kakabadse, A., Ludlow, R. and Vinnicombe, S. (1988) *Social Working in Organisations,* London: Penguin Business.
London Borough of Lambeth (1987) 'Report of the Public Inquiry into the Death of Tyra Henry', London Borough of Lambeth.
MacDonald, S. (1991) *All Equal under the Act? – A Practical Guide to the Children Act 1989 for Social Workers,* London: Race Equality Unit.
Morrison, T. (1993) *Staff Supervision in Social Care,* London: Longmans.
Social Services Inspectorate (1995) *The Challenge of Partnership in Child Protection: Practice Guide,* London: HMSO.
Stevenson, O. (1995) 'Case Conferences in Child Protection', in K. Wilson and A. James (eds), *The Child Protection Handbook,* London: Bailliere Tindall.
Thoburn, J., Lewis, A. and Stemmings, D. (1995) *Paternalism or Partnership? Family Involvement in the Child Protection Process,* London: HMSO.
Tuckman, B.W. (1965) 'Developmental Sequence in Small Groups', *Psychological Bulletin,* LXIII: 384–99.
Vernelle, B. (1994) *Understanding and Using Groups,* London: Whiting and Birch.

# 6 Core groups and partnership: three models and a case study

*Alastair Christie and Helle Mittler*

In this chapter, consideration is given to:

- the development of partnership approaches in post-registration work;
- three different models of partnership and their application to the core group;
- the nature of family involvement in decision making;
- the needs and strengths of families in the partnership process; and
- the voluntary–involuntary nature of partnerships within core groups.

Numerous and complex relationships exist between practitioners, parents/carers[1] and children within child protection social work. These relationships are constantly being reshaped by professional practice, organisational procedures and, not least, by government legislation and guidance. The last decade has seen the introduction and implementation of the Children Act 1989 which has placed relationships between practitioners, parents/carers and children under the broad heading of 'partnership'. The notion of partnership does not appear in the Children Act itself, and it is only overtly referred to in the accompanying guidance and regulations. As well as constructing child protection work, the introduction of the concept of partnership has redefined relationships between the state and the family (Morrison, 1996) with a post-Cleveland emphasis on reducing the power of the state to intervene in the private lives of parents/carers and young children.[2] Whilst partnership has gained a new prominence in the vocabulary of practitioners and policy makers, the concept is not new. Social workers have previously pursued partnership under various labels such as 'client self-determination', 'empowerment', 'user involvement', 'the rights of clients' and 'community participation'.

In this chapter we discuss the development of partnership approaches in post-registration child protection work. We then draw on three models of partnership in order to analyse a case study of work in core groups. The models raise questions about the nature of parent/carer involvement in decision making, the needs and strengths of parents/carers in the partnership process and, finally, the voluntary/involuntary nature of 'partnerships' within core groups. We complete the chapter by suggesting that the use of particular concepts of partnership have implications for the ways in which practitioners, parents/carers and children work together in core groups.

## Current developments in partnership within the core group

Partnership is an ambiguous and yet popular and readily accepted concept. Hughes (1992) suggests that 'partnership of any kind is assumed to be a good thing, like apple pie and cream, intrinsically wholesome and, almost certainly, guaranteed to satisfy'. Howe suggests that 'partnership is one of those promiscuous words; everyone is for it and it is bad not to be in favour of it' (Howe, 1992: 40). Whether 'wholesome' and/or 'promiscuous', working in partnership with colleagues, parents/carers and children is now generally accepted as central to child protection work. However, when we say generally accepted, that is at the level of policy makers and social workers; service users may have a different view of their relationships with practitioners and the child protection process (see Christie, 1992).

Current developments of partnership in core groups have been largely driven in practice by social workers and other front-line workers who have for some time advocated that parents/carers and children be included to a greater or lesser extent in the discussion and/or decision making in post-registration work. Calder and Horwath's (forthcoming) survey of 43 Area Child Protection Committees (ACPCs) as described in Chapter 2, revealed that 69 per cent of ACPCs invited parents to attend core groups, compared to 18 per cent of ACPCs which sometimes invited involvement and 6 per cent which rarely invited parents to attend core groups. While 77 per cent of ACPCs said that social services would provide help for parents to attend core groups, the amount and type of help varied. Support for parents to attend core groups included offering transport, child care, interpreters and flexibility about the timing of the meetings. Calder and Horwath found that ACPCs were less welcoming to carers (as opposed to parents) and to children, with only 56 per cent of ACPCs inviting carers and only 8 per cent of ACPCs always inviting children. The research suggests a greater degree of ambivalence when it comes to retaining partnership with carers and even more ambivalence about children as partners.

## Factors influencing workers' attitudes towards partnership

While the development of core groups has largely been practice-led within individual social work agencies, this important practice development needs to be understood within the wider social context. These developments include, first, the legacy of child abuse enquiries in the 1970s and 1980s which raised questions about working relationships between parents/carers, children and front-line workers. Some inquiries criticised some social workers for working too closely with parents and carers, whilst others criticised workers for not listening to parents/carers and children. Social workers were criticised for not intervening to protect, as in the case of Jasmine Beckford, and for being overzealous in the use of their statutory powers, as in the cases considered by the Cleveland Inquiry. Second, social workers and researchers have become increasingly aware of the limitations of removing children from the care of their parents/carers. More recently, abuse by men, some employed as social workers, has dramatically shown that the safety of children cannot be automatically guaranteed in residential and foster care. Third, parents/carers have formed their own organisations to draw attention to and represent the views of parents/carers and their rights and needs. Groups such as the 'Family Rights Group' and 'Parents Against Injustice' (PAIN) publish research findings, appeal to public opinion, lobby government and demand that front-line workers take more account of parents'/carers' and children's views and rights. These groups appealed to the Conservative government's familial ideology (in the 1980s and early 1990s) which employed and encouraged family maintenance and self-reliance in the context of severe constraints on public spending. Fourth, European and international law has increasingly supported the rights of parents to be consulted and involved in decisions that affect the lives of family members. In particular, the rights of children are acknowledged within the United Nation's Charter on Children's Rights (1989). All the above factors underpinned the Children Act 1989 and encouraged the trend towards the active participation of parents/carers and children in child protection decision making as well as influencing the attitudes of practitioners.

## What is partnership?

Whilst partnership is considered a 'good thing', the underlying assumptions about partnerships between families, parents/carers, children and front-line workers are rarely made explicit. Calder argues that much of recent writing on partnership has been a 'repackaging of old social work ideas accompanied by the trendy notion of empowerment. It is arguably a cosmetic packaging for a new form of social control' (Calder, 1995: 753). He goes on to suggest that, rather than developing partnerships with parents/carers, some social work practice can best be described as paternalistic, with practitioners making judgements in the 'best interest' of parents/carers and child that are not based on their involvement/consultation in the decision-making process. More contentiously, Allsopp (1994) suggests that partnership is a social deodorant that anaesthetises the nostrils but does not get rid of the smell of social control. Both these views acknowledge that professionals have the potential to abuse power within partnerships. It is important, therefore, to deconstruct what is actually meant by partnership, how it is operationalised and in whose interests.

A number of researchers have also identified benefits of partnership for parents/carers, children and the practitioners themselves. For example, Shemmings and Thoburn (1989) argue that parental participation increases parents' understanding of child protection processes and also helps them to understand the concerns that front-line workers might have about their child. The Family Rights Group (1991) suggests that participation encourages parents to be more committed to the child protection process. Thoburn *et al.* (1995) found that social workers wanted to work with parents because they believed it made their interventions more effective. At an operational level, Atherton (1991) suggests that parental participation speeds up the process of assessment. Mittler's research (1993) identified parents' significant contributions to greater accuracy of information and to a wider range of options for intervention. She argues that parental participation in decision making increases parents' ability to protect their children. The government recommends that:

> a co-operative working relationship between the helping services and families is essential if the welfare of the child is to be ensured. This co-operative relationship is more likely to be achieved if parents are encouraged to take as large a part as possible from the outset in decisions about the protection of their children and the appropriate services needed to ensure that the child remains safe. (DoH, 1995a)

Calder and Horwath (forthcoming) have identified four sets of reasons provided by the government (in *Messages from Research* (DoH, 1995b) and *The Challenge to Partnership in Child Protection* (DoH, 1995a)) for workers to operate in partnership with parents/carers and children. They identified these following an evaluation of the two governmental documents. Partnerships are expected:

1 to increase the effectiveness of social workers' intervention;
2 to encourage parents/carers to provide professionals with information;
3 to give parents/carers some 'rights' to hear what is being said about them and influence decision making; and
4 to empower parents/carers through being engaged in the process of decision making.

As Calder and Horwath (forthcoming) have identified, these policy changes on the part of government is both a pragmatic and an efficiency-led development rather than the principle and ethics-led initiatives that have been taken up by professional social workers in their own practice.

*Messages from Research* (DoH, 1995b) noted that inter-agency cooperation falls post-initial case conference, with the social worker often left 'holding the baby' (Hallett, 1995). This finding has serious implications for the idea of partnership when applied to the constituent agencies involved in child protection. Social services have a lead responsibility under the 1989 Act to 'investigate'. Other agencies have a duty to collaborate with social services departments but, because of their different priorities (Hallett, 1995), often withdraw from involvement after the formal, high-profile child protection conference. We could say that, as research emphasises the continuing importance of inter-agency perspectives, it is important that social workers continue to seek to engage other agencies. As long as social services adopt a lead agency attitude it is inevitable that the other agencies will have to adopt a position of 'feeding in', rather than taking particular responsibilities for child protection. This is an issue that social service agencies and social workers need to bear in mind when involved in the setting up and maintenance of partnership with other professional agencies.

Government encouragement in the direction of partnership and the benefits claimed by researchers do not, of course, mean that the process of developing partnerships is straightforward or easy to achieve. Even though the experience of actually including family members in child protection conferences and core groups has greatly lessened the fears of many front-line workers, there are still many questions about what is meant by partnership. Core groups provide spaces which are less constrained by institutional procedures (Mittler, 1997), in which workers, parents/carers and children can develop a wide variety of partnerships. This freedom to develop good practice places an onus on workers to reflect on the nature of partnership and the ways in which their practice might be oppressive and/or liberating.

To encourage this reflection, or reflexive practice, we present three models of partnership which we then use to analyse a case study drawn from the practice experience of one of the present authors. We then go on to suggest some of the ways in which practitioners' concept(s) of partnership may influence their day-to-day practice. In the next section of this chapter we describe these theoretical models of partnership in order to set the scene for the analysis of post-registration.

# Three models of partnership

## Parents'/carers' participation in decision making

The models discussed under this heading emphasise decision making as a central locus of 'participation'. Early examples of this model of partnership can be found in research on parents' involvement in their children's education and in the educational system. These early models tended to focus on the degree to which parents/carers could participate in decision making within the school. For example, Burman *et al.* (1983) developed a model based on a survey of parental participation in special education. The authors describe a continuum of involvement in decision making in the educational system. At one end of the continuum, parents and teachers share basic information about the child's educational progress. At the other end of the continuum, parents are involved in joint service planning, selection of staff, lobbying for resources and representation on various professional and local government bodies. Pugh (1981) suggests that partnerships between parents/carers and practitioners in pre-school education can be characterised in four steps, the fourth of which results in full participation: non-participation, support, participation and partnership/control. Partnership, then, is represented by Pugh as a high level of involvement and potentially incorporating control of decision-making outcomes.

Thoburn *et al.* (1995) has developed the concept of a continuum of participation in decision making in child protection work by drawing on the community development work of Arnstein (1969). Their model is represented in Table 6.1. This 'Ladder of Participation in Child Protection' suggests that non-participatory approaches can be manipulative and placatory. They identify three ways that parents/carers can be involved in decision making which Thoburn regards as tokenistic and Calder (1995) as paternalistic. Thoburn *et al.* argue that involvement, consultation and participation can each be tokenistic. Partnership is only achieved when parents/carers are involved in designing the child protection services and have some delegated power to influence service provision. Thoburn *et al.* set high standards by which partnerships between parents/carers and workers are judged. On these criteria, not all workers will be able to be full partners. This model supports the Family Rights Group (1991) definition of partnership as:

> marked by respect for one another, rights to information, accountability, competence and value accorded to the individual input. In short, each partner is seen as having something to contribute, power is shared, decisions made jointly, roles are not only respected but also backed by a set of legal and moral rights. (Family Rights Group, 1991: 1)

**Table 6.1 Ladder of participation in child protection**

| Consequence | Type of participation |
|---|---|
| Delegated power<br>Involvement in service design | Partnership |
| Participation<br>Consultation<br>Involvement | Tokenism |
| Placation<br>Manipulation | Non-participation |

*Source*: Thoburn *et al.* (1995).

While this definition may offer the ultimate goal of 'true partnership', it may not be realistic for day-to-day work with specific parents. It raises the expectation that parents should be involved in developing child protection systems and places the onus on practitioners to explain why parents/carers are not involved. The development of partnership arrangements requires an 'ideal type' of partnership which in turn forces social workers to identify the specific reasons why the ideal may not be reached in certain circumstances. The reasons may range from resources available to the specific circumstances of parents/carers and so on.

## Parents'/carers' strengths and needs in partnership

In this section we consider a model based on the professional assessment of the strengths and needs of parents which complements the approach by Tibbets and Raynes (Chapter 3) and Calder (Chapter 7). A model suggested by Christie (1992) again builds on Arnstein's (1969) work and on research into parents' participation in the educational system (Hornby, 1990). Rather than focusing on parents' involvement in decision making, the model is based on the assumption that parents have both strengths and needs which influence the process of participation. Parents/carers contribute to the child care system as well as being potential beneficiaries. Practitioners need to be aware of both parents' needs and strengths in developing participation in child care systems.

As shown in Table 6.2, this model implies a hierarchy of strengths but acknowledges that all parents/carers can provide workers with information about their children. Most of the parents/carers will have some knowledge of child care based on their own experience. Many parents/carers have knowledge and ability in child care that they are able to share with other carers and children. However, it is likely that only some parents/carers will have the ability, time and interest to be involved in developing all aspects of child care services.

Nonetheless parents/carers have particular needs. All parents/carers are likely to need basic information about child care services, their legal rights and responsibilities. Most parents/carers are going to be involved in some form of negotiation with a variety of services. A 'partnership' approach is going to demand that professionals facilitate liaison between parents/carers and various agencies. Many of the parents/carers who are referred to child care agencies are likely to need some form of emotional support as parents/carers and in other aspects of their lives. Only a few parents/carers and children are likely to need intensive therapeutic and counselling support. Christie's model indicates that parents/carers who can participate in service/policy development may only have needs for basic information. On the other hand, in a situation where intensive work has to be undertaken with parents/carers and children, parents/carers may only be able to provide information on their own children.

This model, as with the other hierarchical models, makes underlying assumptions about the nature of partnership and the potential strengths of parents/carers. It is assumed that full partnerships are difficult to achieve and are likely only to include a few parents/carers. This pragmatic approach may lower the expectations of workers and discourage them from seeking to work in partnership with all parents; however, this model encourages social workers to think of parents/carers as active participants and to recognise that parents/carers have skills, information and knowledge to bring to partnerships. The strengths and needs of children are not addressed in this model. The strengths and needs of children in relation to the way in which their interests might be served through fuller participation offers one direction in which this model could be developed and expanded. Such an assessment might introduce more subtle and nuanced approaches to child protection assessment.

**Table 6.2 Parents' strengths and needs**

| POTENTIAL FOR CARER INVOLVEMENT | PARENTS'/CARERS' STRENGTHS |
|---|---|
| Some | Service/policy development |
| Many | Work with other parents/carers and children |
| Most | Variety of experience in caring for children |
| All | Information on the children they care for |
| All | Information (e.g. services, rights, responsibilities) |
| Most | Liaison with service providers |
| Many | Support as an adult and as a carer |
| Some | Intensive work with carers and children |
| | PARENTS'/CARERS' NEED |

*Source*: Christie (1992).

## Parents'/carers' involuntary and voluntary participation

The extent to which participation in core groups is voluntary or an increasingly 'required' activity is addressed in Howe's (1992) model of participation in child protection work represented in Table 6.3, identifies two particular dimensions of partnership: the willingness or otherwise of workers to adopt a partnership approach and the extent to which parents are voluntary or involuntary recipients of child protection services. When workers do not adopt a partnership approach and the service recipients prefer not to have contact with social services, Howe suggests that both workers and parents/carers develop a strategic approach in obtaining their own goals. When the service recipient does not want social work help but professionals nevertheless seek to adopt a 'partnership approach', Howe argues that social workers adopt a 'play fair' approach. He suggests that the social worker in this situation will

**Table 6.3 Participation in core groups**

| | SERVICE RECIPIENT | |
|---|---|---|
| PROFESSIONALS | Involuntary | Voluntary |
| Partnership approach absent | Strategic | Paternalistic |
| Partnership approach present | Play fair | Partnership |

be hoping that the parents agree to contribute to the professional assessment. Thoburn suggests that most child protection cases fall within the 'play fair' category because 'although the parent does not request social work help, nevertheless the worker tries to be open and honest about the process and the parent understands the position and co-operates in order to make the process as painless as possible for all concerned' (Thoburn, 1992: 209).

When the parents seek help but are excluded from the decision making process, Howe characterises this relationship as paternalistic. Social workers constructing a paternalistic relationship assume that they are able to judge the best interests of the service recipients without involving the latter in the decision-making process. Howe characterises the relationship as one of partnership when service recipients seek help from a social work agency, and are involved in assessing their problem and deciding on various courses of action.

From his model, Howe identifies two different sets of arguments supporting partnership. First, participation can be supported on the grounds of social justice. Service users should be informed of their rights and be involved in any decisions that affect their lives. Howe (1992) suggests that service users often know too little about their legal and welfare rights. This lack of information, he argues, encourages them to adopt a strategic approach to social work intervention and to avoid participatory involvement. Second, Howe argues that partnership can be justified on therapeutic grounds. A psychological rather than political rationale can be provided for partnerships with service users; that is, therapeutic interventions are seen as more effective when the service users participate in their own 'treatment'. The assumption is that it is only possible to develop partnership with service recipients when they receive the service on a voluntary basis. This is likely to place considerable limits on developing partnership in core groups where a child's name will have been placed on the child protection register indicating potentially involuntary aspects of the relationship. In such circumstances parents/carers know that their non-cooperation with professional agencies may result in social workers using their statutory powers to ensure the welfare of the child.

## Applying the models to partnership within core groups

All three models raise questions about partnership arrangements in core groups. The first model considers the operational levels of working together, ranging from manipulation to partnership. The second model is based on the characteristics of parents/carers and suggests a more pragmatic model whereby partnership may be developed. The third model valorises voluntary involvement as a key ingredient of productive partnerships. The variety of concerns and levels of partnership examined in each model points to the complexity of such working relationships in the field of child protection. We use these models to explore partnership arrangements in the following case study.

---

**Case Study**

Emma, a ten-year-old white girl, lives with her mother and stepfather. She has a younger brother, Robert, from her mother's previous marriage and two younger sisters from her mother's present marriage. Emma and Robert's father lives in a neighbouring town. He maintains regular contact with Emma and Robert, which includes Emma and Robert spending weekends with him and their paternal grandmother.

While on one of these weekend visits, Emma told her grandmother that her stepfather had come into her bedroom when she was undressing and had touched her in a way she did not like. Emma's father and grandmother contacted their local social services department which resulted in a formal investigation of the case. When questioned by the police, Emma's stepfather denied that he had inappropriately touched Emma.

Emma's mother and father attended the initial child protection conference, when it was agreed that Emma's name should be placed on the child protection register and that Emma and Robert would continue to live with their father and grandmother, where they had remained since the allegation of abuse. A core group was established to support the immediate situation and to develop a longer-term protection plan. Emma attended some of the core group meetings.

At one of the first core group meetings, Emma said that she enjoyed living with her father but that she missed seeing her mother and friends. At this meeting it was agreed that Emma would live with her maternal aunt. This allowed Emma to have far more contact with her mother and local friends, and to attend her school. It was agreed that Robert would return to live with his mother.

During the following core group meeting it was discovered that Emma was being bullied at school. Emma had discussed this with one of her teachers; however, it was not discussed with her mother, stepfather or father. Social workers and others discussed with Emma whom she trusted to confide in and how she could feel safe enough to confide in the family members. This then became an issue that Emma's mother and father discussed regularly with her. Emma's mother liaised with the school on this and other issues.

Emma's stepfather was invited to attend the initial child protection conference, child protection reviews and core groups meetings, but did not do so. He was sent copies of the minutes of the conferences and meetings. Core group provided an opportunity in which the issue of bullying and school concerns could be discussed.

After Emma's stepfather left home, Emma's mother was able to express unreserved belief in Emma's allegation. Social workers felt confident that Emma's mother would be able to protect Emma, so it was agreed that Emma should return to live with her mother. Emma's name was removed from the child protection register.

Emma's stepfather's departure caused other tensions within the family, as Emma's younger brother blamed Emma for their father's absence. Members of the core group continued to work with all the children in the household and to support Emma and care of the children.

---

This case study raises questions, not only about the level at which parents/carers can participate with social workers in decision making, but also about who should be members of core groups. There are a number of people identified in this case study. Models of partnership tend to focus on parents and workers as partners, but, as this case study suggests, the provision of child care is often more complex, with a variety of parents/carers and children providing child care. Four key parents/carers are identified in this case study: birth mother, birth father, stepfather and grandmother. The initial child protection conference decided who should be invited to be members of the core group. Emma's stepfather was invited to the initial child protection conference and core group meetings, but did not take up the offer, thereby preventing any possibility of partnership with him. Emma's brother and stepsisters were not invited to take part. As the ACPC had no local procedures for making decisions on whether children should be included, the social worker made the decision not to invite them.

Emma attended some of the core group meetings. The Children Act 1989 indicates that there is a moral, legal and practical obligation to involve children in decisions about their welfare (Barford and Wattam, 1991). The shift from parental rights to responsibilities in the Children Act 1989 reinforces the view that children should not be treated as possessions of their parents but as having their own individual rights. This places a new emphasis on organisations that work with children to include them in their decision making (Lyon and Parton, 1995). In this case study, Emma attended the core group and was able to provide information about being bullied at school, which was an important, additional factor, as research suggests that abused children are more vulnerable to recurrent abuse.

Emma, her mother and birth father participated fully in the child protection procedures, and they were involved in the assessment, child protection conference and subsequent core group meetings. For Thoburn *et al.* (1995) partnership could only be achieved if Emma and her mother and birth father participated in the development of child protection services. One simple way of involving parents/carers and children in the development of services would be to ask them to complete exit questionnaires, indicating their positive and negative experiences of the process. They could also participate in confidential interviews undertaken by a worker/researcher from an independent agency, as a means of evaluating the service they received and their experiences of partnership. This could be developed as another part of the role for *ad litem* guardians. However, it may be unrealistic to expect parents/carers and children who have been part of a core group to be more publicly involved in service development. The stigma of having the child's name placed on a child protection register may reduce the possibility of parents/carers and children becoming 'full' partners, while still involved in working through current child protection issues. However, this might be possible and, indeed, may be welcomed at a later stage. Indeed, survivors of abuse contribute to social work training courses and see this as a positive step in their personal development.

The above case study gives some indication of the strengths and needs of parents/carers and children participating in the child protection process and, in particular, the core group. Emma and her birth parents showed their ability to participate in the core group meetings, bringing with them expertise about their own circumstances and aims in relation to parenting. However, the difficulties for parents/carers and children of participating in core groups should not be underestimated. The case study suggests Emma and her birth parents needed basic information and support in order to participate. This requires a proactive approach by workers. If parents/carers are unaware of the potential of such therapeutic or practical support, it is difficult for them to request it.

In this case study parents/carers and Emma were relatively willing and voluntary members of the core group. Despite the significance of the stepfather in this case, however, he withheld his cooperation and remained outside the core group. Involuntary 'participation' may involve no contact at all with professionals. The models of partnership, as well as research (Reder *et al.*, 1993) suggest that non-cooperation with workers is likely to put children at risk of harm and legal disposals would have to be actively considered (Calder, 1995).

If, for example, Emma's stepfather became a member of the core group, this might have made it difficult for Emma to speak freely and participate. Child protection conferences may involve parents/carers taking part in separate meetings outside the conference and/or being invited to particular sections of the meeting. Such an arrangement may be overelaborate for core groups; instead, social workers may have to make pragmatic decisions in consultation with parents/carers and children about the membership of core groups.

While front-line workers may have to decide who will be asked to participate in the core group, social workers may also need to work with parents/carers and children who are not willing to participate in the core group. Christie (1992) found that some social workers make assumptions about parents'/carers' non-attendance. In this case study, it is easy to assume that Emma's stepfather sexually abused Emma and refused to attend the child protection conference and core group meetings because of his guilt. However, in other cases of non-attendance, Christie (1992) found social workers often judged parents/carers as 'uncaring' and 'irresponsible' if they did not attend child protection conferences. Such judgements are often based on limited knowledge and may affect the possibilities of future involvement and development of worthwhile 'partnerships'. Many researchers and practitioners concerned with issues of partnership emphasise the importance of perseverance and creativity in trying to engage parents and carers in child protection work by stressing the value and importance of their contribution (Mittler, 1993; Thoburn *et al.*, 1995).

Parents'/carers' and children's compliance with workers' requirements is often assumed to be an indicator of voluntary participation in child protection procedures. However, there is a need to be conscious of what Calder and Horwath (forthcoming) call 'passive partnerships with families' in which debate is discouraged and family members are expected to comply with professionals' assessment of the problems. In the above case study there appears to have been agreement between all parties who attended the core group regarding the issues. It is unclear, however, how the models of 'partnership' address disagreement between individual professionals and between parents/carers and children.

The models described above offer no means of analysing how structural inequality affects partnership. Milner (1993) and O'Hagan and Dillenburger (1995) describe how men exclude themselves and are excluded as parents/carers from child protection procedures. Both policy and, often, professional practice can conspire to reinforce women's position as the carers of children. Structural inequalities based on class, race and ethnicity are also likely to influence the development of partnerships on any kind of equal footing. Likewise, none of the models addresses ways in which disagreement or conflict between the family and professionals can be managed to promote partnership. Although providing only a sketchy picture of a complex family and professional scenario, the case study points to the many limitations of existing models of partnership. Our analysis of the case study may also indicate the impossibility of developing a model that incorporates the many diverse relationships, whether structural, professional or personal, all of which have an impact on core groups.

## Concluding comments

In this chapter we have discussed current attempts to improve the workings of core groups by introducing the concept of partnership. We described three models of partnership developed in the field of social work in order to elucidate the ways in which this concept might operate in practice. A case study of child protection work was presented and then discussed in relation to the three models. The use of models to describe and analyse human behaviour is always likely to be very crude. However, the models discussed in this chapter raise questions about social work practice in core groups and the kinds of goals that are being set for both workers and service recipients. Whilst acknowledging that partnership may be a valid and desirable aim, we draw attention to some of the extenuating circumstances which may make it a difficult goal to implement in practice. The factors affecting the implementation of a reciprocal kind of partnership are many and complex, including the characteristics of the case, agencies involved and the blurred boundaries between voluntary and involuntary involvement of service users. Some acknowledgement of these factors is important if core group members are to be set achievable goals which recognise that partnership in theory does not quite coincide with partnership in practice.

## Notes

1 We use the term 'parents/carers' to indicate that, while parents have particular responsibilities for their children's care, a wide variety of other individuals, who may be part of an extended family, are involved in the day-to-day care of children. We recognise that the use of this inclusive term does not reflect the gendered nature of caring and may obscure women's positions as the main carers of children.

2 It was only after the Cleveland Inquiry that the government recommended parental participation in case conferences, in the final version of *Working Together* (DHSS, 1988, para 6.14).

# References


Allsopp, M. (1994) 'Four Faces of Partnership and the Welfare of the Child', presentation to the Second National Congress on Child Abuse and Neglect, University of Bristol, 5–8 July.

Arnstein, S. (1969) 'A Ladder of Citizen Participation', *Journal of the American Institute of Planners*, **35** (4).

Atherton, C. (1991) *Client Participation in Child Protection Procedures and Conferences*, London: Family Rights Group.

Barford, R. and Wattam, C. (1991) 'Children's Participation in Decision-making', *Practice*, **5** (2).

Burman, L., Farrell, P., Feiler, A., Heffernan, M., Mittler, H. and Reason, R. (1983) *Report on Parental Involvement in Special Education*, Manchester: Manchester LEA.

Calder, M.C. (1995) 'Child Protection: Balancing Paternalism and Partnership', *British Journal of Social Work*, **25** (6): 749–66.

Calder, M.C. and Howarth, J. (forthcoming) 'Passive Partnerships with Families: The Core of Post-registration Practice?' submitted for publication.

Christie, A. (1992) 'Putting Carer Involvement in Child Protection Conferences into Practice', in H. Ferguson, R. Gilligan and R. Torode (eds), *Surviving Childhood Adversity*, Dublin: Social Studies Press, Trinity College Dublin.

Department of Health (1995a) *The Challenge of Partnership in Child Protection: Practice Guide*, London: HMSO.

Department of Health (1995b) *Messages from Research*, London: HMSO.

Department of Health and Social Security (1988) *Working Together: A Guide for Inter-agency Co-operation for the Protection of Children from Abuse*, London: HMSO.

Family Rights Group (1991) *The Children Act 1989: Working in Partnership with Families*, London: HMSO.

Hallett, C. (1995) *Inter-agency Co-ordination in Child Protection*, London: HMSO.

Hornby, G. (1990) 'The Organisation of Parental Involvement', *School Organisation*, **10** (2).

Howe, D. (1992) 'Theories of Helping, Empowerment and Participation', in J. Thoburn (ed.), *Participation in Practice – Involving Families in Child Protection: a Reader*, Norwich: University of East Anglia.

Hughes, B. (1992) 'Partnership in Local Government', *Community Care*, 2 (July): 24–5.

Lyon, C. and Parton, N. (1995) 'Children's Rights and the Children Act 1989', in C. Cloke and M. Davies (eds) *Participation and Empowerment in Child Protection*, London: Pitman.

Milner, J. (1993) 'A Disappearing Act: The Differing Career Paths of Fathers and Mothers in Child Protection Investigations', *Critical Social Policy*, **38** (13).

Mittler, H. (1993) 'The Participation of Children and Young People in Child Protection Core Group and Review Meetings: An Evaluation of Practice in a Northern Metropolitan Borough', MSc thesis, Manchester University.

Mittler, H. (1997) 'Core Groups: A Key Focus for Child Protection Training', *Social Work Education*, **16** (2).

Morrison, T. (1996) 'Partnership and Collaboration: Rhetoric and Reality', *Child Abuse and Neglect*, **30** (2).

O'Hagan, K. and Dillenburger, K. (1995) *The Abuse of Women within Child Care Work*, Buckingham: Open University Press.

Pugh, G. (1981) *Parents as Partners. Intervention Schemes and Groupwork with Families of Handicapped Children*, London: National Children's Bureau.

Reder, P., Duncan, S. and Gray, M. (1993) *Beyond Blame: Child Abuse Tragedies Revisited,* London: Routledge.

Shemmings, D. and Thoburn, J. (1989) *Parental Participation in Child Protection Conferences,* Norwich: University of East Anglia.

Thoburn, J. (1992) 'Some Issues of Decision-Making in Child Protection', in H. Ferguson, R. Gilligan and R. Torode (eds), *Surviving Childhood Adversity,* Dublin: Social Studies Press, Trinity College.

Thoburn, J., Lewis, A. and Stemmings, D. (1995) Paternalism or Partnership? *Family Involvement in the Child Protection Process,* London: HMSO.

# 7 Towards anti-oppressive practice with ethnic minority groups

*Martin C. Calder*

In this chapter, consideration is given to:

- the current framework for assessing need and harm in ethnic minority groups;
- the profound difficulties and current limitations in engaging with, and assessing, families from ethnic minority groups;
- findings from a small-scale study;
- the adoption of the strengths perspective to the post-registration phase of child protection work;
- providing tools and techniques for worker use; and
- working with interpreters.

## Introduction

Britain is a multicultural, multiracial, multi-faith society whose diverse population includes just over 3 million people (slightly over 5.5 per cent of the population) who can be defined as black. Of the black British population, 75 per cent are UK-born and at least a quarter of a million are of mixed origin (Macey and Moxon, 1996).

This chapter aims to provide a preliminary framework within which workers and their agencies can begin to formulate an anti-oppressive response to ethnic minority groups in the post-registration arena. Whilst the text concentrates solely on ethnic minority groups, the general principles and practice are transferable to other minority groups, such as people with learning disabilities.

It has been argued that:

> social work is 'Eurocentric', underpinned by white–middle-class, Christian values of godliness, thrift, industriousness and cleanliness. It is also 'ethnocentric', giving status to the world view or experience of a dominant ethnic group at the expense of others. Eurocentrism in social work is described in terms of 'exclusion' (where the existence of black people is denied), 'tokenism' (where the experiences of black people are simply added on as an afterthought), and 'pathology' (where black people are construed as inherently problematic). (Grimwood and Tombs, 1995)

The chapter begins by offering some definitions before moving on to consider the current context of child protection practice with ethnic minorities groups and some important findings from a Department of Health sub-study on child protection work carried out in a multiracial context (Owen and Farmer, 1996). Consideration is then given to models of empowering families from ethnic minorities in child protection work, before an examination of the potential application to the various stages of post-registration practice.

## Definitions

Throughout this book, the following terminology is used and is to be interpreted as follows:

1 An ethnic minority group – can be seen as a sub-group that experiences oppression and discrimination, not as a result of their race or ethnic background, but as a response to the cultural and social norms of the majority group. It is an umbrella phrase which hides the cultural, ethnic and genetic diversity of the population.
2 Black and white – used simply to denote racial identity.
3 Oppression – this is concerned with power relationships and the abuse of power at both the individual and the structural level. It is a process by which life chances are constructed and maintained to work in favour of some groups and to the disadvantage of others (Jones, 1993: 76). There are several clearly identifiable components of oppression: inequality, social justice, domination, stereotyping, discrimination and accessibility to services (Phillipson, 1992). Whilst oppression can be specific to any one of these components, they frequently interconnect.
4 Anti-oppressive practice – this seeks to achieve a fundamental realignment of these power differentials, values and relationships, starting with

the acknowledgement that structural inequalities exist and have a major impact on both groups and individuals. Dalrymple and Burke have defined anti-oppressive practice as 'recognising power imbalances and working towards the promotion of change to redress the balance of power' (Dalrymple and Burke, 1995: 15).

## Contextualising the problem

Although each person's experience of oppression is unique, black children can experience stigmatisation due to society's attitudes which label them as 'second class' citizens. Research also highlights the fact that the child care and child protection systems can disempower black children; for example, black female children with disabilities can experience the interlocking nature of oppression due to age, race, disability and gender and we know that black female children are less likely to disclose sexual abuse for fear of a racist response as well as the additional consequences for both their family and the community (Mars, 1989). There is also a danger that fewer ethnic minority children are being protected as workers are often driven by a belief that any response will be construed as racist (Bogle, 1988; Droisen, 1989; Mars, 1989; Westcott and Cross, 1996).

The Sukina Hammond Inquiry Report (The Bridge, 1991) pointed out that:

> when professionals are faced with matters of child protection, then it should be the needs of the child that are paramount and any investigation of suspicions of injury, neglect or any form of ill-treatment should be equally vigorous in every case, irrespective of the racial or cultural characteristics of the family. (The Bridge, 1991: 84)

The available statistics do not reflect this approach being adopted in practice. In England and Wales there are distinctions between different ethnic groups: for example, there is an underrepresentation of children from Asian communities on child protection registers and in local authority care (Luthra, 1997) while Caribbean youngsters are overrepresented (Armstrong, 1995; Luthra, 1997). Generally, in England and Wales, Barn (1993) found that black children were likely to be admitted into care more quickly than white children in cases of socioeconomic and family difficulties and they were also less likely to be treated with an 'open mind' than similar 'white' cases. She argued that social workers' negative views about black families led them to be unnecessarily cautious, tending to adopt a 'rescue mentality'. Such reactivity can sometimes lead to misdiagnosis. Luthra (1997: 272) also reported on very clear differences in the patterns of rehabilitating black and white children home, with white children being rehabilitated home twice as often as black children.

There are some parallels and differences, that can be drawn from experience in the USA, where Levine *et al.* (1996) reported that Asian Americans are disproportionately represented on child protection caseloads compared to numbers in the general population, and put forward three hypotheses to account for this. Firstly, they argued that this could be accounted for by the disproportionate numbers of minority families living in poverty, with its proven direct and negative impact on the family. Secondly, poverty renders minority families more vulnerable to the kind of social problems that will bring them to the attention of social care agencies. Finally, worker values, professional judgements and biases (oppressive practices) may be related to the overrepresentation of substantiated cases.

There is always the potential for workers to misunderstand culturally specific child-rearing practices or to allow ethnocentric or culturally insensitive values and biases into their investigations of minority families. 'Abuse is not condoned by any racial group. We should not seek excuses for abuse. Children need to be protected. To work effectively and assess whether abuse is taking place we need to understand the context' (Black and White Alliance, 1989/90: 1). All cultures have standards for acceptable and unacceptable treatment of children and some individuals in all cultures violate these standards or are at risk of violating them (Korbin, 1993). While all cultures have parameters and standards of care, not all cultures define optimal or deficient care in precisely the same way. What appears to be abuse in one culture is often not seen as a problem in others. It is also likely that individuals within each culture will also view the same situation very differently, as with, for example, the acceptance or disapproval of physical chastisement.

Korbin (1991) has pointed out that the cross-cultural variability in child rearing beliefs and behaviours has left a dilemma, as no universal standard for optimal child care exists. Failure to allow for a cultural perspective promotes an ethnocentric position in which one's own set of cultural beliefs and practices are presumed to be preferable and superior to all others. On the other hand, a stance of cultural relativism, in which all judgements of humane treatment of children are suspended in the name of cultural rights, may be used to justify a lesser standard of care for some children (such as Jasmine Beckford). Here the members of one culture, such as white, middle-class social workers, struggled to criticise members of another culture: black, working-class parents. This left workers preferring to believe in the concept of 'natural love' (a belief that the relationship between a parent and a child is instinctual and grounded in human nature), thus accepting the parents' accounts of events without question. This uncritical position left the child unprotected, with fatal consequences.

## The Children Act 1989

The Children Act 1989 sought to recast the balance between family autonomy and state intervention so that there is a 'simultaneous emphasis on partnership with parents, support to families and strong protection with a minimum reliance on a court order' (Adcock, 1991). It thus aimed to empower families while not compromising the protection of the children.

Removing children from home can impair the life chances for many children by compounding their earlier experience of structural oppression (Jones, 1993), whilst any failure to intervene could be construed as oppressive as it leaves children in abusive home environments where they are vulnerable and powerless. Whilst the Act can provide a framework for protecting children from both majority and minority groups, the basic difficulty facing workers is 'how?'

In summary, the Act requires a consideration of a child's racial origin and culture, religion and language, when providing services, (s.22(5) and s.74(6)) although few suggestions have been articulated on how to operationalise these. Section 22(3) also states that a local authority must make use of facilities and services available for children to be cared for by their own parents. Where this is not possible, they should help children to maintain contact with groups in black areas, local temples, churches or mosque groups.

Historically, social services have offered a reactive service in the field of child care. Unfortunately, the Children Act encourages this stance to continue, advocating intervention in only the most acute and extreme of circumstances, thus militating against communities who are deprived or disengaged. This contrasts with recent research (DoH, 1995) which shows that a greater degree of intervention is needed in the provision of child care services, at an earlier stage, to support families who are in vulnerable situations.

## Messages from research

The recent battery of Department of Health-endorsed research projects (DoH, 1995) highlighted the tokenism of the current response systems and in particular the different (more punitive) responses to black families. They also highlighted the reality that we are not very good at listening and accurately assessing or considering their needs.

Farmer and Owen (1995) conducted some research on decision making, intervention and outcome in child protection work, which was extended to a metropolitan area to include a sub-sample of black children on the child protection register, reported by Owen and Farmer (1996). The aim of the research was to examine the impact of the child protection procedures on black and ethnic minority groups, and to consider whether they were seriously disadvantaged by problems of communication. The main focus of the study was to examine the management of child protection cases over time, taking into account the perspectives of parents, children and supervising social workers. In the early stages, 120 initial child protection conferences were attended, and an intensive follow-up sample of 44 children was drawn from them. The research was prospective, over a 20-month period.

The sub-sample was restricted to ten 'index' children (one from each of ten different families), for several reasons: it proved difficult to locate cases of black children on the child protection register and it was sometimes difficult to match parents with an interviewer who spoke their language; or the families were wary about participating, for two reasons. Firstly, they feared intervention by white-dominated agencies, with attendant fears about racist treatment and the possibility of unwanted surveillance. Secondly, women withdrew under pressure from male family members. A further restriction came because of an inability to conduct follow-up interviews because of resource constraints, thus depriving the researchers of any data which would have allowed them to analyse the effect of interventions over time. It is significant that this study lacked priority and status within the overall research programme. This study comprised children, aged 4–14 years, with two African-Caribbean, six Asian and two white main carers. The research findings are summarised below. The quality of information often depended on the availability of an interpreter, and this lack of reliable or useful information also served to disempower the social workers involved.

## Pre-conference phase

No child in the study directly contacted the authorities about what had happened to them, and none of the families appeared to be in touch with social services at the time of the referral. The families were hurt and distressed when cases were referred without their being informed or involved. In most cases, the investigation and its aftermath were experienced as 'social policing'. There was little recognition that this could be the start of a helpful period of intervention, or that listing on the child protection register would initiate services. Half of the investigations led to no firm conclusions about what had happened, leading to ambiguities in the assessment of risk, giving any intervention a very diffuse focus.

## Conference and registration

Parents in the study failed to grasp what happens when a child's name is placed on the register. In common with others in the child protection system, many of the ethnic minority families with children on the register were fairly isolated, lacking good support networks, and the families tended to be strongly male-dominated unless there was a lone mother. At the conference, there were fears expressed by workers that the interpreter would take on the role of family advocate and there was often no acknowledgement of the ethnic composition of the attendees and its impact on the family. Where a child was registered, it was important to match the social worker and the family to enhance the engagement and ultimately the outcomes for the child, and this was achieved in 70 per cent of the cases examined. The progress of the child was enhanced when there was successful matching across the three dimensions of race, gender and culture.

### Assessment and planning

In some Asian languages, the words necessary to describe sexual abuse do not exist. Language barriers clearly added to the complexity of the work, necessitating the use of an interpreter. In some families, more than one language was spoken. The interviews suggested that the attitudes and expression of some workers was perceived by families as patronising or marginalising, and the structural inequalities of power were felt more acutely and sometimes became focused on language skills. A lack of understanding was easily linked with feelings of ignorance and inadequacy. Language was often used in subtle ways, to include or exclude participants.

The assessment and planning stages were frequently complicated by a lack of information, not helped by the barriers of secrecy which some families had constructed around themselves because of their fear of racially motivated interventions.

Workers need more ethnically sensitive services to provide an adequate service, indicated by the authors' findings 'that the long-term welfare of the most disadvantaged children and families had not infrequently been sacrificed in the drive towards child protection' (Owen and Farmer, 1996: 311). This message rings true for more recipients of the child protection service.

## Adopting useful theories to guide our interventions: empowerment in child protection work

'Empowerment', like 'partnership', is a current buzzword which often appears in the literature surrounding work with black families. It is a concept which can enhance our work for children on the child protection register generally, so a selective summary of the relevant material will be offered here for this purpose. In the 1990s, 'empowerment' has been used to describe a movement towards greater equality of the parties who relate to each other. Like the concept of partnership, this is not to do with equal power, but with sharing, showing respect for one another and accountability, with each person having something to contribute to planning and the eventual outcome. It represents a recognition of client strengths. Child protection based on anti-oppressive premises needs to believe that families have the ability to define their own problems, set their own goals and take their own action for change; a commitment to basing this change on a broader social analysis than is commonly the case with most professional intervention; and a style of working in partnership with people which facilitates and empowers them to move in the direction they choose (Ward and Mullender, 1991: 12). Boushel and Lebacq (1992) identified certain elements required of a model of empowerment for child protection work which could usefully underpin post-registration practice (see Box 7.1).

**Box 7.1 Empowerment**

Support the right of service users to choose the social roles they wish to fulfil (for example, mother, daughter, carer, partner).
Support the right of service users to undertake those roles in ways that do not jeopardise the welfare of others.
Facilitate an awareness of the ways in which the dynamics of structural and interpersonal oppression operate in the service-user's situation.
Acknowledge and, where possible, build upon service users' previous attempts to protect themselves and/or others from child protection work.
Provide information on the range of resources and options available to service users and their possible consequences.
Support and facilitate service users in their expression of equivocal feelings about interventions, issues and problems.
Generate an awareness in service users of the power exercised by welfare professionals on behalf of the state and their rights of redress.
Facilitate service users in challenging paternalistic or discriminatory welfare provision.

*Source*: Boushel and Lebacq (1992: 45–6).

## A model for intervention: the strengths perspective

The strengths approach is one model which has proved useful in engaging resistant families. Understanding how to assess strengths and intervene in ways that strengthen and support family functioning is of particular importance in child protection work, and it has huge potential if applied to work with ethnic minority groups. It can help professionals work effectively with families in a way that protects the child but does not oppress the family: 'To assess the power of the individual to create change, it is necessary to focus on their strengths as well as the problems. This focus can lead to interpretations of behaviour as coping abilities or survival strategies' (Rodwell and Blankebaker, 1992: 159).

The strengths perspective clearly demands that we adopt a different way of looking at individuals, families and communities. All must be seen in the light of their capacity, talents, competencies, possibilities, visions, values and hopes, however dashed and distorted these may have become through circumstance, oppression and trauma. Personal qualities and strengths are often forged in the face of abuse and oppression (Saleebey, 1996). Table 7.1 usefully contrasts the strengths approach with conventional, pathology-based approaches. The strengths perspective is rooted in the belief that people can continue to grow and change; that many of the barriers people labelled as belonging to 'disadvantaged groups' face in meeting basic needs for shelter, food and positive community participation tend to come from educational, political and economic exclusion based on demographic rather than individual characteristics.

> One of the most noteworthy strengths among Blacks is the biculturality that they exhibit. Blacks are able to walk and function in two worlds. They are forced to know the language, values, norms and habits of the dominant culture and how to function in their own world as well. This fluidity and adaptability are important assets that should be noted and credited. They often walk in two cultures at the same time and are forced to shift back and forth at any given moment. (Leeder, 1994: 36)

For social workers to shift towards the strength approach, they need to have some understanding of its underlying beliefs. They must also not lose sight of the need to take appropriate action to protect children whenever necessary. The following summary is offered to workers in this context, as the strengths approach cannot be adopted on a blanket basis without reference to individual circumstances. The social worker does not change people, but aims to act as a catalyst for clients' discovering and using their resources, to accomplish their goals (Saleebey, 1992). This makes it less likely that workers will 'rescue' clients and more likely that they will reinforce their strengths, even in a crisis.

Any proactive approach to child protection focuses on family strengths and capability in a way that supports and strengthens family functioning. All

**Table 7.1 Comparison of pathology and strengths**

| Pathology | Strengths |
|---|---|
| Person is defined as a 'case'; symptoms add up to a diagnosis | Person is defined as unique; traits, talents, resources add up to strengths |
| Therapy is problem-focused | Therapy is possibility-focused |
| Personal accounts aid in the evocation of a diagnosis through reinterpretation by an expert | Personal accounts are the essential route to knowing and appreciating the person |
| Practitioner is sceptical of personal stories, rationalisations | Practitioner knows the person from the inside out |
| Childhood trauma is the precursor or predictor of adult pathology. | Childhood trauma is not predictive; it may weaken or strengthen the individual |
| Centrepiece of therapeutic work is treatment plan devised by practitioner | Centrepiece of work is the aspirations of family, individual or community |
| Practitioner is the expert on clients' lives | Individuals, family or community are the experts |
| Possibilities for choice, control, commitment and personal development are limited by pathology | Possibilities for choice, control, commitment and personal development are open |
| Resources for work are the knowledge and skills of the professional | Resources for work are the strengths, capacities and adaptive skills of the individual, family or community |
| Help is centred on reducing the effects of symptoms and the negative personal and social consequences of actions, emotions, thoughts or relationships. | Help is centred on getting on with one's life, affirming and developing values and commitments, and making and finding membership in or as a community. |

*Source*: Saleebey (1996: 298), reprinted with the permission of the author.

families have strengths and capabilities. If we take the time to identify these qualities and build on them rather than focusing on correcting deficits or weaknesses, not only are families more likely to respond favourably to interventions, but the chances of making a significant impact on the family unit will be enhanced considerably. A major consideration as part of strengthening families is promoting their abilities to use existing strengths for meeting needs in a way that produces positive changes in family functioning. This can be achieved by using empathy or attempting to promote some mutual agreement. Any social worker adopting the strengths approach should believe that: most children should grow up in their own families; people have the potential for change; people do their best when empowered; and instilling hope is a central part of the child protection remit. In order to cultivate these beliefs, they must emphasise personal and environmental strengths, understand matters from a client's point of view, promote mutual agreement between clients and themselves, use empathy, and avoid blaming (DePanfilis and Wilson, 1996).

Using the principles of the strengths perspective with abusing families may be the only chance to empower families to change their behaviour. Yet uncovering strengths cannot be accomplished in a simplistic manner, as they 'are not isolated variables, but form clusters and constellations which are dynamic, fluid inter-related and inter-acting' (Otto, 1963: 80). Developing a strengths-based practice involves a paradigm shift from a deficit approach to a positive partnership with the family, and will involve the following:

- reframing the relationship between a worker and a family from an adversarial one to a helping alliance and partnership with the family – suggesting a major emphasis on the engagement phase.
- empowering individuals and families to discover and use the resources and tools within and around them.
- integrating a knowledge of resilience in workers as it may be crucial to families in overcoming future risks (DePanfilis and Wilson 1996).

In considering ethnic minority families a fourth point must be added – identification with the community. This community can consist of: religions; media; political, neighbourhood or recreational affiliations; positive racial identity; biculturalism (that is, adhering to values, beliefs, attitudes, customs, language and behaviours of at least two cultures); and maintaining and transmitting cultural or family traditions (for example, celebrations, rituals, food, clothing). If the ethnic identity of a family's neighbourhood is present and positive, the family demonstrates leadership in the community or is affiliated with a religious group, the nuclear family is part of an active extended family that provides material resources, child care, supervision, parenting and emotional support to both the child and the family, and mutual aid and support are accessible to it, the ability of the family to cope with stress and crises is increased.

Although the child abuse field has just begun to apply the strengths perspective to its repertoire, there is a catalogue of documented benefits to date, shown in Box 7.2.

**Box 7.2 The Strengths Perspective**

An emphasis on strengths as well as on risks increases the opportunity for developing a helping alliance – a crucial element in achieving positive treatment outcome and risk reduction.
Positive reinforcement for positive conditions and behaviours is more effective than trying to convince or coerce individuals to alter negative conditions or behaviours.
Cultivating strengths offers the opportunity for more permanent change.
Emphasising strengths helps family members build in successes in their lives, which in turn should help them more effectively to manage crises and stress.
Helping families through short-term positive steps empowers families to take control of their lives.
Celebrating successes changes the tone of treatment, for both client and helper.
Communicating a true belief that a family can change destructive patterns helps to promote more long-lasting change.

*Source*: DePanfilis and Wilson, 1996.

Whilst we should shift towards a strengths-led approach to children's services, we cannot overlook or shirk our statutory responsibilities continually to assess risks and danger to those children we are seeking to protect (Clark *et al.*, 1990).

## Interviewing for client strengths

Identifying family strengths creates a non-threatening atmosphere in which the client-worker relationships can be established. It also helps workers determine interventions that will build on client strengths. DeJong and Miller (1995) have described several interviewing questions that a worker can use to uncover client strengths related to the goals of clients.

### *Exception-finding questions*

These are used to discover a client's present and past successes in relation to the client's goals. Eventually, these successes are used to build solutions, as with an alcoholic who has tried of his or her own volition in the past to stop drinking, but has lapsed. Most families can offer one exception and the worker can then explore how this happened, particularly how the client contributed to this.

### *Scaling questions*

These are a clever way to make complex features of a client's life more concrete and accessible for both client and worker. They usually take the form of asking the client to give a number from nought to ten that best represents where the client is at some specified point: for example, Do you accept the need for social work help to resolve the problem? This scale can be used repeatedly at different points of the process. The responses form the basis of the follow-up questions from the worker that should aim to uncover, affirm and amplify the client's strengths.

### *Coping questions*

These questions accept the client's perceptions of their situation (however desperate) and then move on to ask how the client is able to cope with such overwhelming circumstances and feelings. As the worker helps the client to uncover coping strengths, their mood and confidence usually improve. Sometimes new ideas for coping emerge that the client has never thought of before. Where clients return to the problem descriptions and associated feelings of discouragement, the worker should listen and/or empathise, before returning to a focus on the exploration and affirmation of strengths.

### *'What's better?' questions*

These are useful in continuing the work of building solutions and uncovering client strengths. They increase the chances of uncovering exceptions and associated strengths that are the most meaningful and useful to the client at the present time. Asking what is better since the last time focuses on the process of work and change.

# From theory to practice: working through the post-registration process with ethnic minority families

## Issues for workers when engaging ethnic families in the child protection process

We know that pre-conference activity significantly affects any subsequent work with the family. Maitra (1995) has listed a number of assumptions often used when approaching interventions with ethnic minority families that can have an impact on any attempt to engage ethnic minority families in the post-registration phase. These are given in Box 7.3.

**Box 7.3 Erroneous Assumptions**

1 That a smattering of English words implies the ability to understand or express complex psychological issues.
2 That Western dress implies a grasp of Western ideas, beliefs or systems.
3 That wives/mothers who do not speak in the presence of their husbands, or who walk five steps behind their husbands, are necessarily timid or do not wield much power in the home.
4 That the submissiveness and excessive politeness of ethnic minority clients, the 'yassuh boss' response set (Griffith, 1977), indicate agreement; this may be a way of testing the interviewer's attitude and interest.
5 That non-verbal behaviours and the intensity of facial expressions of emotion have equivalent meanings across cultures.

Lynch (1992: 19–21) set out five reasons for the difficulty that workers can experience when they try to understand or function in a culture other than their own, and which workers need to address to offset any personal impact it may raise:

1 Cultural understanding in one's own culture occurs early and is typically established by age 5.
2 Children learn new cultural patterns more easily than adults.
3 Values are determined by one's first culture and may have to be revised to be effective in a second culture.
4 Understanding of one's first culture introduces errors in interpreting the second culture.
5 Long-standing behaviour patterns are typically used to express one's deepest values.

The key to working effectively with children 'at risk' is the detailed and accurate assessment of their needs from the time the case is opened. Such assessments must take account of the needs of the whole child – social, health, educational, racial, cultural and religious. In addition, effective assessments should include creative approaches to communicating with families, so that an accurate assessment of their parenting capacity can be made as well as creative approaches to working with children, so that their views can be both expressed and heard. Such assessments can then act as a backcloth against which parents can be measured and help can be provided to enable parents to care for their children as well as ensuring that protection is given to the children in any circumstances where risks of abuse have been identified (The Bridge, 1991: 71).

Communication and working relationships between people who differ in terms of race and ethnicity are often hard to initiate or sustain, despite the presence of common interests and shared goals. Where there is some disagreement over the initial diagnosis, as can occur where worker bias, prejudice or lack of familiarity with their particular ethnic group exists, the potential for any effective future partnership is clearly compromised. There is a danger that workers who fail to examine and alter their practice will 'blame' clients by labelling them non-compliant or resistant. Many families often request a professional from the same cultural background as themselves, as they feel they will be better understood. Lynch has suggested that communication effectiveness is significantly improved when workers respect individuals from other cultures, make continued and sincere attempts to understand the world from others' point of view, are open to new learning, are flexible, have a sense of humour, tolerate ambiguity well and approach others with a desire to learn (Lynch, 1992: 51–2).

Dungee-Anderson and Beckett (1995) have offered a model designed to help social workers become effective multicultural workers. Their first three steps are as follows. First, acknowledge cultural differences. Contrary to some workers' fears, an open discussion of differences does not suggest a racist orientation or reflect racism or other discriminatory behaviour. Discussion of cultural differences with the client sensitises the worker to differences among clients and values, learning about other cultures as an important practice component. If the worker ignores the client's cultural values and behaviours, he or she negates the client's individual and cultural identity. Cultural differences influence family organisation, family interaction and individual behaviour, and they are key factors in the experience of persons of colour. Understanding cultural differences helps to reduce workers' stereotypical responses and enhances their ability to recognise heterogeneity within an ethnic group.

Second, know yourself, particularly your own cultural values and beliefs. Because these customs are internalised, we do not distinguish on a daily basis the feelings, behaviours and congruent thought that flow from feelings and behaviours. Moreover, individuals belong to multiple cultures: occupational, regional, of gender, and so on. Self-knowledge requires a measure of cultural attention to the multiple cultures in which one lives. Workers also need to be cautioned against overgeneralising or characterising all members of a cultural or ethnic group as alike.

Third, workers have to know about other cultures. They will never be experts in many different cultures, but rather should be aware of cultural values and patterns that motivate their own and their clients' behaviours. They need to be sensitive to differences so as not to project their own internalised cultural responses onto their practice responses. Workers do need to ask about customs or values with which they are not familiar. There are other excellent papers on working together across differences, such as Narayau (1989) and Valasquez *et al.* (1989), and the reader is encouraged to use these for personal learning and practical application.

Engaging ethnic minority families is more important when you consider that there is a disproportionately higher rate of discontinuing social work services by these groups (Levine *et al.*, 1996). This may be because they do not perceive what services they are offered as helpful or that the partnership that ideally evolves from engaging a client in a positive, purposeful relationship does not develop. It comes as no surprise, therefore, that post-registration work should focus on mobilising resources to deal with specific, observable problems, with outcomes clearly stated; building on identified family strengths; ensuring family preservation; and actively engaging clients in evaluating progress towards the stated goals (Leung *et al.*, 1994).

The final five steps identified by Beckett and Dungee-Anderson are the need to identify and value differences; identify and avoid stereotypes; empathise with persons from other cultures; adapt rather than adopt, and acquire recovery skills. For a fuller discussion of these final steps, the reader should refer to Beckett and Dungee-Anderson (1993).

## Using interpreters

Many families have reported having a greater understanding of what the worker has said and feel more assured in their ability to communicate with the worker when an interpreter is available. It is also courteous for discussions to be conducted in their first language and can help make the clients feel more comfortable with the process. Lynch (1992: 52) has suggested that an interpreter should be someone who is:

1 proficient in the language, including specific dialect of the family as well as that of the worker;

2 trained and experienced in cross-cultural communication and the principles (and dynamics) of serving as an interpreter;
3 trained in the appropriate professional field relevant to the specific family–worker interaction; and
4 able to understand and appreciate the respective cultures of both parties and to convey the more subtle advances of each with tact and sensitivity.

A number of guidelines have been suggested (see, for example Lynch, 1992) for workers to follow when working with an interpreter. Box 7.4 lists some of these.

**Box 7.4 Working with an Interpreter**

Learn proper protocols and forms of address (including a few greetings and social phrases) in the family's primary language, the name they wish to be called, and the correct pronunciation.
Introduce yourself and the interpreter, describe your respective roles, and clarify mutual expectations and the purpose of the encounter.
Learn basic words and sentences in the family's language and become familiar with special terminology they may use so that you can selectively attend to them during interpreter–family exchange.
During the interaction, address your remarks and questions directly to the family (not the interpreter); look at and listen to family members as they speak and observe their non-verbal communication.
Avoid body language or gestures that may be offensive or misunderstood.
Use a positive tone of voice and facial expression that sincerely convey respect and your interest in the family; and address them in a calm, unhurried manner.
Speak clearly and somewhat more slowly than usual, but not more loudly.
Limit your remarks and questions to a few sentences between translations and avoid giving too much information or long complex discussions of several topics in a single session.
Avoid technical jargon, colloquialisms, idioms, slang and abstractions.
Avoid oversimplification and condensing important explanations.
Give instructions in a clear, logical sequence; emphasise key words or points; and offer reasons for specific recommendations.
When possible, reinforce verbal information with materials written in the family's language and visual aids or behavioural modelling, if appropriate.

Before introducing written materials, tactfully determine the client's literacy level through the interpreter.
Be patient and prepared for the additional time that will inevitably be required for careful interpretation.

*Source*: Lynch (1992: 55–6).

Workers have to negotiate carefully the introduction of an interpreter as this changes the dynamics of the worker–family interaction, often making it more complex. There should be a clear decision taken as to whether he or she is to act as a straightforward interpreter, being a community worker (providing interpreting services from within the community), being a link worker (supporting clients to make informed choices about services and to identify and understand the needs of the clients in addition to providing an interpreting service) or being an advocate for the client (Raval, 1996). Where mutual respect and good cultural understanding exist between the worker and the interpreter, this may help to nurture a more equal power relationship between them. Raval found that workers used interpreters as they enhanced their cultural understanding of the family, increased their level of communication and engagement with the family and allowed them to elicit more information about the family by discussing a greater variety of topics, particularly family beliefs and marital problems.

## The initial child protection conference and registration

Workers emerge from the initial child protection conference with perceptions about each other, and how the families perceive both the system and the workers. Stevenson (1989) has suggested that conflict between professionals over cultural relativism may arise at conferences in three ways: they may vary in their awareness of the significance of professional differences, they may differ in their views as to the extent to which certain behaviour is normal in a particular culture, and they may differ as to what weight should be given to these cultural variables in the decisions that are made – often for fear that they could be interpreted as racist.

The initial child protection conference has to address the issues identified in Box 7.5 to minimise family oppression.

Virdee argued that the conference should consider the relevance of race, ethnicity and cultural issues to the case; a definition from the family on their ethnicity; what their views are of their culture, values, norms, lifestyles, child-rearing practices and how these are related to the particular case in question; and language – so that jargon and pejorative terms are avoided and there is a recognition that black and ethnic minority families may use terms that convey a different meaning (Virdee, 1992: 53–4).

**Box 7.5 Avoidance of Conflict**

*Language and communication* Translating and interpreting issues, signing, and so on need to be introduced. We need to use materials that will maximise the opportunity of accurately interpreting non-verbal cues and communication. Indirect comments and gestures which are oppressive need tackling (Moore, 1992). Farmer and Owen (1995) have noted difficulties with interpreters at conferences.

*Access issues* These include where the conference is held, in which community and venue, and physical access for disabled participants.

*Presumptions over carers/availability* Many make an assumption that the female is the primary carer without embracing the males in the intervention. Research is highlighting that we struggle to engage men in the process, particularly beyond the point that their own agenda has been met (Egan, 1994). There are also issues about professional collusion with abuse in middle-class families, particularly where their financial resources tap into private services which may be acutely resistant to following child protection procedures (Calder and Waters, 1991).

*Power relationships* These are very real between workers and families, as well as between the professionals themselves, and there is a need for the chairman to address these issues to keep the intervention safe and child-focused (Hallett and Stevenson, 1980).

*Racism* The strengths of black families may be missed and there may be an inference that sexual and physical abuse is a natural part of the family culture of a particular race group (Moore 1992).

Wilson (1995) set out various questions for the conference to consider when deciding on the membership of the core group:

- Does the group reflect the child's family images?
- Does the group reflect or have an understanding of differing family patterns and lifestyles?
- Is there an opportunity for family members to request support or representation at core group meetings – particularly when many areas restrict numbers for management purposes?
- Can additional services such as interpretation or translation be provided at core group meetings? Alternatively, can meetings be held in the family's first language having translation for professionals?
- Are the roles and tasks for each core group member made clear,

achievable and recorded? Are professionals listening to what black parents have to say – not just making tokenistic or patronising agreements?
- Does the group have a clear understanding of what is available as 'black resources' in their geographic area?
- Have community leaders been consulted about the issues of local resources?

## Core groups

Wilson (1995) set out some key principles for anti-oppressive core group practice. She argued that a corporate perspective should be developed by the core group membership to take account of individual values, experiences and beliefs, as well as systems to strive towards eliminating injustice and disadvantage in providing services. She advises us to consider the following issues when deciding on the membership of and issues for the core group as families from different cultures may have very different ways of participating in interventions for their children.

1. Brief the family about the meeting, its purpose and who will be present, well in advance of the meeting. What will facilitate their participation? What does a meeting mean to them? What terminology do they understand? How can we fully explain the process to them in a way that helps them feel they want to be involved?
2. Reduce the number of professionals present unless the family has requested that others be present.
3. Incorporate practices that are culturally comfortable for the family (for example, serving tea), taking time to get acquainted before beginning the more formal aspects of the meeting, or, for some families, conducting the meeting in a highly formal manner.
4. Does the group reflect or have an understanding of differing family patterns and lifestyles? What are the social and cultural expectations of the family/child, and what are the family roles for women, men and elders?
5. Is there an opportunity for family members to request support or representation at core group meetings, particularly when many areas restrict numbers for management purposes? Families should be encouraged to bring along people who are important to them, such as relatives or friends.
6. Can additional services such as interpretation or translation be provided at core group meetings? Alternatively, can meetings be held in the family's first language, with translation for professionals?

7 Be sure that family input is encouraged without creating embarrassment. If it is felt that family members will not interact comfortably in such a public forum, be sure that the worker who knows the family best has spoken with them ahead of time and can represent their perspective at the meeting.
8 Are the roles and tasks for each core group member made clear, achievable and recorded? Are professionals listening to what black parents have to say: not just offering tokenistic or patronising agreements? Are the goals, objectives or outcomes that are being developed matched to the family's concerns, priorities and needs?
9 Does the group have a clear understanding of what is available as 'Black resources' in their geographic area? Are resources being used, that are designed for, or are a part of, the family's cultural community: for example, child care sponsored by the religious group to which they belong or a referral to a health care provider who shares the same language and culture?
10 Have community leaders been consulted about the issues of local resources?
11 Allow time for questions, but be prepared to comment on questions that other families have often asked. This allows questions to be answered without having to be asked.
12 What are the family strengths? It is important to focus on their situation, culture, community, lifestyle, parenting style and so on.
13 What is the impact of race, class and social position on the family/child?
14 How will further assessment/work be undertaken within the context of the above points?

*Source*: Adapted from Lynch and Hanson (1992) and Wilson (1995).

Empowerment work would seem to be more feasible during the core group phase, where workers try to restore a sense of control to families. The checklist from Boushel and Lebacq (1992) cited earlier can be usefully applied when formulating the core group. As a result, families become empowered and are more likely to deal with problems and change. Self-determination by parents is enabled when workers provide the necessary climate for change to occur, and the strengths focus reinforces this process. Once the climate for self-determination has been established, case planning can proceed in an empowering way. It is often very important to address the structural as well as individual factors, embracing poverty, homelessness and health care. Whilst workers do not control social policies which determine the resources available to families, they have greater access to resources than most clients, as well as better information in relation to the availability of goods and services (McCallum and Prillentsky, 1996).

## Planning and the use of written agreements

Written agreements should promote an exchange of views, minimise understandings and counter some of the negative effects of being a recipient or user of social services (Braye and Preston-Shoot, 1992). If used within a relationship that is based on partnership, they will be a useful practice tool (MacDonald, 1991) which will empower those we work with, because it promotes user involvement and control (Croft and Beresford, 1994). Yet they can also be disempowering as they are unlikely to be based on equal power relationships. They can be used to control and maintain the power base of the worker. In child protection work, they can be used as the means to ensure that parents reach a standard that has been defined by the worker as acceptable to them. If the parents fail to reach the required standards then the worker has the evidence in the terms of the 'failed' agreement to take to court to prove the case against them. However, setting people up to fail is by no stretch of the imagination empowering. Nor is it a recommended method of making and sustaining working relationships. Liz Wilson has noted that:

> it should come as little or no surprise to hear that failure of protection plans is more likely to be attributed to 'parental failure' to co-operate with professionals rather than professionals recognising a somewhat flawed plan in meeting the child's needs and family's expectations. (Wilson, 1995)

She noted that inter-agency child protection plans are often drawn up with little or no thought for their appropriateness for black families. If agreements instigated by workers are to be successful then those workers have to be aware of their own value base. They can utilise the strengths approach as a mechanism to neutralise any excessive social control aspects of the planning process. They also have to be able to acknowledge the power they have as workers and then decide on the extent to which they are prepared to share power (Dalrymple and Burke, 1995: 68).

Written agreements have a better chance of succeeding if the parties can share a common understanding of the problems, have a degree of mutual trust, have a common way of expressing themselves, have a shared understanding of time, and have a broadly similar view of the context in which the problems have arisen (MacDonald, 1991).

Leung *et al.* (1994) identified a number of issues needing to be addressed when formulating a written agreement (see Box 7.6).

We must remember that any plan will only be as effective as those who are implementing it. It follows, therefore, that each person who will be involved in its implementation 'buy into' the plan. We should acknowledge that families from different cultures may not expect or prefer to have such an active role,

**Box 7.6 Formulating Written Agreements**

Attitudes – for example, to what extent do ethnic differences influence how I approach the contracting process with this family? Will I be more authoritarian or indifferent? Do I assume ethnic differences might influence the family's level of understanding, resistance or effort in contracting? To what extent does fear of being perceived as racist influence me?

Knowledge – for example, are the goals and objectives for this family ethnically sensitive? Have I concentrated on ethnically specific services – formal and informal? Have I selected means that are ethnically appropriate and sensitive in measuring the family's progress towards goals and objectives?

Skills – for example, to what extent have I been ethnically sensitive in assessing the following. Who will be included in the planning process? What role does each member of the family play? Is an interpreter needed and, if so, how do I arrange for one? Are goals and objectives stated in language and behaviours that are understandable to this family? Are they built on the particular strengths of the family's ethnic context?

Are desired outcomes stated in ways that can be achieved within the ethnic framework of the family?

Are their potential ethnic barriers to achieving the goals and objectives in the plan? (Leung *et al.*, 1994: 713–16)

and workers are then faced with rethinking established practices with regard to how or whether to ensure proactive involvement. They must also be clear about targets for change and how to achieve them, as workers' assumptions about race dynamics can have an impact on the making and measurement of plans. Once constructed, plans need to be accessible if they are to be effective, although we should acknowledge that written communication should not be imposed without prior negotiation. Implementing the plan is potentially the area for greatest cultural conflicts. If family members had a different understanding of the goals, if they viewed their roles in implementation differently than did the workers, or if they were simply too polite to disagree at the time the goals were being written, conflicts may arise. Workers may need to introduce a cultural advisor to reformulate the plan to maximise the implementation prospects. Lynch and Hanson (1992) argue that implementation can be made more effective by incorporating the following into the process.

1 Put a lot of time and energy into ensuring that the goals and outcomes proposed are those that are of primary importance to the family.
2 Adjust typical goals to match the family's priorities, behaving in cooperative rather than competitive ways and learning words in the language of the home – for example, encouraging sleeping and napping in the parent's bed rather than alone, and using terms such as using the potty rather than going to the toilet independently.
3 Involve the family to the extent that they choose to be involved in all aspects of the programme.
4 If families choose to take a less active role, continue to provide them with information about the programme and their children's progress through cultural mediators, photos, and/or videotapes, as appropriate.
5 Create a programme that fits into the cultural communities that it serves. Use the multicultural aspects of the programme to strengthen its implementation through a community centre where people want to be, and partnering other community services such as child care and health clinics.
6 Involve the various cultural communities' leaders in the programme and invite their participation and advice through advisory boards (Lynch and Hanson, 1992: 367–8). This needs to be carefully managed, given the need for confidentiality in situations which do not compromise the child's protection, such as domestic violence in an Asian home. Workers need to review the plans if families disengage or if they cannot be sufficiently engaged in the process from the outset.

## Assessments

### *Cross-cultural assessments: planning issues*

Leung *et al.* pointed out that 'assessment is a process of gathering pertinent information about family needs, problems, resources, strengths and analysing information to determine risk, for the purpose of developing a service plan to bring about change' (Leung *et al.*, 1994: 709). We should never overlook the reality that we can still uncover strengths when assessing for risks. Seabury has argued that a good assessment identifies the salient issues and difficulties facing the family which all concerned agree need to be addressed, as well as identifying the major strengths and resources the family bring to bear on the issues (Seabury, 1985: 348). It is not a matter of assessing their deficiencies, but it does need to embrace the political, social and economic arena if it is not to be skewed (Okine, 1992: 115). Boushel found that we have not developed an approach to assessment that integrates the multiple aspects of structural and personal disadvantage, while at the same time acknowledging cultural diversity (Boushel, 1994: 174).

There are various useful points to consider when approaching cross-cultural assessments.

1 Anticipate and plan for a greater number of interviews than usual, possibly of somewhat longer duration if other professionals are to be present.
2 Consider making at least one assessment interview in the family home; however, it is important to confirm that the family are comfortable with outsiders visiting.
3 Arrange the assessment at a time that allow the people important to the child/family to be present. For example, although the father may not have any direct care-giving responsibilities for the child, it may be important for him to be present during an assessment. In fact, it may be the father, or another family member such as the grandmother, who holds the decision-making powers in the family with respect to the child's education or treatment.
4 The family may want to assess your attitude towards their cultural/ethnic group, and to assess your independence from other professional agencies. Repeated explanations are likely to be necessary to explain the entire process of assessment and your part in it, as well as the specific responsibility you may have in making reports to the court. Explanations may need to be made in several different ways.
5 If the family's use of the English language is limited or not proficient, work with a trained interpreter who can interpret language as well as cultural cues, and follow the guidelines suggested for working with interpreters presented earlier: remember that what is not said can be as meaningful in some cases as what is said. Use a professional interpreter rather than a child, member of the family or family friend. This is not a simple matter as the interpreter, too, may arouse anxieties about confidential family matters being made available to the minority community. It is very important to confirm for yourself the training and experience of the interpreter.
6 Gather only the data necessary to begin work with the child and family. Limit the numbers of forms, questionnaires, and other types of paperwork.
7 Include as few assessors as possible. Additional observations or information can be obtained at another time.
8 Gather information in those areas in which the family has expressed concern. Tending to the families' issues first is a sign of respect for all families. (Adapted from Lynch and Hanson, 1992; Maitra, 1995; Thanki, 1994.)

## *Process issues*

Phillips and Gonzalez-Ramos (1989) argued that we should emphasise a number of areas in the assessment process (see Box 7.7).

**Box 7.7 Assessment Process Issues**

*Stress and risk factors* How well does the family cope with stress? Does stress overload affect the parents' ability to care for their child? Are episodes of abuse triggered by stress? What supports exist that can help the family diminish or better cope with stress? Do parents feel a sense of hopelessness? How well does the family handle basic activities of daily living?
*Sociocultural background and values* A basic knowledge is required, and workers should be aware of those aspects of the culture in which the client takes pride; culturally prescribed roles and expectations; accepted child-rearing practices; attitudes towards problems and accepting help; valuable support systems; and religious and culturally sanctioned beliefs and practices.
*Knowledge and values regarding child development and child management* The tasks for the worker are to ascertain the family's degree of understanding of children's developmental needs and how children should be raised; to determine whether the family's understanding, attitudes and behaviour are appropriate to foster the child's growth and development; and to determine the family's motivation and capacity to expand their understanding and adopt alternative ways of managing their children.
*Ego functioning and coping mechanisms* This entails exploring the context in which a punishment occurred, the client's state of mind, the severity of the punishment, how similar or different this client is from clients of similar cultural background, and how the client behaves in other areas of his or her life. It is impossible to make an accurate ego assessment without considering what is an appropriate culturally based coping pattern.
*The life-cycle stages of the abused child* For example, the parents will have problems dealing with the child at particular phases of their development and with the behavioural patterns they manifest. They may have unrealistic expectations that a child will fulfil the aspirations they could not achieve.

*Source*: Phillips and Gonzalez-Ramos, 1989: 132–5.

## *Assessment tools and questions*

When selecting commercially available assessment instruments, choose only those that are appropriate for the language and culture of the child and family. The government guide *Protecting Children* (DoH, 1988) implicitly acknowledges that children from minority groups receive a culturally insensitive service. In doing so, it outlines a number of basic needs of children which are distinctly Eurocentric and which can skew the risk assessment process. For a comprehensive and critical analysis of this guide, the reader is referred to Phillips and Dutt (1990).

There is no simple checklist of questions which can be used to assess child abuse in ethnic minority families, but Box 7.8 gives useful suggestions from the available literature.

**Box 7.8 Assessment Questions**

What are the social and cultural expectations of the family?
What are the ethnic expectations of family role and interaction?
What are the family roles for women, children, men, elders?
What is the response to ethnic history?
What is the impact of racism?
What is the impact of class and social position?
Is the family integrated/marginalised/powerful/powerless?
What belief systems and value orientations influence role expectations, define and set limits of acceptable behaviour?
What are the structures relevant to authority and decision making in the family?
Which are the key kinship patterns? Which are the key relationships with important supportive functions?
What is the relevant family network?
What life-cycle phase is this family at? What are the risks and challenges?
What are the traditional solutions used to manage conflict and to what extent are they operational in this family? How is the family organised to enable essential tasks to be performed?
What traditional networks and activities have maintained and supported structural relationships in the family?
Which traditional networks and activities have been lost, and with what consequences?
What significant stresses and losses arise from the family's own experience, from the country of origin, from adaptation to the UK? What racial or cultural factors confer advantage or disadvantage on the individual/family in the UK?
What is the impact of isolation from their own family, roots and ethnic reality?
What are their understanding and coping abilities, regarding racism, discrimination, oppression and so on?
What part do the social support system and network play in their life?

(Adapted from the Black and White Alliance, 1989/1990; Lau, 1991.)

Two very helpful articles exist which explain how to use the culturagram (Congress, 1994) and genogram (Hardy and Laszloffy, 1995) to collect useful information in the process of assessment. The reader is referred to the full texts in order to equip themselves to use them in their practice.

It is important that we do not ignore the risks at the expense of family strengths. As DePanfilis and Wilson (1996) have noted, 'we need to focus our assessments on the complex interplay of risks and strengths related to individual family members, the family as a unit, and the broader neighbourhood and environment'.

### *Assessment questionnaires/tools*

There are a number of emerging assessment instruments that focus on developing and measuring the achievement of positive outcomes or strengths over time and which include the following:

- Family Strengths Inventory (Stinnett and De Frain, 1985),
- Family Strengths Scale (Olson *et al.*, 1983),
- Family Hardiness Index (McCubbin and Thompson, 1987),
- Family Functioning Style Scale (Deal *et al.*, 1994),
- Family Resources Scale (Dunst and Leet, 1987),
- Support Functions Scale (Trivette and Dunst, 1988b),
- Family Needs Scale (Dunst *et al.*, 1988),
- Personal Network Matrix (Trivette and Dunst, 1988a),
- Family Strengths Profile (Trivette *et al.*, 1988).

Charles Cowger (1992) has written an excellent paper on the assessment of client strengths which provides an assessment framework and a useful checklist is provided. Finally, Wayman *et al.* (1990) have produced a set of guidelines that can be used to learn more about a family's cultural values and references, and which includes questions on family attitudes, beliefs and practices.

## Summary

The whole area of child protection requires further research in an ethnic context, and this has become more apparent to the present writer in the course of reading for this chapter. In the absence of a substantially revised pre- and post-qualifying training programme addressing the issue of working with ethnic minority families in the area of child care/protection, there is a huge personal and supervisory responsibility to nurture and apply an anti-oppressive approach. The broad framework does exist in statute, but a considerable amount of work needs to be done to translate the theoretical potential into a practice reality. It is clear that the adoption of a strengths approach is a useful foundation for this pursuit and it should be extended to work with all families, whatever their culture. It is clear that a full text is now necessary to consolidate more comprehensively the information and assessment materials and then utilise these as the basis of the way forward. It is hoped that this chapter can act as a catalyst for research and practice activity in this much neglected area of work.

## Key points for workers to consider

1. Britain is a kaleidoscope of cultures, and services to children and their families should always reflect this.
2. Workers can strive for anti-oppressive practice by adopting a strengths perspective in their work, underpinned by a philosophy of empowerment and partnership, and supported by the Children Act 1989.
3. Workers should believe that families have the ability to define their own problems, set their own goals and take their own action for change. They may need support to achieve these outcomes and coercion may sometimes be needed – but only at a level commensurate with protecting the child.
4. Workers need to learn how to engage and work with families and cultures other than their own; this should include respect for other cultures, a sincere attempt to understand other people's points of view, flexibility and amenability to learning and change. These are the building blocks to becoming an effective multicultural worker.
5. We can learn to tailor our interventions to the individual circumstances of each case, and some preliminary guidelines have been set out above to assist workers in the post-registration phase.

## References

Adcock, M. (1991) 'Significant Harm: Implications for the Exercise of Statutory Responsibilities', in M. Adcock, R. White and A. Hollows (eds), *Significant Harm: Its Management and Outcome*, Croydon: Significant Publications.

Armstrong, H. (1995) *Annual Reports of Area Child Protection Committees 1994/5*, London: HMSO.

Barn, R. (1993) *Black Children in the Public Care System*, London: Batsford.

Beckett, J. and Dungee-Anderson, D. (1993) *A Framework for Teaching Multicultural Intervention*, Richmond Va.: Virginia Commonwealth University, School of Social Work.

Bell, M. and Sinclair, I. (1993) *Parental Involvement in Initial Child Protection*, York: University of York.

Black and White Alliance (1989/90) *Race in Child Protection: A Code of Practice*, London: Race Equality Unit.
Bogle, M.T. (1988) 'Brixton Black Women's Centre: Organising on Child Sexual Abuse', *Feminist Review*, **28**: 132–5.
Boushel, M. (1994) 'The Protective Environment of Children: Towards a Framework for Anti-oppressive, Cross-cultural and Cross-national Understanding', *British Journal of Social Work*, **21** (2): 173–90.
Boushel, M. and Lebacq, M. (1992) 'Towards Empowerment in Child Protection Work', *Children and Society*, **6** (1): 38–50.
Braye, S. and Preston-Shoot, M. (1992) 'Honourable Intentions: Written Agreements in Welfare Legislation' *Journal of Social Welfare and Family Law*, November (6): 511–28.
Calder, M.C. (1995) 'Child Protection: Balancing Partnership and Paternalism', *British Journal of Social Work*, **25** (6): 749–66.
Calder, M.C. and Waters, J. (1991) 'Child Abuse or Child Protection: What's in a Name?', keynote presentation to the APT conference on child abuse, University of York, 18 June.
Clark, B., Parkin, W. and Richards, M. (1990) 'Dangerousness: A Complex Practice Issue', in Violence Against Children Study Group (eds), *Taking Child Abuse Seriously*, London: Unwin Hyman.
Congress, E.P. (1994) 'The Use of Culturagrams to Assess and Empower Culturally Diverse Families', *Families in Society*, November: 531–40.
Courtney, M.E., Barth, R.P., Berrick, J.D., Brooks, D., Needell, B. and Park, L. (1996) 'Race and Child Welfare Services: Past Research and Future Directions', *Child Welfare*, **75** (2): 99–137.
Cowger, C. (1992) 'Assessment of Client Strengths', in D. Saleebey (ed.), *The Strengths Perspective in Social Work Practice*, New York: Longman.
Croft, S. and Beresford, P. (1994) 'A Participatory Approach to Social Work', in C. Hanvey and T. Philpot (eds), *Practising Social Work*, London: Routledge.
Dalrymple, J. and Burke, B. (1995) *Anti-oppressive Practice: Social Care and the Law*, Buckingham: Open University Press.
Deal, A.G., Trivette, C.M. and Dunst, C.J. (1994) 'Family Functioning Style Scale', in C.J. Dunst, C.M. Trivette and A.G. Deal (eds), *Supporting and Strengthening Families*, Cambridge, Mass: Brookline Books: 139.
DeJong, P. and Miller, S.D. (1995) 'How to Interview for Client Strengths', *Social Work*, **40** (6): 729–36.
Depanfilis, D. and Wilson, C. (1996) 'Applying the Strengths Perspective with Maltreating Families', *The Apsac Advisor*, **9** (3): 15–20.
Department of Health (1988) *Protecting Children: A Guide for Social Workers Undertaking a Comprehensive Assessment*, London: HMSO.
Department of Health (1995) *Messages from Research*, London: HMSO.
Droisen, A. (1989) 'Racism and Anti-semitism', in E. Driver and A. Droisen (eds), *Child Sexual Abuse: Feminist Perspectives*, London: Macmillan.
Dungee-Anderson, D. and Beckett, J.O. (1995) 'A Process Model for Multicultural Social Work Practice', *Families in Society*, **76** (8): 459–68.
Dunst, C.J. and Leet, H.E. (1987) 'Measuring the Adequacy of Resources in Households with Young Children', *Child: care, health and development*,**13**: 111–25.
Dunst, C.J., Cooper, C.S., Weeldreyer, J.C., Snyder, K.D. and Chase, J.H. (1988) 'Family Needs Scale', in C.J. Dunst *et al.* (eds), *Enabling and Empowering Families: Principles and Guidelines for Practice*, Cambridge, Mass.: Brookline Books.

Egan, E. (1994) 'Does Partnership Exist in Child Protection Decision-making?', presentation to the Second National Congress (BASPCAN), 'Working in Partnership', University of Bristol, 5–8 July.

Farmer, E. and Owen, M. (1995) *Child Protection Practice: Private Risks and Public Remedies. Decision-making, Intervention and Outcome in Child Protection Work*, London: HMSO.

Griffith, M.S. (1977) 'The Influence of Race on the Psychotherapeutic Relationship', *Psychiatry*, **40**: 27–40.

Grimwood, C. and Tombs, J. (1995) 'Anti-racism Training: Time to Explore the Conflicts', *Professional Social Work*, November: 4.

Hallett, C. and Stevenson, O. (1980) *Child Abuse: Aspects of Interprofessional Co-operation*, London: HMSO.

Hardy, K.V. and Laszloffy, T.A. (1995) 'The Cultural Genogram: Key to Training Culturally Competent Family Therapists', *Journal of Marital and Family Therapy*, **21** (3): 227–37.

Jadeza, K. (1997) 'Relationship problems', *Community Care* (inside supplement), 29 May–4 June: 5.

Jones, A. (1993) 'Anti-racist Child Protection', *Race and Class* **35** (2): 75–85.

Kakar S (1982) *Shamans, Mystics and Doctors : A Psychological Inquiry into India and its Healing Traditions*, London: Unwin Hyman.

Korbin, J. (1991) 'Cross-cultural Perspectives and Research Directions for the 21st Century', *Child Abuse and Neglect*, **15** (1): 67–77.

Korbin, J. (1993) 'Cultural Diversity and Child Maltreatment', *Violence Update*, **3** (11): 8–9.

Lau, A. (1991) 'Cultural and Ethnic Perspectives on Significant Harm: Its Assessment and Treatment', in M. Adcock *et al.* (eds), *Significant Harm*.

Lawrence, D. (1996) 'Race, Culture and the Probation Service: Groupwork Programme Design', in G. McIvor (ed.), *Working with Offenders*, London: Jessica Kingsley.

Leeder, E. (1994) *Treating Abuse in Families: A Feminist and Community Approach*, New York: Springer Publishing.

Leung, P., Monit Cheung, K.F. and Stevenson, K.M. (1994) 'A Strengths Approach to Ethnically Sensitive Practice for Child Protective Service Workers', *Child Welfare*, **733**: 707–21.

Levine, M., Doueck, H.J., Freeman, J.B. and Compaan, C. (1996) 'African–American Families and Child Protection', *Children and Youth Services Review*, **18** (8): 693–711.

Luthra, M. (1997) *Britain's Black Population: Social Change, Public Policy and Agenda*, Aldershot: Arena.

Lynch, E.W. (1992) 'From Culture Shock to Cultural Learning', in E.W. Lynch and M.J. Hanson (eds), *Developing Cross-cultural Competence: A Guide for Working with Young Children and their Families*, Baltimore: Paul H. Brookes Publishing Co.

Lynch, E.W. and Hanson, M.J. (1992) 'Steps in the Right Direction: Implications for Interventionists', in E.W. Lynch and M.J. Hanson (eds), *Developing Cross-cultural Competence*.

MacDonald, S. (1991) *All Equal under the Act: A Practice Guide to the Children Act 1989 for Social Workers*, London: Race Equality Unit.

Macey, M. and Moxon, E. (1996) 'An Examination of Anti-racist and Anti-oppressive Theory and Practice in Social Work Education', *British Journal of Social Work*, **26**: 297–314.

Maitra, B. (1995) 'Giving Due Consideration to the Family's Racial and Cultural Background', in P. Reder and C. Lucey (eds), *Assessment of Parenting: Psychiatric and Psychological Contributions*, London: Routledge.

Mars, M. (1989) 'Child Sexual Abuse and Race Issues', in BAAF (ed.), *After Abuse Papers: Papers on Caring and Planning for a Child who has been Sexually Abused*, London: BAAF.

McCallum, S. and Prillentsky, I. (1996) 'Empowerment in Child Protection Work: Values, Practice and Caveats', *Children and Society*, **10**: 40–50.

McCubbin, H.I. and Thompson, A.I. (1987) *Family Assessment Inventories for Research and Practice*, Madison, Wis.: University of Wisconsin–Madison.

Moore, J. (1992) *The ABC of Child Protection*, Aldershot: Gower.

Narayau, U. (1989) 'Working Together Across Differences', in B.R. Compton and B. Gallaway (eds), *Social Work Processes*, 4th edn, Belmont, Cal.: Wadsworth Publishing.

Okine, E. (1992) 'A Misassessment of Black Families in Child Abuse Work', in J. Moore (ed.), *The ABC of Child Protection*.

Olson, D.H., Larsen, A. and McCubbin, H.I. (1983) 'Family Strengths Scale', in D.H. Olson, H.I. McCubbin, A. Larsen, A. Muxem and M. Wilson (eds), *Families: What Makes Them Work*, Beverley Hills: Sage.

Otto, H.A. (1963) 'Criteria for Assessing Family Strengths', *Family Process*, **2**: 329–37.

Owen, M. and Farmer, E. (1996) 'Child Protection in a Multi-racial Context', *Policy and Politics*, **24** (3): 299–313.

Phillips, L.J. and Gonzalez-Ramos, G. (1989) 'Clinical Social Work Practice with Minority Families', in S.M. Ehrenkranz, E.J. Goldstein, L. Goodman and J. Seinfeld (eds), *Clinical Social Work with Maltreated Children and their Families*, New York: New York University Press.

Phillips, M. and Dutt, R. (eds) (1990) *Towards a Black Perspective in Child Protection*, London: Race Equality Unit.

Phillipson, J. (1992) *Practising Equality: Women, Men and Social Work*, London: Central Council for Education and Training in Social Work.

Raval, H. (1996) 'A Systemic Perspective on Working with Interpreters', *Clinical Child Psychology and Psychiatry*, **1** (1): 29–43.

Rodwell, M.K. and Blankebaker, A. (1992) 'Strategies for Developing Cross-cultural Sensitivity: Wounding as Metaphor', *Journal of Social Work Education*, **28** (2): 153–65.

Saleebey, D. (ed.) (1992) *The Strengths Perspective in Social Work Practice*, New York: Longman.

Saleebey, D. (1996) 'The Strengths Perspective in Social Work Practice: Extensions and Cautions', *Social Work*, **41** (3): 296–305.

Seabury, B.A. (1985) 'The Beginning Phase: Engagement, Initial Assessment and Contracting', in J. Laird and A. Hartman (eds), *A Handbook of Child Welfare: Context, Knowledge and Practice*, New York: Free Press.

Stevenson, O. (1989) 'Multi-disciplinary Work in Child Protection', in O. Stevenson (ed.), *Child Abuse: Public Policy and Professional Practice*, London: Harvester Wheatsheaf.

Stinnett, N. and De Frain, J. (1985) *Secrets of Strong Families*, Boston: Little, Brown and Co.

Thanki, V. (1994) 'Ethnic Diversity and Child Protection', *Children and Society*, **8** (3): 232–44.

The Bridge (1991) *Sukina: An Evaluation of the Circumstances Surrounding her Death*, London: The Bridge Child Care Consultancy.

Trivette, C.M. and Dunst, C.J. (1988a) 'Personal Network Matrix', in C.J. Dunst *et al.* (eds), *Enabling and Empowering Families*.

Trivette, C.M. and Dunst, C.J. (1988b) 'Support Functions Scale', in C.J. Dunst *et al.* (eds), *Enabling and Empowering Families*.

Trivette, C.M., Dunst, C.J. and Deal, A.G. (1988) 'Family Strengths Profile', in C.J. Dunst *et al.* (eds), *Enabling and Empowering Families.*

Valasquez, J., Vigil, M.E. and Benavides, E. (1989) 'A Framework for Establishing Social Work Relationships across Racial/Ethnic Lines', in B.R. Compton and B. Gallaway (eds), *Social Work Processes,* (4th edn), Belmont, Cal: Wordsworth Publishing: 312–16.

Virdee, G. (1992) 'Issues of Ethnicity and Participation', in J. Thoburn (ed.), *Participation in Practice: Involving Families in Child Protection,* Norwich: University of East Anglia.

Ward, D. and Mullender, A. (1991) 'Making Empowerment Work', *Youth Social Work,* **4**, Summer: 11–13.

Wayman, K.I., Lynch, E.W. and Hanson, M.J. (1990) 'Home-based Early Childhood Services: Cultural Sensitivity in a Family Systems Approach', *Topics in Early Childhood Special Education,* 10: 65–6.

Westcott, H. and Cross, M. (1996) *This Far and No Further: Towards Ending the Abuse of Disabled Children,* Birmingham: Venture Press.

Wilson, L. (1995) 'Race Equality/Equal Opportunity Issues in Core Groups', keynote presentation to the national conference, 'Core Groups: central to child protection: myth or reality?', Manchester Town Hall, 14 July.

# 8 Core groups: a catalyst for change?

*Tony Morrison*

In this chapter, consideration is given to the following:

- the current context of collaboration for core groups;
- the role of the core group in the process of encouraging change within families;
- exploring the link between partnership and change;
- how core groups can create the conditions for change and what 'messages from research' tells us about this;
- looking at how change occurs, and how to enhance parental motivation for change;
- adopting Protchaska and DiClemente's model of change to the core group.

## Introduction

The discussion in this chapter focuses on the concept of the core groups as a catalyst for change. As Gibbons *et al.* (1995) have pointed out, surveillance, monitoring and practical help for abused children are insufficient both to 'get to grips with the forces that produce maltreatment and to compensate for its effects on the child'. It is clear, therefore, that whatever else collaborative post-registration work might achieve, if it does not create the conditions in which change can occur, it will be failing to meet the needs of the majority of children on child protection registers. The question as to how far post-registration responses can be organised so as to be therapeutic is a critical one for all involved in the child protection system, and is pivotal to the approach taken in this book about the role of the core group.

This chapter examines the role of the core groups as a catalyst for change by exploring a number of related issues. What is the collaborative context in which core groups operate? What is the relationship between social justice and therapeutic notions of partnership? What does research from child protection say about conditions for creating change? How does change happen and what is the nature of motivation? What is the role of core groups in facilitating and sustaining parental motivation for change? What is a comprehensive model of change?

## Context of collaboration for core groups

Previous chapters have considered the impact of organisational change on multidisciplinary working (Chapters 1 and 4), the lack of central government guidance on core group roles and responsibilities (Chapter 2) and of group dynamics on core group processes (Chapter 6). The child protection system operates in a rapidly changing and, in part, increasingly fragmenting, organisational context. Key features of this include the separation of purchasers from providers and the emergence of multiple providers; contracting of services which may cut right across traditional Area Child Protection Committee (ACPC) boundaries; the local management of schools and GP fundholding, making accountability for child protection responsibilities far more diffused and diluted. In this environment, collaboration is increasingly dependent on the strength and commitment of multidisciplinary relationships between individuals as opposed to inter-agency relationships between organisations. While good multidisciplinary working between individuals is of course essential, if collaboration is entirely dependent on this, it becomes dangerously vulnerable when such individuals depart.

This of course reminds us of another very important facet of collaboration, which is that formal requirements to collaborate work best when embedded within a wider network of strong informal networks, at both senior and local levels (Hallett and Birchall, 1992; McFarlane and Morrison, 1994). Thus it is likely that the functioning of core groups will reflect the quality or otherwise of pre-existing relationships at all three levels: inter-agency, multidisciplinary and networking. If core groups are to work, they cannot be considered in isolation from the background of the local collaborative culture.

However, a further dimension to the core group's context is its position along the continuum of case management, after referral, investigation/ inquiries, initial child protection conference, and sometimes after court proceedings and other placement and statutory review meetings. In other words, core groups make their entrance fairly late in the day. This is a very significant factor because, as the research by Farmer and Owen (1995) showed, the influence of the early attitudes and decisions taken, particularly by those investigating concerns about possible abuse, has been found to have considerable effect on the subsequent management of the case. Farmer and Owen found that the initial recommendations of the investigating professionals are rarely reversed by the initial child protection conference, and even less likely to be challenged by child protection review. In other words, by the time the core group is established, the shape, direction and dynamics of the case are highly developed and resistant to redirection, even when initial child protection conference plans are unrealistic, unprotective or unviable. Thus the gradient that the core group will then be operating on may well be very steep, creating conditions that may not be propitious for therapeutic change. In addition, research by Hallett (1995) shows how frequently, by the time the first core group meets, other agencies have often withdrawn, leaving the social worker as the principal direct worker and social services as the main provider of services, assisted by monitoring through the health visitor, and sometimes the school, as explored later in this book by Appleton and Clemerson (Chapter 10) and Peake and Turner (Chapter 11).

What all of this adds up to is a clear message that the core group cannot easily undo failings of assessment, planning or partnership when they occur earlier in the process, and that the potential for the core group depends significantly on the quality of what has gone before. In other words, the core group's role is more effective in transforming the investigative and forensic aspects of child protection into a therapeutic opportunity than in challenging what has already occurred. In order to explore the role of the core group, its place must therefore be understood within the wider process of inter-agency collaboration.

Challis *et al.*'s definition (1988) of the ingredients of effective collaboration is particularly useful. They describe collaboration as having three key elements upon which the outcomes in terms of actual benefits to service users of collaborative effort depend: (1) machinery (structures, procedures and so on), (2) the process of working and learning together, and (3) outputs in terms of services to users – in this case, children and families. Taking Challis *et al.*'s definition, the role of the core group in terms of effective collaboration can then be framed as follows:

> Core groups operate as part of the machinery of the Child Protection System, in order to assist the process of professionals and families working together, with the purpose of assessing, planning, and co-ordinating the outputs to abused children and their families, so as to facilitate outcomes that protect children and promote their welfare.

However, if core groups are to fulfil their potential in transforming collaborative effort into meaningful changes in families, there must be a shared understanding about what 'partnership' under the Children Act 1989 does and does not mean, and what are the links between partnership practice and therapeutic processes.

## Revisiting 'partnership': social justice versus therapeutic meanings

While Christie and Mittler have discussed the issues around partnership in Chapter 6 of the present volume, there is a need to focus here on the link between partnership and change. The Children Act 1989 and the associated emergence of the partnership principle, in order to reduce the need for statutory intervention, have clearly been hampered by resource constraints, particularly with regard to its preventative aspects. However, they have also been constrained by a lack of clear definition about what partnership is meant to be, and the absence of related theoretical frameworks to guide the details of partnership practice (Calder, 1995). It is one thing to subscribe to the philosophy of partnership, quite another to know what that should look like in an interview, and yet another thing to develop shared consensus across agencies about the nature of partnership practice. In this regard, the 1995 Department of Health practice guide *The Challenge of Partnership in Child Protection* (DoH, 1995a) was a welcome publication. It acknowledged that partnerships with families occur across a continuum of dynamic and changing relationships, and operate at different levels of intensity, power sharing and reciprocity. The guide described four levels of partnership: (1) providing information, (2) involvement (being present), (3) participation (influencing what is going on), and (4) partnership (shared working, but not necessarily equality). With regard to the last point, the document openly states: 'Words such as equality, choice and power have limited meaning at certain points in the child protection process.' Helpful though this publication has been, it does not resolve all the dilemmas about the nature of partnership in child protection matters.

Work by Fox-Harding (1991), Howe (1992) and Sainsbury (1989) has sought to unravel some of the philosophical and practical complexities of partnership, and remind us that there remains a necessary paternalistic element to child protection legislation and practice. The use of authority, the reality of conflict and the consequent limits on what partnerships can be forged in child protection work must all be incorporated in any realistic framework for practice. As Howe (1992) states: 'It might be that clients experience participation as fair rather than helpful, or that empowerment is a weasel word in child protection if good practice is to be characterised by honest dealings.'

Howe (1992) makes the very important distinction between partnerships based on 'social justice' principles and partnerships based on 'therapeutic' principles. Thus 'social justice' partnerships are based on notions of fairness and natural justice: respect, sharing, openness, contracts, clarity of roles, powers, responsibilities, information, involvement in decisions, service provision and opportunities for redress. In contrast 'therapeutic' partnerships are based, not on a political contract, but on a psychological contract between the parties for change. Whilst all our dealings should be based on social justice principles, if it is interpersonal change that is sought in the dynamics of abusive interactions, or in the development of parenting skills, or the recovery of self-esteem, a social justice contract will not suffice. Without a therapeutic and psychological partnership for change, the social justice partnership remains a necessary but insufficient condition for interpersonal change. This echoes Gibbons *et al.*'s conclusions (1995) that environmental manipulation, such as surveillance and material aid, are not enough to achieve the therapeutic goals of partnership. There is a need for a fourfold approach which combines both material and interpersonal help.

1 Services to assist parenting and children's development.
2 Strategies to compensate for poverty and alleviate stress.
3 Skilled interpersonal help to improve family relationships.
4 Individual help for family members to recover from trauma and bolster self-esteem.

If core groups are to be vehicles for engaging families in these areas, and forging therapeutic contracts for change, it will be vital that sufficient consensus is achieved between the different professionals on the general conditions and processes that are most likely to facilitate such change. Without this, at best we may fail to recognise parental motivation when it is present, or at worst may be unwittingly offering contradictory interventions, leaving the family either perplexed and unchanged or perhaps even worse off than before. We require a framework for change if we are satisfactorily to explain our actions to families, ensure that our interventions are congruent and, when called upon, be able to justify our actions publicly. After all, which of us would accept drugs from a doctor who, when asked, could not explain the nature of the drug, its ingredients, what it was intended to cure, the possible side-effects of taking it and the other options available?

## Creating the conditions for change: involuntary status of service users

However much we seek to work in partnership with families, the fact that the vast majority of families in our child protection system are psychologically involuntary clients is a critical factor as a context for change. Moreover, as Farmer's research found (1993), in the large majority of cases, even after the investigation and initial child protection conference, there remained fundamental disputes between the family and professionals about three key areas likely to affect the prognosis for change: (1) commission – who perpetrated the abuse, (2) culpability – who is to blame, and (3) risk – whether the child is still at risk, and whether therapeutic work is needed.

Farmer (1993) found in her survey of 44 cases that there was agreement on all three criteria in less than a fifth of the cases, and disagreement on all three dimensions in just over a third of cases. Disagreement of this extent on such key dimensions of problem definition is a major inhibitor in any model of change. Interestingly, the 18 per cent of cases where there was a high degree of agreement concerned seven sexual abuse cases where the mothers agreed that the abuser should be out of the home, and one case of a physical abuse referred by the mother herself. In contrast, the most disputed cases were physical abuse, neglect and emotional abuse, and those where both parents remained at home (O'Hagan, 1997).

## Conditions for change

What, then, does child protection research tell us about the conditions most likely to facilitate change in these families? Firstly, both Gibbons *et al.*'s (1995) and Farmer and Owen's (1995) recent research remind us of the crucial relationship between good planning based on analysis of risks and needs, and positive outcomes. Secondly, both underline the fact that the quality of the worker's relationship with the client is absolutely critical, particularly with regard to accurate empathy (Miller and Rollnick, 1991). It is essential that we do not lose sight of the centrality of the skilled helping relationship, which at times is in danger of being submerged or even drowned by the current culture of outputs, tasks and turnover (Fisher, 1995). We need to understand and work with process as well as outcome, which requires the skills to work with troubled family and intrapersonal dynamics, including such features as splitting, projection and transference. Other factors associated with good outcomes include the following:

- maximising the involvement of families in decision-making processes (DoH, 1995b);
- early allocation of workers (Gibbons *et al.*, 1995); avoidance of delay;
- change of workers where there is antagonism (Farmer and Owen, 1995);
- mobilising of appropriate practical and specialist help for families to enhance the general quality of the child's life (Gibbons *et al.*, 1995);
- attending to the needs of the primary carers, including the provision of emotional understanding and support (Farmer and Owen, 1995);
- identifying family strengths and needs as well as risks and problems, which has been discussed in Chapter 7 of the present volume;
- not leaving families abandoned in the period between a child protection investigation and an initial child protection conference while they are in a state of crisis (Farmer and Owen, 1995); and
- confronting dangerous adults and taking decisive protective action (Gibbons *et al.*, 1995).

## How does change happen and what is motivation?

Looking more widely at the change process itself, the therapeutic literature emphasises the need to promote three things: self-esteem, self-efficacy and constructive dissonance (Miller and Rollnick, 1991). Although self-esteem and self-efficacy are clearly related, they are also distinct. No matter how much you tell me I have dignity and self-worth, my belief in my own competence is in the end an internal process, based on how I have experienced and construed the world around me. Self-esteem is thus a product of the interplay between a person's internal and external world. In this way sociocultural factors, such as class, gender and ethnicity, interact with interpersonal factors, feelings, attitudes and self-esteem. This is why partnerships with service users must contain both social justice elements, such as openness and participation, and therapeutic elements. If not, the experience of the child protection system will simply add to previous oppressions, and damage any opportunities to improve both self-esteem and self-efficacy. Social justice and therapeutic partnerships are therefore interdependent.

Constructive dissonance can be a powerful change agent, as long as it is contained within a positive helping relationship. It occurs when we are presented with evidence that shows our beliefs about ourselves or others, such as my belief that I am a good parent, to be at odds with our behaviour, as when, for example, observations of my relationship and attachment behaviours with my child reveal repeated instances of cold and punitive interactions. This process is not a question of labelling people or being confrontational, but of offering feedback to people based on close observation of both behaviour and attitudes. The role of cognitions in the change process is one of the most overlooked aspects of child protection work. As Miller and Rollnick (1991) state: 'the model is not personal combat and the object in motion is not a body but perception'. This involves eliciting both rational belief systems, what people intellectually believe, and emotional belief systems, what people believe in their hearts from experience. These two types of belief systems can often be in conflict with each other, producing incongruent behaviours. Feeding back these observations in the course of an assessment process can act as a potent catalyst for change. The catalyst lies in the fact that all of us need to believe that our beliefs and behaviours are congruent and consistent in order to maintain a reasonable sense of self-identity and integrity. Any discovery of serious discrepancies between the two provokes discomfort and an urge to resolve this gap, through changing either our beliefs or our behaviours. Constructive dissonance can be utilised in the course of an assessment process as families are invited to reflect on their functioning and the different and conflicting perceptions, feelings, needs and strengths of family members.

Therefore change can be seen as a matter of balance, so that, in relation to any demand/wish to change, a person is more or less motivated. Motivation, then, is a fluid state and not a personality trait. People are not simply 'motivated' or 'unmotivated', but are always more or less motivated. The job of the worker is positively to encourage, enable and exploit the positive forces for change and, as far as it is within their influence, to diffuse and remove barriers to change, whether material, interpersonal or perceptual: in other words, motivating families towards change is a central part of the task. It is wrong to assume that family members' motivation resides solely within them as individuals, for motivation exists in an interpersonal context, in which the child protection worker is a significant component, alongside extended family, friends and community. Indeed, these almost certainly are, for better or for worse, the most salient part of the family's motivational network.

This appreciation is also one of the therapeutic reasons behind the inclusion of members of the extended family in work, either within the formal child protection process, including core groups, or through the use of family group conferences, in seeking positive support for change within the family's wider motivational network. These wider networks are also of crucial importance for the professionals' understanding of the family in their own context, especially so in relation to families from ethnic minority groups, where extended family and other community influences such as religious leaders can be particularly important. Space does not permit a detailed discussion of the role and management of family group conferences (FGCs), but it is important to note that, even though the same family members may be present at a child protection conference or core group and at a FGC, the balance of power in the FGC is significantly different, in that the family have far more control of the agenda, the process and the outcomes of a FGC by comparison to a conference or a core group.

## Prochaska and DiClemente's model of change

Recognising that we as professionals cannot change the family, that task must lie with the family. Our task is to establish the conditions in which change can occur. This usually requires some combination of material assistance, therapeutic help and careful monitoring over a period. Even then this does not always guarantee that change will follow. Jones's research (1991) has shown that the prognosis for positive change in a small minority of abusing parents is very poor indeed. Whatever the prognosis for the family, the workers need to be guided, not only by a framework of clear planning and task allocation, but also by some underpinning framework of the process of change. Without this, workers from different agencies may be providing well-intentioned but contradictory responses to the family. For instance, at a core group in which an argument between the parents began, the health visitor leapt in to stop the argument developing, whilst the social worker felt that some enactment of the couple's relationship difficulties might be potentially very productive in helping the couple accept the need for work in this area. This was a good example of a situation where one worker's model of change clashed with another over the role of discomfort in the change process.

One very useful general model of change comes from Prochaska and DiClemente (1982). Its value lies in the fact that their model (Figure 8.1) offers an overarching framework of change, within which a wide variety of intervention methods can be contained. These may be coordinated through case conferences and core groups and be delivered by different professionals, according to the need of individual families. In this model there are four main stages of change described, each of which is explained below: contemplation, action, maintenance, and relapse. However, these are preceded by an initial stage, called 'pre-contemplation'.

### Pre-contemplation stage

This stage is characterised by blaming others, denying responsibility or simply being unaware of the need to change, perhaps because of depression and so on. Whilst people are in this stage, no change is possible: change can only start once they are in contemplation, accepting that they are part of both the origin and the potential solution to their problems. Unfortunately, the vast majority of families enter the child protection system on an involuntary

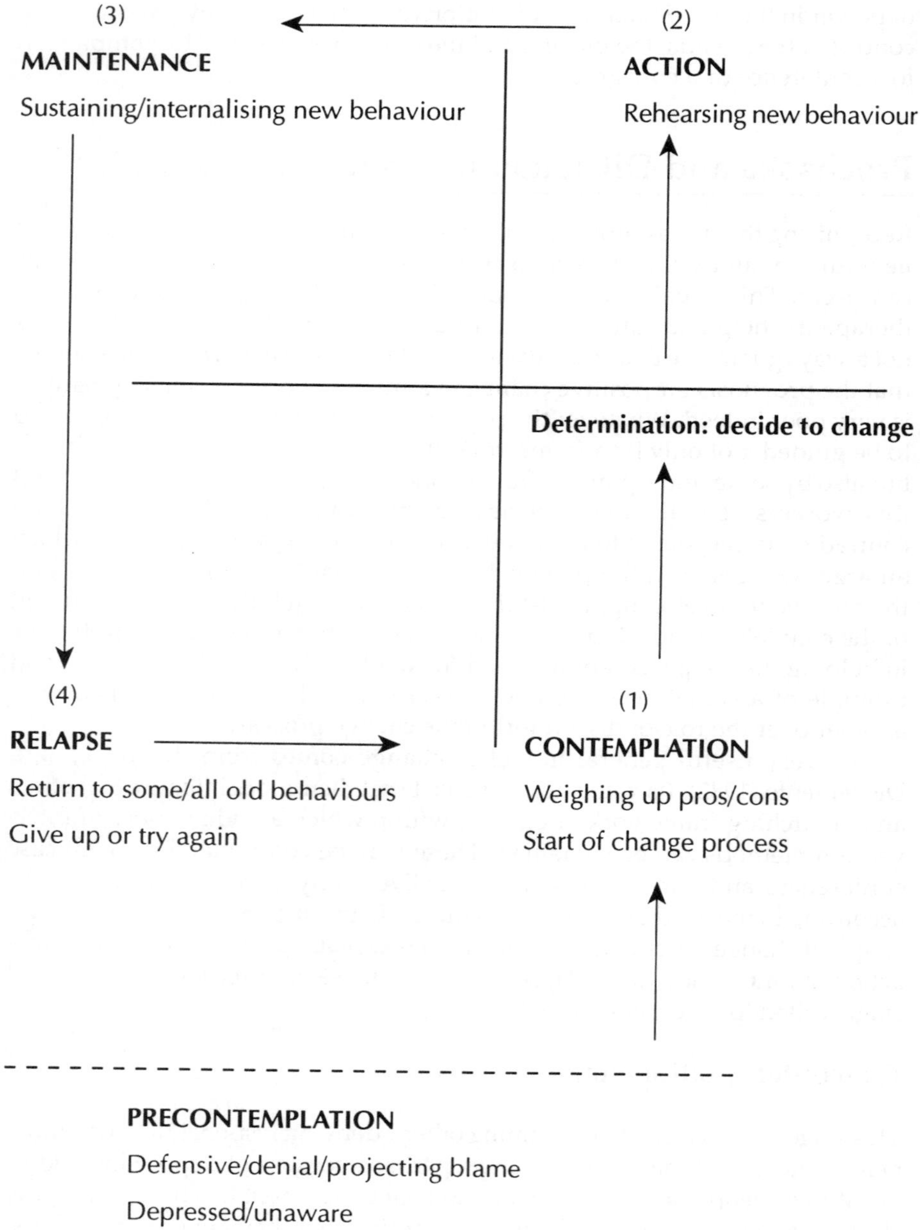


**Figure 8.1 Prochaska and DiClemente's model of change (1982)**

basis at this pre-contemplation stage: 'the only problem we've got is you (the worker)'. Pre-contemplation is thus the point at which most initial assessments take place.

It is here, particularly, that social justice principles of partnership (openness, fairness and so on) need to be combined with emotional support and understanding (Farmer and Owen, 1995) and high-quality interviewing skills, such as those described in motivational interviewing approaches (Miller and Rollnick, 1991). Investigative approaches on their own will not enable families, where abuse has clearly occurred, to begin the painful process of moving out of pre-contemplation to the first stage of change, contemplation.

Workers' expectations about how far families can move by the time of the initial child protection conference also need to be realistic. For instance, are most families realistically in a position to engage, through the child protection plan, in any meaningful process of change? Too often anxiety, pressure of other cases, and procedures can drive agencies prematurely ahead into the action phase while the family are barely out of pre-contemplation. This is a scenario that is doomed from the outset, because family and professionals are not working from the same stage of the change process. The result can be that the family's response is compliance rather than change. We need, therefore, to be very clear at this early stage about the distinction between coordinating plans for safeguarding the child and therapeutic planning.

## Contemplation stage

During the contemplation phase the goal is to help families look at themselves, to identify strengths, needs and risks, consider the consequences of their actions, understand options for the future and come to believe in the possibility that they can change. This approach strives to maintain both self-esteem and self-efficacy at the same time as the family is being confronted by very difficult issues. Maintaining a dual focus on needs and risks and identifying family strengths is vital if both problems and potential solutions are to be owned. This stage may well take a considerable amount of work, whatever the strength of any external mandate on the family.

It is important to identify the different elements within the contemplation stage in order to avoid a simplistic analysis of motivation, which may lead to either overly pessimistic or overly optimistic, and premature judgements about a family's capacity to change. Understanding parental motivation is probably the single most important factor in child protection planning, for it is on this that the judgement about the level and viability of partnership with parents rests.

Miller and Rollnick (1991) describe motivation as much more than the promise of cooperation, when they state: 'Motivation is the probability that a person will enter into, continue and adhere to a specific change strategy.' Do we inadvertently set some families up to fail by a well-intentioned, but uncritical, acceptance of the 'promise to work with us', perhaps under threat of losing their child. Motivation to change must be based on a realistic weighing up of likely gains and losses.

A more careful and specific assessment of motivation can be achieved when the contemplation stage itself is broken down into seven distinct steps (Morrison, 1998). These seven steps can be used to identify the family's, or an individual's, level of motivation, which is essential in making a realistic contract for change in preparation for the action stage. Alternatively, this seven-step assessment may reveal that the family simply cannot make sufficient changes, and that an alternative protection plan is needed for the child:

1 I/we accept there is a problem.
2 I/we have some responsibility for the problem.
3 I/we have some discomfort about the problem and my/our part in it.
4 I/we believe that things must change.
5 I/we can see that I/we can be part of the solution.
6 I/we have choices to make.
7 I/we can see the first steps towards change.

This framework can enable workers and families, together, to assess where family members are and how this is changing over time, and to plan their interventions in the light of this. For many families, working through these steps may take months, not weeks, and may well constitute the task to be undertaken by the core group between the initial child protection conference and the first child protection review. Thus, by the first child protection review, the family will be much more prepared to engage in a programme of change. Some may reply that contemplation work is 'doing an assessment', but this is not always the same thing. Considerable information about the family can be gathered, whilst the family's motivation remains unclear, and unchanged since the concerns first arose. The assessment process itself should be a catalyst for motivating families, not simply observing or finding out information about them. Doing this will transform the quality of the assessment as the family engages in self-assessment. The core group plays a key role here in leading, directing and coordinating this detailed assessment work, whose endpoint, it is hoped, will be to establish engagement with, and a clear contract for work to address, needs and risks that family and workers have jointly identified.

In many cases the reality is that parts of the family will be at different stages of the contemplation process, and therefore engaging at different levels of partnership. For some, in pre-contemplation, partnership may be limited to information giving, whilst others will be engaged in a much more comprehensive working relationship involving changes in behaviour and relationships.

A number of other points about the seven steps should be noted.

- It is essential to distinguish between admission and responsibility. People can admit to doing something, but blame others, and show little or no remorse.
- Discomfort is not simply a matter of emotional distress or anger at the actions of agencies. It refers to Miller and Rollnick's (1991) concept of dissonance: that there is a conflict within the person/family between behaviour and beliefs. At some level the behaviour towards the child is in conflict with parents' beliefs about what they believe, or would like to believe, about themselves as parents. Discomfort represents internal tension between how they see their behaviour and their sense of identity and self-belief.
- The step that is most easily overlooked is the fourth step, 'I believe that I can be part of the solution', which concerns the individual's level of self-efficacy and degree of competence to control and direct her/his life. For many parents who come into the child protection system, their previous life experiences have done considerable damage to their sense of self-efficacy. Becoming an involuntary client in the child protection process can easily serve to exacerbate this. Workers, sensitive to this, can sometimes skip exploration of this key step, believing that, if someone is distressed (step three), says she/he need to change (step four) and the worker believes she/he can change, this will be enough. Whilst exploration of self-efficacy can be painful, it can also be very productive.
- Delays between steps six and seven – for instance, waiting for a place in a family centre or to join a therapeutic group – can set the whole process back.

## Action stage

In the action stage the focus is on learning, exploring and rehearsing new ways of relating, thinking, behaving and feeling. Indeed, all change is essentially a combination of these four basic human processes. However, the focus here is on understanding and regaining control of historical and harmful patterns, and trying out new ways of relating in safe settings based on modelling, education or problem-solving techniques, or learning specific skills. The importance of modelling and teaching parental and relationship skills needs to be stressed. For many families, change is not a possibility until they see it. The role of family centres in this regard is central. From the above it can be seen how a wide range of intervention strategies can be accommodated in this change model: verbal and behavioural work; educational and teaching work; individual therapy and group work. Here the work of the core group is to provide and coordinate the different intervention strategies, trying to ensure that families are not overwhelmed or confused about the number of different appointments they may be asked to keep, and providing a central point of reference to hear and give feedback from the family.

## Maintenance stage

Assuming progress, the next stage, maintenance, occurs when the new ways of relating and behaving become internalised and generalised across different situations. They do not now depend on the presence of the workers, but become consolidated and owned by the individual/family as part of themselves. This is vital if, as a result of the strategies and services adopted during the action stage, the family's sense of self-efficacy has been increased. If this does not happen, positive changes in behaviour achieved, for instance, during a family centre's programme, will quickly run aground when confronted by unchanged patterns of thinking that deep down continue to tell the parents that they are no good at anything or that they are useless. The new behaviours may well be no match for the old thinking. For instance, a parent may make clear behavioural progress by improving a range of child management skills, as a result of which her child is removed from the child protection register. However, if little work has been done on the parent's cognitions and self-efficacy, she may still consider that she is a poor parent, despite these gains. Then, when the first crisis with her child comes along, away from the reassuring support of the family centre, whose level of service has also been reduced, there is a relapse into the old ways of responding to her child, thus confirming the unchanged internal thinking that 'I am a useless parent.'

This model demonstrates why deregistration should not be the cut-off point for services, for the change process is not complete at the end of the action stage, and can easily be undermined if maintenance work is not done. If deregistration does occur, the core group may well need to continue in another form, in order to provide a period of maintenance. This allows time for the family to consolidate its progress and new-found confidence. Relapse prevention work is required at this point so that families can identify situations, feelings or relationship factors which may trigger a lapse or relapse. If this is not done, some of the best work done at the action stage, for instance in family centres, founders because of the pressure for turnover.

## Lapse or relapse stage

The model proposes, however, that under stress there will be pressures to 'lapse', for example, to get into high-risk situations such as drinking excessively, which is a precursor to parental arguments, or to relapse when the old behaviour pattern reappears in full: for example, with further abuse. Relapse may quickly lead to a loss of all or most of the earlier gains, a sense of rapidly losing control, resulting in a 'giving up', and a return to pre-contemplation. The sense of associated failure, guilt and shame may itself feed into a return to abusive behaviours. By contrast, in the case of a 'lapse', if the dangers are realised quickly enough as a result of the earlier relapse prevention work, and help is urgently sought and available from friends, family or professionals, all is by no means lost. Thus, using the earlier example, the family will realise that a return to previous patterns of heavy drinking is a known danger signal and an indication that feelings are being avoided. Realising this, the parents can utilise their relapse prevention strategy, which might for instance include asking a member of the extended family to come and mediate between them, or giving each parent some time out. This might also lead to a return to the contemplation stage and to further work. Failures to identify 'lapses' in known child protection cases have often been greater than failures to identify the original abuse. Thus at this point the core group's role is to help the family identify their own relapse prevention plan, which could include relatives, friends, neighbours or professional services that they can seek out urgently if they begin to recognise signs of lapse.

One of the values of this model is that it integrates the 'lapse' as part of a normative and incremental process of change: two steps forward and one back. However this has implications in terms of the need to prepare families very carefully for the possibility of relapse, through the identification of stresses and triggers, and the creation of a specific relapse prevention plan. This should involve not just professionals but wider family, and community networks, for it is they who are most likely to spot the early signs of lapse and who will provide most of the day-to-day support. Thus the core group's role should include mapping the family's wider social support system, to identify those who may be able to play a part in the relapse prevention process.

As the model has been described, various tasks for the core group have been identified. In the following section a summary of the role of the core group as a catalyst for change is provided.

## The role of the core group as a catalyst change

Core groups, less formal and smaller than child protection conferences, provide for a closer, more relationship-based than procedure-based partnership between workers and families. It is within this kind of relationship that parental motivation can be more fully assessed, enhanced and sustained. Adapting

Miller and Rollnick's (1991) eight key factors for enhancing motivation, a practical agenda for the role of the core group in facilitating change can be identified.

1 Advice: core groups can provide practical information about services, procedures and so on.
2 Barriers: core groups can reduce practical barriers to getting help, via information, child care assistance, travel and so on.
3 Choice: core groups can help families weigh and consider a range of options and their potential consequences, and can help generate alternatives.
4 Desirability: core groups can work with families to increase their perceptions/experiences of the benefits of change, and to decrease their fears about perceived costs of change.
5 External leverage: core groups can act in a cohesive way to exert pressure where appropriate for families to change; core groups can also advocate resources and services for families.
6 Feedback: core groups can provide specific, regular, balanced feedback to families, as well as seeking feedback from families about services in order to identify shortfalls or unhelpful responses.
7 Goal: core groups can work with families to devise specific, incremental, realistic goals for change.
8 Helping attitude: above all, core groups can work with an empathic, open, firm and affirming style to engage families in processes of change.

## Conclusion

This chapter has sought to establish a relationship between procedures for coordinating services and safeguarding children, with processes for facilitating change. It has argued that practical support and surveillance are insufficient in tackling the dynamics of abuse and its effects. It has suggested that the purpose of the child protection plan at the initial child protection conference needs to be reconsidered, on the basis that it will normally be premature, and potentially confusing, to include 'therapeutic' goals for change at that stage. It is also suggested that core groups have considerable potential to act as a bridge between protection and therapeutic activities; problem identification and problem resolution processes; formal and informal processes; and between social justice and psychological notions of partnership. However, these considerable benefits will only be achieved if the role and functioning of core groups are clear and valued by all the agencies involved. In addition, achieving these aspirations for core groups also has implications for multi-agency training. There is a need to incorporate models of change, and to equip workers with an understanding of, and skills in, motivational interviewing approaches, if partnership philosophy is to be fully translated into partnership practice.

Finally, if all of this is to become a reality, agencies, too, must seek to create the organisational conditions in which change-producing practice can occur. That means attending to staff needs for professional self-esteem and self-efficacy. Such climates exist in organisations in which staff are not expected to 'do' but where thinking and feeling are also legitimised, a theme which is pursued in the following chapter.

## References

Calder, M.C. (1995) 'Child Protection: Balancing partnership and paternalism', *British Journal of Social Work*, **25** (6): 749–66.

Challis, L., Fuller, S., Henwood, M., Klein, R., Plowden, W., Webb, A., Whittingham, P. and Whistow, G. *Joint Approaches to Social Policy – Rationality and Practice*, Cambridge: Cambridge University Press.

Department of Health (1995a) *The Challenge of Partnership in Child Protection: Practice Guide*, London: HMSO.

Department of Health (1995b) *Child Protection: messages from research*, London: HMSO.

Farmer, E. (1993) 'The Impact of Child Protection Interventions: The Experiences of Parents and Children', in L. Waterhouse (ed.), *Child Abuse and Child Abusers*, London: JKP.

Farmer, E. and Owen, M. (1995) *Child Protection Practice: Private risks and public remedies, Intervention and Outcome in Child Protection Work*, (The University of Bristol Team), London: HMSO.

Fisher, T. (1995) *A Systemic Knowledge Base in Child Protection: what knowledge do social workers use?*, University of York: Department of Social Policy and Social Work.

Fox-Harding, L. (1991) 'Underlying Themes and Contradictions in the Children Act 1989', *Justice of the Peace*, 15 September.

Gibbons, J., Conroy, S. and Bell, S. (1995) *Operating the Child Protection System*, London: HMSO.

Hallett, C. (1995) *Inter-agency co-ordination in child protection*, London: HMSO.

Hallett, C. and Birchall, E. (1992) *Co-ordination in Child Protection: A Review of the Literature*, Edinburgh: HMSO.

Howe, D. (1992) 'Theories of helping, empowerment and participation', in J. Thoburn (ed.), *Participation in Practice – Involving families in child protection*, Norwich: University of East Anglia, Social Work Development Unit.

Jones, D. (1991) 'The Effectiveness of Intervention' in M. Adcock, R. White and A. Hollows, (eds), *Significant Harm*, Croydon: Significant Publications.

McFarlane, T. and Morrison, T. (1994) 'Learning and Change: Outcomes of Inter-agency Networking for Child Protection', *Child Care in Practice: Northern Ireland Journal of Multi-disciplinary Child Care Practice*, **1** (2): 33–44.

Miller, W. and Rollnick, S. (1991) *Motivational Interviewing*, London: Guildford.

Morrison, T. (1998) 'Partnership, collaboration and change under the Children Act', in M. Adcock and R. White (eds), *Significant Harm*, 2nd edn, Croydon: Significant Publications.

O'Hagan, K. (1997) 'The problem of engaging men in social work', *British Journal of Social Work*, **27**: 25–42.
Prochaska, J. and DiClemente, C. (1982) 'Transtheoretical Therapy: Towards a more Integrative Model of Change', *Psychotherapy: Theory, Research and Practice*, **19** (3).
Sainsbury, E. (1989) 'Participation and Paternalism', in S. Shardlow (ed.), *The Values of Social Work*, London: Tavistock/Routledge.

# 9 The role of the social services first-line manager

*Sharon Anne Cooke*

In this chapter consideration is given to:

- the current working environment for first-line social service managers;
- what supervision means within a social services context;
- issues for first-line managers;
- a framework for effective supervision in terms of post-registration practice; and
- the role of the first-line manager within the core group.

## Introduction

The role of the social services first-line manager is pivotal to effective multidisciplinary child protection practice. First-line managers must attempt to create and sustain a working environment in which professionals and families can work together. In addition they supervise and manage the keyworker, and occasionally intervene in post-registration practice to resolve conflict and tackle any dangerous practice, as well as ensuring that all planning is clear and up-to-date. First-line managers undertake a number of delicate balancing acts in this area of practice. Firstly, they are responsible for ensuring that children are protected by the social workers they manage, through the implementation of departmental procedures and statutory responsibilities. This is undertaken in a climate of continuous change and diminishing resources and in the knowledge that they and themselves are pilloried by the media and the general public if they fail to protect children (such as Jasmine Beckford) or are perceived as being too interventionist (as in Cleveland). Secondly, they must manage a balance between investigative work that retains more resources and post-registration work. This chapter will aim to look in detail at the role of the first-line fieldwork manager in social services departments.

## The current working environment for first-line social service managers

The last decade has seen the role of first-line social services managers both change and expand. Not only are they responsible for the supervision of team members but the destructuring and delayering that has occurred in many social services departments have meant that they are now responsible for significant budgets and for the management of additional staff. This has had an impact on supervision. Marsh and Triseleotis (1996: 351) noted that 25 per cent of staff in social services reported that they had received no supervision within their first year of practice and for many others it was unplanned and erratic. Horwath (1997) commented that the pressures placed on first-line managers meant that decisions were made 'on the hoof' as they rushed from one meeting to another. She also noted that many managers found they did not have the time to read case files in detail, and were increasingly dependent on social workers to give them verbal details, which could lead to subjective assessments.

Managers are also operating in a climate of changing philosophy, where the dominant view is one of taking a 'wider, more holistic view of the needs of vulnerable children and their families' (DoH, 1995: 335, iii). Burton (1997) reported the findings of a study which highlighted the impact of this changing philosophy on first-line managers. She noted that managers had a number of concerns. These centred on anxiety over the ability to balance support and protection, fear regarding the management of risk, low professional esteem and lack of emphasis on enhancing the professional knowledge of managers and budgets structured in favour of intervention. She noted the need for a general acknowledgement that while team managers are pivotal in changing practice, they cannot do it without concerted effort at all levels within the organisation.

It is against this backcloth that the first-line social services manager is expected to provide supervision. Before we can consider the impact of these changes on the way that supervision is provided around post-registration practice, it is necessary to consider what is meant by supervision in a social work context.

## The supervisory task

> Supervision has been defined as a forum where a worker can talk about cases, look and ask for guidance, express his/her feelings, learn about procedures, policies and methods, and evaluate practical and emotional needs. The line manager has a duty to listen, facilitate, teach and organise ways of filling the gaps in knowledge and experience. (Pritchard, 1993: 218)

Supervision implies guidance, advice, correction, encouragement, teaching and support. Supervisors have been identified as teachers, enablers, consultants and managers. Their roles reflect the reality that managers must bridge the worlds of management and practice in everything they do. For a first-line manager it feels at times that they must be all things to all people. Traditionally, there are four interrelated functions of supervision: managerial, developmental, supportive and mediatory. These will be considered in the context of post-registration practice.

### Managerial function

Here the aim is to scrutinise the overall quality of the performance of the worker, ensuring that the agency policies and child protection procedures are observed. In terms of the management of the keyworker, this means evaluating the way in which they work with the family and other professionals in the core group. The supervisor should ensure that child protection plans are formulated and carried out within prescribed time scales, that the short- and long-term objectives are linked to projected outcomes, and that they are reviewed and reformulated where appropriate. The supervisor, in this role, becomes a quality controller, responsible for ensuring that prescribed standards set by the agency are kept. Supervisees are accountable for what they do and the way that they do it. However, within post-registration practice, there is often a lack of clarity regarding expected standards. As Calder and Horwath set out in Chapter 1 of the present volume, these standards provide direction for workers in the post-registration phase.

The supervisor also needs to ensure that the keyworker is managing his or her administrative tasks. As highlighted earlier, there is an increasing bureaucratisation of the child protection process (Howe, 1992). Managers must ensure that the worker is recording relevant information and completing the appropriate documentation.

## Developmental function

The developmental role of the supervisor is to enable staff to reflect on their performance and use their experiences to develop their practice. The manager also has a responsibility to provide opportunities for staff to develop their knowledge, values and skills. Recognising the pace of change in child protection work, it should be acknowledged that the manager cannot aim to know everything themselves; their role is to identify sources and create opportunities for professional development, such as training courses. They also have a responsibility to ensure that their supervisees have opportunities to reflect and apply learning from training courses within their work setting.

## Supportive function

The supportive role of the supervisor is to help staff identify and manage the stresses and risks associated with child protection work, particularly where other agencies' roles may be reduced whilst agency and conference expectations of the keyworker increase.

Social workers working in the area of child protection can feel particularly vulnerable, for a number of reasons. 'Social worker bashing' is a frequent aspect of media reporting and places social workers and their managers in a defensive mode. The impact of organisational change can unsettle staff and lead to fears about job security. Staff who deal with child protection experience anxiety and stress on a daily basis. The emotionally charged work can be physically and psychologically draining, and emotional fatigue can affect judgement and alertness. Workers cannot leave their feelings at home when they come to work, and vice versa. Child protection work often creates a bridge across the personal–professional divide. Staff care needs to be an integral part of the manager's remit and not an occasional reactive response when staff problems become too acute to ignore (Murphy, 1997: 250). Managers who offer support to staff can expect a return, which includes critical reasoning and analysis, higher motivation, improved working relationships and reduced staff stress (Morrison, 1997).

## Mediatory function

On occasions, the supervisor also has a responsibility to act as a mediator on behalf of the worker. This can occur when the worker requires additional resources to implement the child protection plan and requests need to be made to senior managers. In addition, the supervisor may act as mediator between the worker and families and/or other agencies in the post-registration phase. The manager can utilise the combination of social work and management skills to intervene and work towards resolving problems. This is discussed in detail later in the chapter.

## Issues for the first-line manager

As has been seen above, meeting the supervisory needs of practitioners is a complex task which is not made easier by the fact that supervision is delivered in a climate of continual change. This raises a number of issues for first-line managers which need to be addressed: first, the need for a framework for supervision that is accepted at all levels within the organisation; second, an acknowledgement that managers require supervision training; and finally, that first-line managers require supervision themselves. Each of these will be explored in detail.

The relationship between fieldworker and first-line manager/supervisor is a critical relationship in the management of child protection cases (DoH, 1991a: 27). The SSI report (1986) identified several difficulties affecting this relationship; these included a lack of supervision policy, supervision tasks being inadequately described in the job description, a lack of time and physical space, interruptions to supervision, case records failing to show any planning, inadequate recording of supervision, a tendency to focus on workload control and current cases, poor awareness of the process of collusion by workers, and supervisors failing to acknowledge their training role. More than ten years after this inspection report, a number of social services departments still have no formal, clear and explicit supervision policy, whilst in others the policy is very limited, providing no clear framework for supervision (Morrison, 1993). Some social services departments may have a policy, but often there is no practice guidance regarding the focus and timing of supervision or agreement on ways in which the outcomes of supervision should be recorded. Without a clear framework, the first-line manager and his or her supervisees are left to determine for themselves the importance of supervision and decide structure and content of supervision sessions on their own. This can lead to infrequent, unstructured supervision sessions or supervision that focuses on certain elements, ignoring others.

It is equally important for organisations to equip their first-line managers for the jobs they are asking them to do. Iwaniec noted that practitioners expect their supervisors to have good knowledge of agency policies, procedures and resources; up-to-date awareness of child protection issues; sound understanding of child development, child care and family work; sound knowledge of child care legislation; understanding of human behaviour; ability to recognise risks and make appropriate judgements; skills to manage workers' workloads; ability to manage and allocate appropriate resources;

ability to use given authority and power when appropriate; ability to pick up workers' stresses and anxieties and attend to them; willingness and capacity to support staff; ability to keep good morale in the team; willingness to address workers' professional and personal needs; ability to represent workers' needs outside the team; ability to promote anti-discriminatory practices; and an ability to establish and promote a multidisciplinary approach to problem solving (Iwaniec, 1993). This is a daunting list and highlights the fact that training has an important role to play in ensuring that managers are aware of current child protection practice in terms of research, professional developments and changes in local and national guidance. In addition, first-line managers need training in supervisory practice enabling them to develop knowledge, values and skills to provide high-quality supervision.

> Supervisors also have supervisory needs themselves, and these are frequently overlooked or the focus is on management and workload rather than providing opportunities for support and development. Front line managers need appropriate supervision themselves, including advice, guidance, clarification, reassurance, assistance, help and support. (Iwaniec, 1993: 203)

It is a costly fallacy that everyone who has reached the first-line manager level can do the job effectively without having their identified needs met. If managers do not receive adequate supervision themselves, there is a danger either that they will turn to their staff for support, thereby confusing roles, or that they may fail to meet the supervisory needs of their team members effectively.

## A framework for effective post-registration supervision

The issues described above can be resolved if there is an effective framework for supervision that exists throughout the organisation, not merely at a practitioner level. This framework should be supported by a comprehensive training strategy that prepares supervisors for their task but also provides opportunities enabling them to develop their skills. Listed below are some components required for an effective framework for supervision, with consideration of ways in which they can be used to supervise post-registration practice.

First, supervision should be formal and underpinned by a written contract which embraces frequency, length, preparation, agenda, written records and access to materials. Written contracts clarify the mutual expectations of supervisor–supervisee, motivate both parties, provide data for later evaluation, particularly in the event of any subsequent disputes, and provide a reminder of what is intended and hoped for. This models what is expected of the keyworker and the core group in their work with families. In constructing these contracts, supervisors should take into consideration the worker's level of experience in child protection work, their confidence and stamina in dealing with conflicts, and their knowledge and skills (Iwaniec, 1993: 210).

Second, a written record of the session should be kept which includes areas covered as well as areas the session has not been able to address, and plans for when these will be discussed. The recommendations for each case should be recorded and signed by both parties and then placed on the case file.

Third, managers should ensure that supervision is conducted in a positive and structured fashion. This means that consideration should be given to where the supervision takes place and that every effort should be made to avoid interruptions.

Fourth, supervisees should be asked to bring their files so that the quality, quantity and frequency of their recording can be monitored. It can also be a check that any previously agreed work has been done, and done within a specified time scale. This allows managers to assume the responsibility for ensuring that work with a family has been undertaken adequately. Recommendations for amendments or completion could be made where the work, the recording, or both, are substandard. Supervision offers a forum for re-focusing upon the child and their needs and how they can best be protected. It is important for managers to monitor the variations in case recording and to offer advice where necessary. Cases before the courts can be a good example of situations where close scrutiny may be invited. Poor quality recording of child protection cases can mean that crucial evidence is lost. Recording should remain child-focused. Occasionally, workers may record in detail their involvement with the family, but without mentioning the child. This can often be the case if the child is of pre-school age and workers are focusing on their work with the parents. Workers need to record when the child is seen, how the child appears, relationships, interaction between child and carer, and the wishes and feelings of the child. This is more difficult with pre-school children, but observations of the child in play should be made, as such information is crucial to the overall assessment.

Fifth, supervisors need to be actively involved in the construction of both the initial and the subsequent child protection plans. This will ensure consistency and quality control of the plan and also that the child and their safety and well-being are the primary focus. By discussing the plan, workers are enabled to deal with the issues it raises, reformulate certain aspects of the plan within their control and qualify any areas of risk. They can also discuss alternative strategies if there are difficulties with other professionals or the family. The supervisor is able to identify where cases are drifting, or might do so, thus preventing the focus of any work getting lost.

Supervision does not necessarily always have to be delivered on a one-to-one basis. The manager also has a number of alternate forums to provide an input to workers.

## Group supervision

This is useful for those staff who feel comfortable enough to contribute in this forum. Ground rules of confidentiality, honesty, support and amenability to constructive criticism are essential in creating a safe learning and reflective environment, as are an agenda and agreed format. Group supervision can facilitate team development and ways of working together. It also allows managers opportunities to identify the particular skills and knowledge of team members as well as their gaps in knowledge, and weaknesses.

## Appraisal

Staff development and training opportunities and needs are addressed in this forum. Using an agreed format and agenda can diffuse any anxieties or threats for the worker. In a climate of starved opportunities, managers can create small but insightful opportunities for staff, such as a number of days out to pursue certain activities or interests related to their work: time with a psychologist, regional psychiatric unit or at the library doing literature searches for a particular area of interest, for instance working with disabled sex offenders, and so on. For the manager, they can elicit information on individual functioning in a more intense way, and look at broader team issues.

## Team development

Team development is essential to the health of the individual workers and the recipients of their services. As well as looking at aims and objectives, sessions can be used to consider more specific issues, such as working together, partnership or levels of intervention. Case studies and recent research can be used to facilitate this work and help the team to trust and be supportive of one another.

## Consultation

This is a supplement to supervision and a professional support system which is increasingly being provided by child protection coordinators, in specialist posts, but with no line management responsibilities. The aim is to utilise the consultant's wider experience, more specialist knowledge and acknowledged expertise. This is crucial when you consider the complexity of child protection work, fuelled by a rapidly changing organisational context, knowledge and practice base. Consultation can provide a forum for problem solving, advice giving, knowledge of services and the law and the acknowledgement of professional anxiety; teach complex skills to apply knowledge of child development and family interaction; help staff weigh the likely outcomes of different courses of action; maintain a focus on the child in all discussions, offsetting the preoccupation by managers with the resource constraints and procedural problems in their team/section; focus on the longer-term outcomes, given the preoccupation with short-term solutions; and resolve conflicts (Rushton and Nathan, 1996). The outcome of such a service is multiple. For example, where workers have difficulties putting aspects of a protection plan into action, the consultant could analyse and unpick the difficulties, posing new questions, altering the focus from the one presented and thereby helping to devise an alternative plan which better ensures the child's safety.

### Coworking

This is important in most child protection work to ensure that the essential observational issues are not overlooked, that the worker is not isolated, stressed or allowed to operate secretly, thus avoiding a duplication of the dynamics in the abusing family, and that there is continuity of case management in the event of sickness, holiday or court time tabling. For the manager, it also allows workers to be paired according to the presenting case, such as issues of equal opportunities or the need to utilise a particular worker's area of expertise, for example Munchausen's Syndrome by Proxy. It is also an incrementally safe way to introduce new staff to a difficult arena, with the aim that there will be a transfer of skills and knowledge. This transplanting of expertise is a crucial modelling of partnership for staff (Calder, 1995).

## The manager within the core group forum

In the Barnsley Metropolitan Borough Council the team leader will chair core group meetings, whilst in other authorities they may only chair difficult meetings, frequently characterised by conflict. Only 20 per cent of managers routinely attend core groups (Calder and Horwath, 1996). The chairing of core group meetings on a routine basis can prove to be an effective way for managers to be proactive and supportive to all professional staff involved in child protection work. It can also ensure that core groups are given status as a formal meeting, but making time available is often difficult, given the competing demands on front-line managers. In the present writer's experience there are many other advantages in managing the core group, including the following.

1 Meetings remain focused: agendas are set, work is reviewed and the focus remains on the child and protection issues.
2 Agencies are held accountable for their role within the plan: this is often more noticeable when a manager is in the chair, and it can relieve the keyworker of considerable anxiety. Conflict can be avoided by not setting up the social worker to manage staff of equivalent level (but frequently higher status).
3 Professional dangerousness and inter-agency dangerousness can be reduced, as the professionals can be challenged by the manager. The Department of Health (1988) set out very clear examples of professional dangerousness. These include situations where a social worker is allowed to operate alone and unsupported and collude with a family in order to avoid the real issues – 'it would damage my relationship' is a phrase commonly used by a dangerous professional – or to act without a theoretical base and a systematic, structured approach to intervention; where he or she maintains unrealistic optimism about families, against all the evidence; becomes overinvolved and overidentified with a family, so that he or she 'can't see the wood for the trees' and misses the significance of family patterns of behaviour by focusing only on the content of events and crises; avoids recognising and dealing with his or her own personal feelings and values, including cultural or religious values; and avoids contact with the child or family because of unacknowledged fears for personal safety. Inter-agency dangerousness is likely when there are undefined boundaries of roles and responsibilities; the absence of clear, written procedures to guide intervention; hidden agendas that affect formal activity; competition and hostility between professionals; or the avoidance of overt disagreement about the management of cases (DoH, 1988: 12–13).
4 Linking core groups to the supervision process: issues may arise during the core group which need following up in supervision. This might include identifying where the worker is struggling to keep his or her focus on the child or to get other core group members to participate and take responsibility for their role in the child protection plan. This may arise when a worker, for example a school or education welfare officer, has agreed to his or her role in the plan, and then persistently fails either to do the work or to attend the core group to report on his or her findings – even though the dates, times and venues may have been chosen to accommodate them. The manager may need to speak to the worker and try to negotiate their inclusion in one way or another.

5 Conflict or difficulties between professionals can be highlighted and monitored: on occasion, two members of the core group may disagree about the risk to the child and the role of the manager is to ensure that all the available information is shared and questioned by the group so that the most informed decision can be made.
6 Managing conflict between parents and professionals: the manager will need to resolve difficulties which are limiting their ability to construct a workable plan or the actual effectiveness of the plan. It sends a clear message to core group participants that the keyworker is not being selective in his or her work or acting independently, without reference to his or her line manager. Families can also hear information on how to make complaints as well as receiving explanations about decision-making processes. They can also be advised about any action which would be taken if they intimidated any staff member.

Managers often have other, less formal, forums to try and facilitate good local working relationships with professional colleagues. For example, local liaison meetings of key agencies (such as social services, education, health, police, probation and voluntary agencies) can be very effective in promoting effective inter-agency communication and cooperation. Professionals who become familiar with each other and therefore gain insight and understanding into each other's roles and responsibilities are more likely to work together closely and this must be beneficial to the children we collectively seek to protect. They are also more likely to raise issues of concern which might otherwise remain festering and unresolved. Fieldwork staff should be able to agenda and discuss issues within these forums. These meetings should take place at least quarterly and could occasionally be used as training sessions to address topics of significance, such as the role of core groups and child protection plans in post-registration work. Case studies can be used to help agencies discuss their roles and consider the importance of sharing information and working together.

## Managing conflict in the core group forum

Conflict is a fact of life for managers and it is not uncommon for them to be faced with a number of disputes simultaneously on the same case, for instance between social workers, colleagues from other parts of the department, other agencies and recipient families. In post-registration work, managers have the responsibility for intervening and resolving any conflict that is impairing the construction, operationalisation or review of the child protection plan. Conflict is any situation or state that is characterised by perceived differences that the parties see as negative.

On occasion conflict can arise if the keyworker believes that he or she has been left to manage the risks and others are simply not cooperating or 'pulling their weight'. This can be illustrated by a case of neglect where inter-agency cooperation was essential but, owing to the overwhelming needs of the parent (health, substance misuse), some core group members were overidentifying with the adults and leaving the difficult child protection issues to the keyworker. This was discussed in supervision and required the chairman of the core group continually to define and redefine roles within the child protection plan, allocate tasks to appropriate professionals and review with them during core group meetings whether these tasks had been completed. The chairman of the core group needed to help the group refocus upon the child in question and support the keyworker in the challenge he or she made to fellow professionals.

Conflicts between agencies have potentially damaging consequences for the workers involved and others involved in the same process. If the core group is the crucible of child protection planning, the manager may be called upon to mediate in a range of situations, such as:

- where the situation needs further analysis, for example where a professional divergence of opinion exists and there is deadlock, or where the group is unsure about how to interpret or respond to a particular issue, such as disclosure of bullying or a child being left home alone;
- where the core group wants want more information on a problem, such as understanding juveniles who have sexually abused or assessing risk where a female has been the perpetrator;
- where an opportunity exists to raise concerns, for example on core group functioning, worker safety, lack of agency responsiveness or dangerous practice;
- where there is a possibility of generating and exploring alternative options, such as concurrent planning or prioritising according to perceived risks and outcomes; considering new strategies to engage families, or new ways of interviewing resistant or hostile families, or where the views of the professionals, parents and child(ren) are all conflicting;
- where authority is needed to take a decision on a particular issue, such as variation of contact arrangements by allowing a mother to resume supervisory responsibility for contact from her schedule one partner, or seeking funding for a mother and baby unit for further assessment purposes.

The following sequence may help managers when approaching an intervention with the core group. (If the matter involves professionals, the meeting should not include the family.) The manager is responsible for convening the meeting and is responsible for the process, whilst the group is responsible for the content and what is discussed during the meeting and the group members retain the authority and responsibility over their willingness to resolve the conflict. They will probably have helped the keyworker define the issues in advance and this is the basis of identifying the need for a mediation meeting. The manager will need to identify who needs to be involved and who is affected so that they can be drawn into the process of finding a solution.

The meeting should be convened in circumstances where there is a conflict that can be negotiated, there are specific issues to be resolved which have been identified, the manager can neutralise the power differential between the parties, and sufficient time exists to work through the process from beginning to end, culminating in some consensual resolution or an agreement of differences. The manager needs to find out who holds the power and use this as the basis of any solutions suggested.

The meeting should be fixed at a venue, date and time when all members can attend.

The manager can adopt the following process of mediation.

- Setting the stage: the manager prepares the environment, does the introductions and explains the ground rules and process. It is imperative that the specific reason for the meeting is made clear from the outset, as this helps focus minds and avoids any confusion.
- Uninterrupted time: for each of the group members in turn.
- Focusing the issues: summarising and clarifying the main issues so that work can begin towards solution. Any solution must resolve the fundamental, rather than the peripheral, aspects of the problem, and managers should openly share their analysis with everyone.
- The exchange: encouraging parties to talk, primarily to each other, about their feelings regarding the issues and their ideas for possible solution. The manager needs to pick out any points of agreement, as well as setting boundaries.
- Generation of potential solutions: brainstorming the possible options as well as removing the obstacles to agreement.
- Agreement building: the group members try to narrow down the potential solutions and then translate these into written agreements that are signed by all parties (see Katz and Lawyer, 1994: 68). People need to agree what the problem is as the basis of 'owning' any proposed solution. In resolving conflict, managers must have an eye on the longer-term implications of their decisions, avoid humiliation for staff who are 'losers' by finding face savers to retain the status of individuals and reduce the chances of division within the group, and set a date for review. It can be

dangerous to assume that things can be resolved and then forgotten. The situation should be reviewed again in a month's time to check that it is working and has not created even more conflict (Walker, 1992).

Overall, the manager should model the skills of good listening, effective summarising, creative problem solving and agreement construction. Failing any solution, the manager may need to reconvene the child protection review or involve the line managers of other agencies.

## Summary

This chapter has highlighted the complex and demanding role of first-line managers in both the management of their social workers and the multi-disciplinary network. They need opportunities to develop their own skills as a prerequisite for their being able to manage the multiple demands made of them. Organisational change and restructuring can increase the demands, as resources and support become more limited and managers are forced to fight for resources, whether material or human. Managers need to try and equalise the status and priority afforded to post-registration work and investigative activity to demonstrate that they are both crucial to effective child protection and desirable outcomes. Post-registration work needs skilled and healthy workers who are given time and supervision to plan and review their work, rather than responding to crises. The test for any manager is to ensure that his or her staff remain child-focused and provide a quality service to children and their families.

The key points may be summarised as follows. First-line managers need to ensure that the focus remains permanently on the child; the risks to the child are monitored, reviewed and reassessed; and work with the child and the family is planned. This can best be achieved by planning; monitoring and reviewing the work and the child protection plan; regular supervision of staff; and support of staff involved in this stressful area of work.

## References

Burton, M. (1996) *Child Protection Issues in General Practice: An Action Research Project to Improve Interprofessional Practice*, Essex: Essex Child Protection Committee.

Byrne, C. (1995) 'The Supervision of Health Visitors in Child Protection', *Child Care in Practice*, **2** (1): 71–8.

Calder, M.C. (1995) 'Child Protection: Balancing Paternalism and Partnership', *British Journal of Social Work*, **25** (6): 749–61.

Calder, M.C. (1996) 'Inter-Agency Working in Child Protection: A Review of Local Arrangements in Salford', *Report to ACPC*, March.
Calder, M.C. and Horwath, J. (1996) 'National Core Group Sample: Analysis of Questionnaire Responses', unpublished paper, Salford ACPC / University of Sheffield.
Casson, S. and Manning, B. (1997) *Total Quality in Child Protection. A Managers' Guide*, Lyme Regis: Russell House Publishing.
Department of Health (1988) *Protecting Children: A Guide for Social Workers Undertaking a Comprehensive Assessment*, London: HMSO.
Department of Health (1991a) *Child Abuse: A Study of Inquiry Reports 1980–1989*, London: HMSO.
Department of Health (1991b) *Working Together*, London: HMSO.
Department of Health (1995) *Child Protection: Messages from Research*, London: HMSO.
Department of Health and Social Security (1975) *Report of the Enquiry into the Provision and Co-ordination of Services to the Family of John George Auckland*, London: HMSO.
Gibbons, J., Conroy, S. and Bell, C. (1995) *Operating the Child Protection System*, London: HMSO.
Hallett, C. (1995) *Inter-agency Co-ordination in Child Protection*, London: HMSO.
Horwath, J. (1997) 'Child Protection Messages from Research: Issues for Inter-agency Practice in the late 1990s', *Child Care in Practice*, **3** (4).
Horwath, J. and Calder, M.C. (1998) 'Working for Children on the Child Protection Register: Myth or Reality?', *British Journal of Social Work*, **28** (6): 879–95.
Howe, D. (1992) 'Child Abuse and the Bureaucratisation of Social Work', *The Sociological Review*, **40**: 491–508.
Iwaniec, D. (1993) 'Supervision and Support of Workers Involved in Child Protection Cases', in H. Owen and J. Pritchard (eds), *Good Practice in Child Protection*, London: Jessica Kingsley.
Katz, N.H. and Lawyer, J.W. (1994) *Preventing and Managing Conflict in Schools*, Thousand Oaks, Cal.: Corwin Press.
Marsh, P. and Triseleotis, J. (1996) *Ready to Practice? Social Workers and Protection Officers: Their Training and First Year in Work*, Aldershot: Avebury.
Morrison, T. (1993) *Staff Supervision in Social Care*, London: Longmans.
Morrison, T. (1997) 'Emotionally Competent Child Protection Organisations: Fallacy, Fiction or Necessity?', in J. Bates, J. Pugh and N. Thompson (eds), *Protecting Children: Challenges and Change*, Aldershot: Arena.
Murphy, M. (1997) 'Delivering Staff Care in a Multidisciplinary Context', in J. Bates *et al.* (eds), *Protecting Children: Challenges and Change*, Aldershot: Arena.
Pritchard, J. (1993) 'Support and Supervision of Social Workers Working in the Child Protection Field', in H. Owen and J. Pritchard (eds), *Good Practice in Child Protection: A Manual for Professionals*, London: Jessica Kingsley: 216–31.
Rushton, A. and Nathan, J. (1996) 'Internal Consultation and Child Protection Work', *Journal of Social Work Practice*, **10** (1): 41–50.
Social Services Inspectorate (1986) *Inspection of the Supervision of Social Workers in the Assessment and Monitoring of Cases of Child Abuse When Children, Subject to a Court Order, Have Been Returned Home*, London: HMSO.
Social Services Inspectorate (1993) *Inspecting for Quality: Evaluating Performance in Child Protection. A Framework for the Inspection of Local Authority Social Services Practice and Systems*, London: HMSO.
Vanstone, M. (1995) 'Managerialism and the Ethics of Management', in R. Hugman and D. Smith (eds), *Ethical Issues in Social Work*, London: Routledge.
Walker, B. (1992) 'A Matter of Mediation', *Community Care*, 17–24 December: 24–5.

# 10 The roles and responsibilities of health service personnel

*Jane Appleton and Jill Clemerson*

In this chapter, consideration is given to:

- the current roles and responsibilities of health service personnel for children on the child protection register, highlighting the many misconceptions which prevail;
- contextualising the child protection work of health staff in the process of providing a range of health services to vulnerable children and their families; and
- outlining the key practice issues currently facing health staff.

## Introduction

This chapter will consider the current roles and responsibilities of health service personnel who are likely to be working with children on the child protection register. Contributing to an inter-agency practice guide provides an ideal opportunity to set the health service contribution in context, albeit briefly. The initial focus on preventative work is deemed extremely important to demonstrate that the skills used by health professionals in the course of clinical practice are the same as those used when working with children and families on the child protection register. Indeed, it is impossible to discuss health workers' roles in core group activity without describing the range of needs-based interventions available to children and families. This chapter will provide an overview of the range of health services available to vulnerable children and their families in a chronological manner, from preventative work to post-registration core group activity. It will outline the key practice issues currently facing health services personnel as well as highlighting the many misconceptions which prevail about the responsibilities of health service staff in this area of work.

## The structure of health services

Before considering the responsibilities of health services personnel in child protection work it is vital to outline the nature of the structures and settings in which health staff operate. In England and Wales the structure of the health service has altered considerably since the reorganisation of the NHS following the introduction of the NHS and Community Care Act 1990. Health services nationally are now separated into organisations responsible for the purchasing of health care and those responsible for the provision of health care services; this is often referred to as the purchaser–provider split (Figure 10.1). The agency responsible for purchasing health services for a local community from both hospital and community organisations is the District Health Authority (DHA), which is accountable directly to the National Health Service Executive through the Regional National Health Service Executive (NHSE) office. The DHA is responsible for identifying the health needs of its local population, which usually spans more than one local authority area, and then purchasing services to provide health care to meet these needs. The majority of provider services are supplied by NHS trusts, which are either acute general hospital-based services or community and specialist services, which include community hospitals, mental health provision, elderly services and community nursing services. A third provider service includes organisations in the private and voluntary sector.

General practice, however, is organised separately, with the majority of general practitioners (GPs) being self-employed and funded directly from the DHA, either as GP fundholders or partners, or as salaried GPs in a practice in receipt of an income. In the latter part of the 1990s, there is a move towards GPs commissioning provider services alongside health authorities; and in a few inner city areas where recruitment to GP practice is particularly problematic, GPs are employed by provider trusts.

## Community services for children

Health services are broadly divided into two groups: those based within district general hospital settings and those within the community (Figure 10.2). The

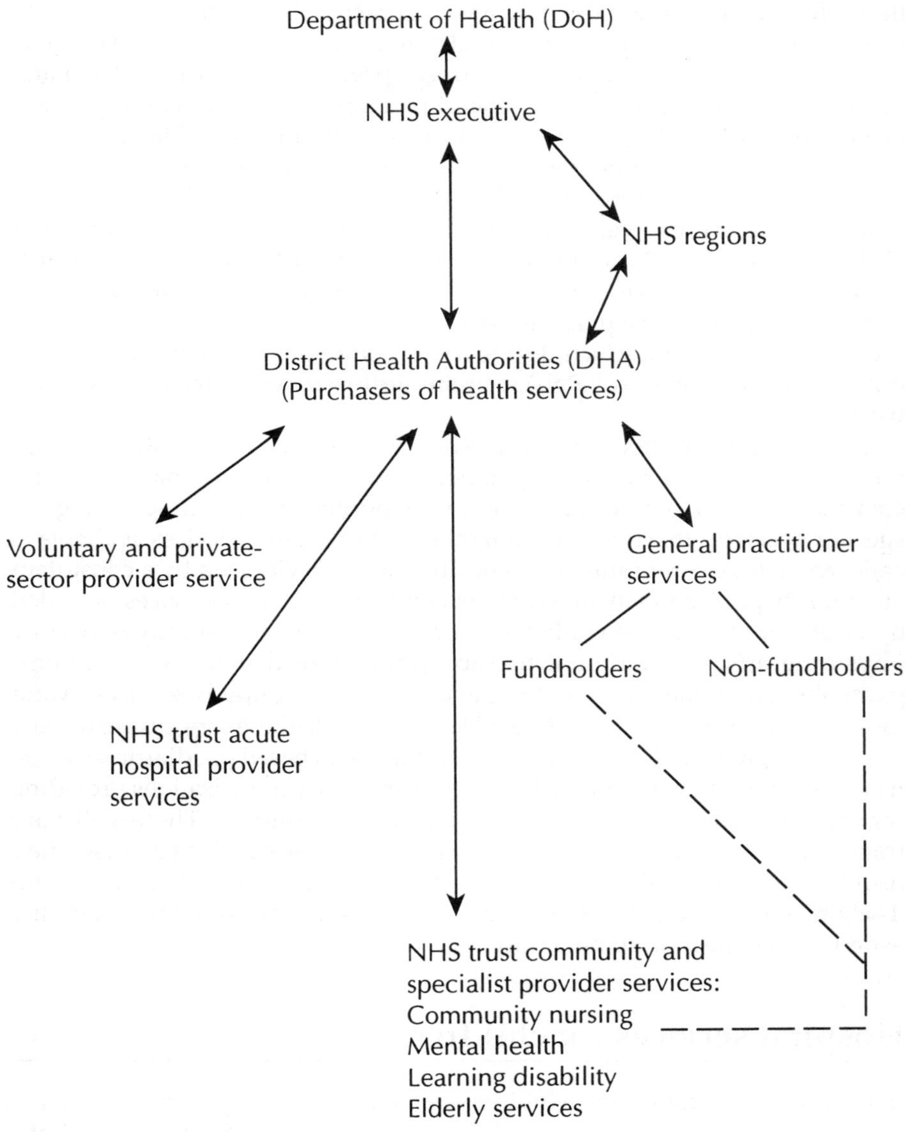


**Figure 10.1 National Health Service structures**

complex nature of the health service does mean that differences in organisational structures occur around the country. However, the first point of contact which most people have with health services is in the community, through contact with services from general practice. Each citizen is entitled to register with a GP and, through general practice, has access to a wide range of health services. These services are termed 'primary health care' (PHC) and the staff working with a GP in general practice are known as the primary health care team (PHCT). Nationally, the profile of a PHCT will include a core team of health visitors, practice nurses, GPs, district nurses, practice managers and administrative/support staff. It is important to point out that team structures are likely to vary from area to area because of the different stages of development of GP fundholding and implementation of PHCT working. PHC workers also have close links with other practitioners who have sessional input into general practice work, but who may not be based within the health centre. These may include midwives, community mental health nurses (until recently known as CPNs), community paediatric nurses and clinical psychologists.

We have described above the core primary health care team; however, these professionals will also make use of other colleagues who form part of a wider community health service and who are important in providing a range of specialist services for children and families. The range of services available to children include community child health doctor services led by a consultant community paediatrician, the child development team and services provided by a number of professions allied to medicine, such as community paediatric physiotherapy, occupational therapy (OT), speech therapy, audiology, psychology, ophthalmology services and children's chiropody services (Audit Commission, 1994; NHS Executive, 1996). Referrals to these services are usually made through the PHCT or sometimes via hospital based paediatric services. It is also important to highlight the range of voluntary organisations providing services for children and families within the community. These will vary from area to area and may include play groups, mother and toddler facilities, respite care services, day care, specialist fostering services for children with disabilities and a range of services, such as Homestart and Newpin, for families experiencing stress or vulnerability.

## Hospital services for children

In the acute hospital setting, children are seen in many departments, such as Accident and Emergency (A and E), orthopaedic services/out-patients, paediatric wards and departments, Special Care Baby Units/neonatal intensive care, dietetic out-patients, labour and post-natal wards. Midwifery and obstetric care are currently organised under the auspices of the district general hospital. However, following the recommendations of the Cumberlege Report – *Changing Childbirth* (DoH, 1993) and the *Maternity Charter* (DoH, 1994), care

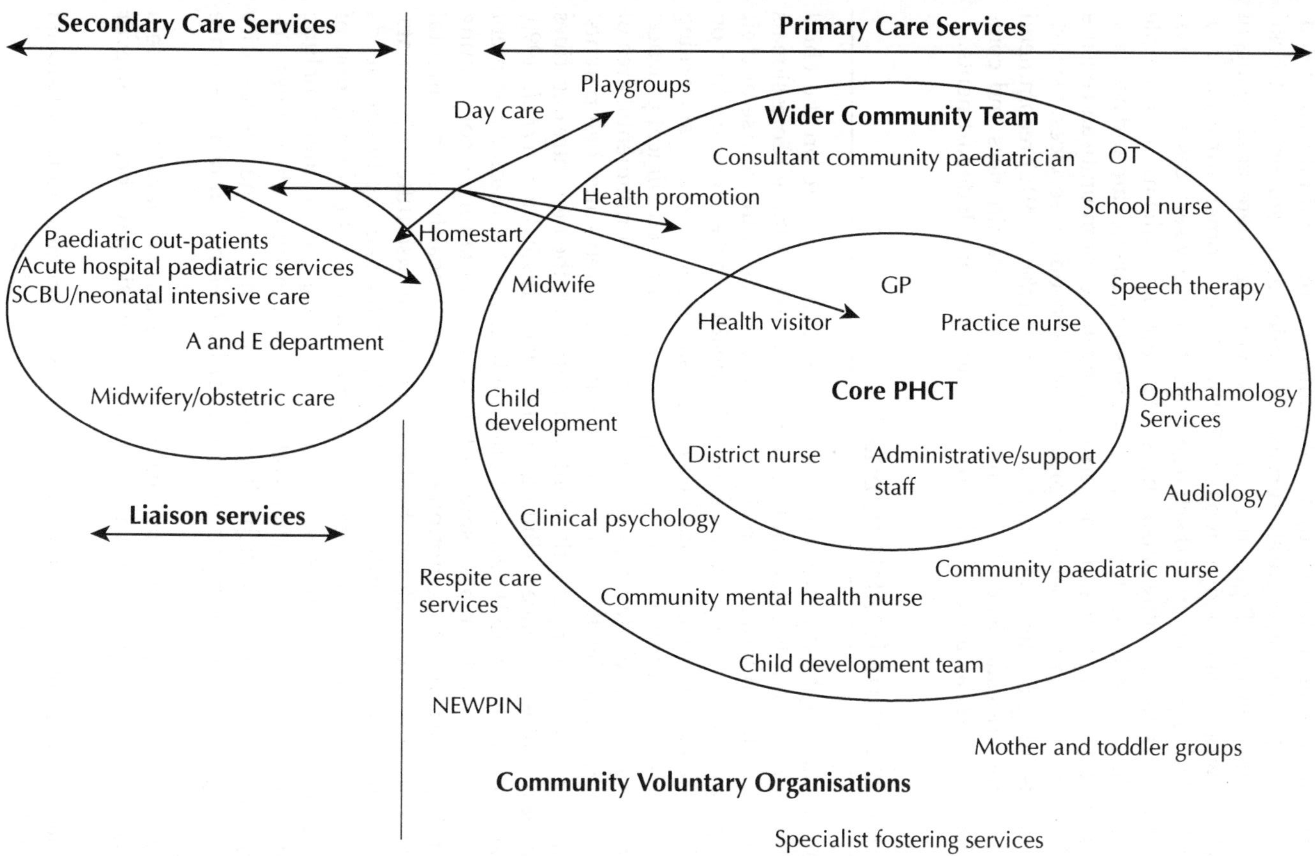


**Figure 10.2 The community/hospital interface health services for children and families**

for pregnant women is becoming more woman-centred and midwifery-led. Rather than there being separate services for ante-natal, delivery and post-natal care, the concept of 'group practices' is evolving where small teams of midwives with a caseload of women follow those women through from identification of pregnancy to discharge from midwifery services at 28 days. Most hospitals also employ liaison nurses for most specialisms, for example paediatric liaison health visitors, outreach nurses for diabetic care and neonatal intensive care to liaise with practitioners working in the community and ensure that links are maintained between primary and secondary services. Department of Health guidelines outlined in *Working Together* (1991a) recommend that systems are established to ensure that general practitioners and community nurses are aware of all children who attend A and E departments.

## Assessment of health needs

When discussing health workers'* work when children are on the child protection register, it is essential to outline the activities these professionals would normally undertake with children and families in the course of their broader roles. This is important as input by health workers for children on the child protection register should be a progression from their normal working practices within a framework of good-quality needs-based clinical practice. The possession of well developed assessment skills is a fundamental area of responsibility for all health workers in order that children's and their parents' health needs can be competently identified. Although the literature describes 'need' as a contested concept (Billings and Cowley, 1995; Buchan *et al.*, 1990; Stevens and Gabbay, 1991) nursing and medical health needs assessment will generally include an assessment of the child and family, incorporating general physical health, emotional health, social health, environmental health and parenting. Different health workers will use different formats, assessment tools and recording methods to undertake the health needs assessment. The outcome of needs assessment will be the formulation of medical or nursing 'diagnoses' and a plan of care which might include input from that practitioner or referral to another, or other disciplines. Although many individuals have health needs from time to time, the majority meet these needs with their own resources or by seeking out health service advice themselves.

It is important to be clear that health workers do not start to provide a service when a child protection issue arises. They will have been, however

* The term 'health workers' is used to refer to any worker from a health background who may be working with children and families.

minimally, in contact with the child/family and will need to reassess the child/family's health needs in the light of the concerns raised.

## Assessment of health needs and the child health promotion programme

The child health promotion programme (Hall, 1996) is implemented in all provider settings in England and Wales by primary health care teams and through the work of GPs, practice nurses and the health visiting and school nursing services. It consists of a programme of contacts with the child and parent(s) to discuss the child's health and development, while recognising the 'central role of parents, and the importance of parent "empowerment"' (Hall, 1996: 17). It is the vehicle through which health workers have contact with children and families and undertake both child and family health needs assessment.

Health visitors in particular have a key role to play with families with children under school age, as they are statutorily notified of the birth of all new babies. Traditionally, health visitors have provided a universal home visiting service to families with young children, which is viewed by many parents as non-stigmatising (Orr, 1980; Mayall and Foster, 1989) and socially acceptable (Machen, 1996). This means that health visitors are potentially in a unique position to identify families experiencing stress (Appleton, 1996). However, it is important to point out that since the mid-1990s, with increasing emphasis on services tailored to need, health visitors' work has been broadened to encompass a more generic role. This has meant that 'routine' home visiting is a thing of the past and, in an attempt to reduce home visiting time by health visitors, many community trusts have introduced protocols which prescribe the numbers of home visits and/or client contacts which health visitors should be making with clients with children under school age (Carney *et al.*, 1996; Appleton, 1997). Despite the National Commission of Inquiry's *Childhood Matters* (1996: 106) recommending that 'the health visiting service should be run as a universal service, and encouraged to undertake preventive work with families', in reality the focus on targeted client contacts and a major reduction in the number of health visitors means that this is unlikely to continue to be the case (Cassiday and Day, 1994; Health Visitors' Association, 1994; Laurent, 1994). There is a frequent misconception that health visitors have a statutory requirement to visit children and families, when this is not the case.

The school health service, which includes school nursing, is provided to all local authority education settings. The health needs assessment is usually undertaken at school entry and is either a universal school health interview for all children or is aimed at those children who have not completed their pre-school child health programme or have an existing health need. These assessments are usually undertaken by the school nurse, with referral to general practice or community child health doctor services if a medical assessment is required. Recent NHS organisational changes have led to a focus on resources. School nursing has had to respond to this new agenda by targeted screening and focusing increasingly on health promotion activities, particularly those which correspond to *Health of the Nation* (DoH, 1992) initiatives. Debell and Everett (1996: 487) suggest that school nursing work is not 'clearly understood ... [by] commissioning authorities' and that if school nurses roles and functions are not clarified between provider trusts and health authorities then this 'workforce potential could well be lost'. This would clearly have a major impact on the health assessment of school-age children.

Debell and Everett (1996: 490) also highlight the fact that, with school nursing activities focused within local authority state schools, there 'is the recognition that some vulnerable children of school age can be entirely missed; for example, some travellers, teenage mothers, school non-attenders, the children of refugees, children excluded or in transit'. It also needs to be recognised that the school health service does not usually provide a service to children in independent schools.

The GPs' role in the child health promotion programme includes a contact with or a home visit to the family shortly after the birth of a baby and the six-week child health developmental review. The child health promotion programme is provided during child health clinics in GP premises or health centres. At a child health clinic it would be usual for a GP to be present to undertake six-week developmental reviews or to see children referred by the practice nurse or health visitor. Health visitors undertake developmental reviews for children at six weeks, eight months, 18 months and three years and offer health educational advice to parents on nutrition and child care. The practice nurse contributes to the child health promotion programme by running paediatric immunisation sessions according to the national vaccination schedule, alongside GPs and health visitors, during child health clinics (DoH, 1996). If the health visitor, through the child health promotion programme, identifies a need for a medical assessment, she or he will refer to the GP. Child health promotion services should be organised so that a child and their carer can see a health visitor, practice nurse or GP as necessary during a child health clinic session.

## Increased health input

The child health promotion programme ensures that there are regular contacts by members of the PHCT with families with young children. This provides the gateway to health needs assessment and increased levels of intervention by health service personnel. Health visitors, in particular, are the key practitioners involved in the child health promotion programme. They are in a unique position to identify the need for home visits and to assess for and undertake short-term preventative work with families experiencing stress, or who are vulnerable. For example, health visitors may initiate a short-term, simple behavioural management programme with parents dealing with a constantly crying baby or a child who will not sleep. This aspect of home visiting to all families regardless of need is unparalleled and means, therefore, that health visitors are in a unique position to identify children in need and children in need of protection (Dingwall, 1977; Barker and Percy, 1991; Sharma and Sunderland, 1988; DoH, 1991b; Health Visitors' Association, 1994; DoH, 1995). However, as highlighted earlier, this universal home visiting service is currently under threat.

It is important to outline the increased health input which a child and family may receive when there is an identified health need. This may involve one or more health workers from the PHCT or from the secondary acute hospital or community services providing increased interventions for a child and/or family. For example, a family which has previously experienced a sudden infant death and is expecting a new baby will be offered a range of support services from both the PHCT and hospital-based services. The midwife, GP, paediatrician and health visitor will be involved in a package of care for such a family which may involve the CONI (Care of Next Infant) programme.

A further example would be where there are concerns about a child's growth, such as in the case of a three-year-old whose height and weight are not progressing along the expected centile lines. The GP and health visitor will initially advise on nutrition and monitor weight and growth. The health visitor may offer extra home visits to observe and advise on mealtime activities and management. A behaviour modification programme may be initiated, using food diary and nutritional and behavioural advice. In the case of a school-age child who is presenting with unmanageable behaviour, the school nurse, GP and child mental health services should be involved in implementing a programme of care aimed at assisting parents and school staff (where appropriate) to manage a child's behaviour appropriately and consistently, both at home and school.

These examples are offered as an illustration of the range of increased interventions which can be offered to children and families where there is an identified health need. Experience would suggest that many social service departments overlook the fact that health professionals have actually attempted this level of work with families with young children prior to child protection registration and core group working. It is crucial that social workers recognise that such attempts have frequently taken place prior to social services contact and intervention with a child and family, yet such care plans/programmes may have not been seen as important by the family, or the family may not have wished to follow the advice given.

## Care plans and exception care planning/documentation

In the preceding section some examples of the increased interventions which can be offered to families with young children have been described. Increasingly, these identified health needs are structured in the form of a care plan, which will be written and shared with the parents and child (if old enough). Care plans can be described as written tools usually used by the nursing profession to identify clients' health needs and the interventions needed to meet those health needs. Care plans aim to detail the steps needed to address or meet an identified health need; they will include advice, detail of any referrals made, changes that the client agrees to undertake and activities the health professional agrees to implement. For families with children under school age, the development of a care plan will be facilitated through the use of the parent-held Personal Child Health Record (Health Visitors' Association, 1991). Where the care plan is solely about the child's health needs, it will be recorded in the parent-held Personal Child Health Record.

However, where the care plan refers to aspects of parenting or the parents' health needs, there will be an exception care plan using different documentation. Each health discipline has its own documentation systems to record work with children and families. Some of this is shared with families; some is solely a record for the professional. Increasingly, in primary health care teams where staff have access to sophisticated information technology, the concept of 'shared records' is growing in popularity. In these cases, the GP practice-based record is used by all health professionals having contact with the child/client and professionals may not maintain their own separate records.

## Identification of children in need or children in need of protection

As demonstrated in the preceding sections, health workers identify and work preventatively with many children and families, yet unfortunately this important aspect of their work does not often appear to be recognised by social services personnel (Appleton, 1996). Indeed, frequently social services personnel do not seem to recognise that other professionals make an assessment of a child and family.

Where short-term work has not resulted in an improved situation or where the family consistently avoids or is unable to achieve an improved situation for the child, there will be a need to discuss the child's situation with a statutory agency: that is, social services. Health workers regularly identify the need for social work intervention and support in such families, but research evidence indicates that social work intervention is only accessible if a referral is described as a child protection issue (Gibbons *et al.*, 1995; Hallett, 1995). Furthermore, communication difficulties between health professionals and social services departments are frequently cited in the literature.

Research by Taylor and Tilley which investigated health visitor involvement in child protection in two community areas identified the ambiguity of the health visitor's role in this area. They found that health visitors 'tended to feel frustrated by their lack of power and influence. They felt that their referrals, opinions and skills were not always valued or taken as seriously as they should have been' (Taylor and Tilley, 1989: 275). Appleton recorded similar findings, with health visitors continually complaining about social services and the lack of assistance from social workers:

> And sometimes you can get stuck – you can't get any help. People don't recognise what you see. Because Social Services are being pressured all the time, they can't cope. So they don't want to see the needs that we're finding out in other families. (Appleton, 1996: 916)

Many health workers appear angry and frustrated over the lack of social services input with some families, particularly in those areas of 'high concern' often described as 'grey areas' (Appleton, 1996). This pushes some health workers, notably health visitors, into trying to bridge the gap of lack of family support resources (Appleton, 1996; Nettleton, 1991; Potrykus, 1990) and couching their referrals to social services using child protection/child abuse terminology to ensure that the referral is accepted (Gibbons *et al.*, 1995). This appears particularly difficult for health workers when concern surrounds emotional issues and chronic neglect. Inevitably, these experiences will influence health workers' expectations of joint working after a child is placed on the child protection register. Some health workers will feel aggrieved that it often takes a child protection incident for their concerns to be acted on by social services. As a consequence, they will be only too pleased to leave the majority of work post-child protection registration to the statutory agency.

Despite these criticisms of social services, health workers must also recognise that they have an obligation to be clear about their concerns, particularly around parenting. Health workers have a responsibility to articulate clearly the health needs of a family. Health workers need to be able to make a decision about the action they require from social services and provide a rationale for that decision.

Following the publication of *Messages from Research* (DoH, 1995) the 'refocusing' debate has highlighted the dilemmas in social work practice as regards working preventatively with children in need of services as opposed to children in need of protection. The suggestion is that we approach referrals as a child 'in need' inquiry unless there is a chronic situation that requires a child protection investigation. Although social services are the responsible statutory agency for children in need inquiries, workers from many agencies who are in contact with the family will have previously assessed the child's needs and can provide that information for social services, thus speeding up the process.

## The child protection conference

It is important to reiterate the significance of preparatory work in ensuring that all professionals can make an effective contribution to a child protection conference. Health staff need to be clear about their health assessment and the needs of the family in written reports as well as in verbal communications within the child protection conference. A health worker's report will be based on his or her knowledge of the family and information from the health records, including health care plans, and should reflect working in an open manner with children and families.

Box 10.1 offers practical guidance for health staff required to write reports for a child protection conference.

## Core groups: health input

It is perhaps useful to clarify at the outset that the ways of working described above are those that the health worker should bring to their work within a core group. It is a misconception that health professionals' work will change following the placing of a child's name on the child protection register. When a professional such as a health visitor holds a caseload of between 350 and 450 families, and school nurses cover a population of 2500 school-aged children, realistically their intervention with families can only be short-term and selective. There cannot be an expectation by the individual health worker or other agencies that health visitors and school nurses will work intensively over a considerable period of time with a child or family.

The role of health workers working with children and their families following child protection registration is to do with meeting health needs identified as part of the health workers' assessment and report to the child protection conference. Therefore a health worker's contribution to the child

**Box 10.1 Child Protection Conference Reports: Guidance Points**

The health professional writing a report for a child protection conference should:

1. refer to local guidance and format;
2. refer to the records available, as well as their own knowledge of the family;
3. refer to the chronology of key events recorded in the records, compiling one if it is not available;
4. include facts: what was said, done, heard and/or observed;
5. include professional opinions, stating clearly how these have been reached;
6. include the conclusions of the health needs assessment on each family member, children and parents;
7. include a summary of the work undertaken with the child/family, referring to the care plan agreed with the child/family;
8. include the strengths and weaknesses in parenting abilities patterns;
9. include significant aspects of the pattern of contact with the family;
10. conclude the report, if possible, with:
    - a summary of the major concerns for the child(ren),
    - the care plans to meet identified health needs,
    - recommendations for services and work which would improve the child's (children's) situation.

protection plan will be directly related to the identified health needs of the child or individuals in the family. Perhaps it is important at this stage to clarify the difference between a care plan and a child protection plan. Whereas a health worker's care plan will focus solely on the health needs of the child and/or family, the child protection plan sets out the overall plan agreed by the core group which should result in an improved situation for the child. This child protection plan negotiated by the core group will make reference to the needs identified by the various professionals who will be part of the core group.

The expectation of other key agencies involved in child protection processes, such as education and social services, tends to be that health workers will be available to 'monitor' the child and family. There is probably a divergence of opinion about what is meant by 'monitoring'. In health professionals' minds, 'monitoring' will mean specific health-related reassessment of an identified health need, rather than regularly keeping contact with a family just to 'keep an eye on things'. There is a need to distinguish between a health and social need and there needs to be a recognition that there may not be a working role for a generalist health care worker with the family. However, it is essential that health workers continue to liaise with the key agencies and personnel involved in carrying out the child protection plan.

In terms of involvement in the child protection core group, different health staff will have varied levels of input and it is worthwhile outlining this input so that other disciplines' expectations are clear. The child protection conference will usually identify core group members, the health workers most frequently directly involved in core groups are health visitors; less frequently, they are school nurses. Other PHCT members need to be kept informed, through written communication and liaison, of changes in plans for the family and in family circumstances. To illustrate this, some examples will be offered.

A midwife will only be involved where there is a woman who is expecting a baby or who has just delivered. Midwives have statutory responsibility for the mother and baby and this continues until 28 days post-delivery. Midwives' work within a child protection core group will include midwifery assessment of care for the woman during pregnancy and delivery and the family's adjustment to the new arrival. Specific interventions which could be part of a child protection plan may include ensuring that parentcraft education is offered and taken up by the parents. Post-delivery, the midwife will assess parenting skills and advise social services of any concerns. A midwife will be able to give information from her or his assessment of the parent(s)' attitude to and preparation for the new baby.

A GP will not normally be a child protection core group member, because he or she will not usually have frequent or continuing contact with the child/family. However, the GP will see family members or the child if they are unwell and must be kept informed of any progress or changes in the child's/family's situation. A GP would report directly to the keyworker or through the health visitor on contacts and health concerns that they identified.

Health visitors will usually be key members of the core group where there is a child under school age. Their input will depend on their assessment of health need as reported to the child protection conference. For example, their input could range from reviewing growth and development during child health clinic sessions, through giving advice to the core group on health matters in the family, to involvement in the management of a specific problem such as sleep difficulties, play and stimulation and child accident prevention.

Practice nurses will not be directly involved in the core group but may have contact with a child under school age through child health clinics. They will usually refer or discuss concerns with the GP or health visitor. For example, if a child failed to attend for an expected contact, this would be reported to the family health visitor, who should then notify the social worker. Paediatricians will not normally be involved in the core group, but a child may be referred to them for an assessment and they will inform the core group of their findings or opinion via the GP or health visitor.

School nurses will only be involved in a child protection core group if there is a specific area of work that is appropriate for their service: for example, if the child has a nutritional problem, an eneuretic disorder or a special health need or disability, or requires continuing ophthalmology or audiology services. Their role will usually be to advise parents or the child and see the parents or child once or twice a term to support them following this advice.

Box 10.2 outlines the responsibilities of health staff attending core group meetings.

**Box 10.2 The responsibilities of health staff attending core groups**

1 Sharing information and opinions openly, both with parent(s)/clients and with other professionals.
2 Respecting and valuing the views of all the other members of the core group.
3 Providing information from their assessment and identification of health needs of the child(ren) and family.
4 Carrying out health needs assessment if this was not available or appropriate prior to the child protection conference.
5 Compiling a care plan with the child/parents(s)/family to meet the identified health needs including the parent(s)' agreed input and their own input.
6 Collation of information from health professionals as agreed with the client and the professionals concerned, such as clinical psychologist, therapy services, specialist team or PHCT colleagues, GP or school nurse.
7 Being realistic about liaison with other health staff and their own health need-focused input to the child protection plan.
8 Health staff should present written reports to core group meetings and sign any agreements regarding their input to child protection plans.

Despite suggestions to the contrary, most other health workers are unlikely to be involved in child protection core groups. However, there is an important, if not vital, liaison and communication function that must be established between other health workers and the core group. It may be helpful for the core group to identify and record which members will undertake this liaison and communication role with specific health workers and departments. For example, the health visitor or school nurse could liaise with the GP, hospital A and E departments and specialist children's services such as the child development team.

Unfortunately, boundaries in core group working are often unclear and in practice this can lead to unrealistic expectations about the potential role and function of health workers in post-registration activity. In an attempt to overcome this problem, a scenario is offered below which outlines the particular components of health workers' work in the core group. It endeavours to illustrate good working practices by giving examples of possible interventions which health staff might undertake with children on the child protection register and their families.

## Health staffs' involvement in core group working: a scenario

### Family composition

The mother is aged 25 years, the father 26 years. (He is father of the two youngest children.) There are two boys, aged six and two and a half, and a girl, aged eight months. The father of the older boy has not been around for the last five years.

### History of input from agencies prior to the child protection conference

At school, the class teacher is concerned about lack of regular attendance and lack of concentration of the six-year-old. Attempts to discuss this with the parents have been unsuccessful, as parents have not come to the school as arranged.

The children have been taken to the GP's surgery and hospital A and E department with minor injuries. This pattern has increased over the last year. A head injury recently to the girl resulted in an overnight hospital stay. The family has been known to the health visiting service for last six years. Concerns about the pattern of parenting, particularly supervision, stimulation and routines for the children, have increased over the last six months.

A day care placement for the two-and-a-half-year-old has been recently arranged, but he has only attended once a week over the last four weeks instead of every afternoon. The six-year-old was found at about 10 pm by the police; he was with a group of older boys and was taken home. The parents did not seem concerned about the time he was out or where he was.

### Previous work with the family

The GP has discussed the pattern of accidents to the children with both parents, reiterating the need to supervise them. The health visitor has advised and offered support on stimulation and supervision of the children, including home safety advice. Bedtime routines and sleep pattern management were discussed and follow-up visits to support change were completed. Patterns of bedtime or supervision did not obviously improve.

Staff from the day centre have visited weekly since the placement was available, to encourage attendance both of the two-and-a-half-year-old and of the mother or parents at the parents' group. Although the parents have said they will bring in the toddler and come to the group, they have not done so.

The outreach teacher from the school has visited the home to explore the six-year-old's poor attendance and pattern of activities, such as reading and constructive play, between him and the parents. This did not result in any appreciable change in attendance or concentration.

Social services have had several 'duty' contacts with the family and have visited them at home on two occasions over the last year and given financial support for a new cot and fireguard.

## Child protection conference

### *Decisions*

1 The children's names are to be placed on the child protection register (CPR) – Neglect.
2 Social services are to appoint a keyworker.

### *Recommendations*

1 The social services are to coordinate and collate a comprehensive child/family assessment.
2 The six-year-old is to attend school regularly.
3 The two-and-a-half-year-old is to attend the day care placement regularly.
4 The eight-month-old is to have a regular pattern and routine for meals, play and sleep.
5 All children are to have a bedtime routine established.
6 Supervision and stimulation of children at home are to improve, resulting in a reduction in minor accidents and the children being able to play constructively.
7 Parents and the social worker, and other agencies as agreed, are to work on improving the relationship between parents and children.
8 Supervision of the six-year-old is to be improved.

Core group members are agreed as follows: parents, social worker, school outreach teacher, health visitor, day care placement representative.

## Child protection plan

During the initial meeting of the core group, after the child protection conference, the views of the parents on their family's situation and functioning must be heard and respected. There must be the acknowledgement of the anger the family may feel about having children on the child protection register and the reiteration by professionals of what in their collective view needs to change.

It may also be important to prioritise the areas of work and agree an overall plan to address each area in turn. The family will be encouraged by success and therefore their priorities and what they see as most achievable are as important as workers' concerns.

There may be support for aspects of the plan from members of the extended family. This must be explored with the parents and agreed as part of the steps taken to achieve change.

## Core group's working plan

### *Comprehensive assessment*

*Assessment* The social worker (keyworker) will collate information from the reports to the child protection conference and complete the comprehensive assessment as per local guidelines. All information and the chronology of life events will be shared, and checked for accuracy, with the family.

*School attendance for the six-year-old* The social worker and school outreach teacher will meet the parents at a place and time agreed by the parents and discuss the parents' perception of the six-year-old's non-attendance, reasons for it, difficulties in getting him to attend school, and the usefulness of school to children and their children.

From this discussion an agreed programme for a return to full school attendance will be drawn up. This will probably include the following:

- discussion with the six-year-old by parents and outreach teacher together;
- support for the six-year-old in socialising in the school peer group;
- a programme to support learning to enable the six-year-old to be on a par with peers; this will include a daily activity of ten minutes between parent(s) and child and activities with the class support teacher.

*Day care placement* The social worker, health visitor and day centre representative will meet parents at an agreed place and time and discuss the parents' perception of the offered place, the need for it, the advantages and disadvantages of the parents' viewpoint.

From this discussion it will be agreed whether a day care place is helpful and supportive to the parents at present. An agreed programme of introduction for the two-and-a-half-year-old and one or both of the parents to the centre can then be arranged.

If it is agreed that the placement is inappropriate at present, support for constructive play and stimulation for the two-and-a-half-year-old will be explored with parents and input from the health visitor and day care staff agreed.

*Eight-month-old's-routines* The parents and health visitors are to meet and agree issues that the parents wish to change in their routine with the girl. The health visitor will advise on long-term results of a lack of change and encourage parents to think preventatively. The health visitor and parents will agree a short-term (4–6 weeks) programme for change in routines mutually agreed as most important. Discussion may include exploring possibilities of support from another professional or team, such as the Child and Family Consultation Service.

*Bedtime routines* The social worker, health visitor and parents will meet and discuss the importance of bedtime routines and the parents' view of this, family patterns of children's bedtimes and potential for change. From this discussion, a shared programme which works towards an agreed bedtime for the children will be set. Support for the programme will be agreed.

*Supervision and stimulation of the children* The health visitor, social worker and parents will meet and discuss the parents' view of the pattern of accidents to the children and their underlying cause; family patterns of discipline and teaching personal safety to children; home safety, including ensuring that there is one 'safe' room for play for the younger children, and deciding which room this is; and use of accident prevention aids.

From this discussion, changes to ensure that accident prevention aids are available and used will be agreed. This will include what professionals will provide and what parents will undertake to do. The discussion will also aim to agree upon what will be the parents' agreed and consistent way of disciplining each child to prevent accidents.

*Family relationships* The social worker and health visitor will discuss family patterns of relating to children with both parents as appropriate and agreed by parents. Suggestions for activities which may promote positive relationships, including short activities with each child and praise for each child when they are doing something the parent is pleased they are doing, will be incorporated in other aspects of the plan, where possible. Support from other professionals or a specialist team may be discussed and included.

*Supervision of six-year-old* The social worker will discuss with both parents their concerns about the six-year-old and their ideas for changing the pattern of supervision. As with the issues to do with family relationships and routines for the eight-month-old, the family may need support from a specialist team. However, the need for this must be agreed by all concerned and the social worker may find it necessary to help parents understand this through offering initial support to a programme agreed with the parents to supervise the six-year-old. Such a programme may include time to 'play out' with peers, the latest time to return home, and informing parents of where he is and who he is with.

## Critical evaluation of core groups

The literature indicates that there are expectations from social services personnel that they wish to share the responsibility of core group key working with other practitioners (Calder and Barratt, 1997; Horwath and Calder, 1998). However, health service staff do not share this perception, as they view social services as the statutory agency for child protection work and therefore as being responsible for ensuring that the work is carried out. Furthermore, this chapter has illustrated the boundaries of health staff work with children on the child protection register as well as giving some indication of current NHS resource constraints.

There appears to be a common view within social work that, just as a social worker's level of work increases when a child is placed on the child protection register, so should the work of health personnel. Social workers may experience frustration that health workers do not have a greater input in the work that needs to be achieved with families. In fact, the opposite often occurs, with health workers finding that their level of work usually reduces once a child is placed on the child protection register. This is because the relevant work to improve the child's situation within the family has to be undertaken within a child protection framework and social services are the statutory agency responsible for ensuring that this work is completed. It must be remembered that health professionals have often worked with a family to try and achieve change for the good of the child or children before making a referral to social services for a child protection investigation. The referral is made because health workers have not been able to achieve change that will prevent further significant harm to the child. Essentially, health workers are only too aware of their non-statutory status, their lack of power and their inability to insist that families change for the good of their children.

However, all workers who are part of the core group need to have 'ownership' and a sense of responsibility for the continuing work for the family and child once the child is on the register. The absence of this appropriate collective responsibility will lead to overburdening of the social worker. Health workers view themselves, and should be viewed, as equal partners with other frontline workers within the core group. This means that, for health workers, core group working should be a continuation of the good practice which was undertaken before the child was registered. If all practitioners who are involved in a core group practise at an optimum level, supported by supervision and specialist advice, difficulties in role and responsibility should not occur.

Child protection conferences need to identify key recommendations. This will enable the core group to establish common goals and expectations of the work that needs to be undertaken. Core group work may fail for three reasons: firstly, because the core group members do not have a common understanding of the child protection issues; secondly, because core groups have not established ground rules about the nature of communication within core group meetings and about work undertaken between meetings; and thirdly, because the goals or steps are not sufficiently detailed or short-term for parents to see their relevance and benefits. A series of short-term goals following a similar theme will be easier for families to relate to than broad conference objectives (see the objectives set in the scenario, above). These short-term goals can illustrate to families that they are taking incremental steps and, it is hoped, achieving positive outcomes. All core groups should have written contracts that cover communication and the agreed goals and tasks to be achieved by the family and the workers.

Another major issue facing the functioning of the core group is the difficulties which arise when workers leave or change. This potentially halts the work during the changeover period, particularly if it involves one of the workers who is undertaking a considerable amount of work with the family. Families may also change, and major crisis can lead to a break-up of family members. Families may decide that children should be cared for by other family members. These changes may be positive or negative in terms of the child protection issues, and the reconvening of a child protection conference may be necessitated.

If, within the negotiations during the core group to arrive at the child protection plan, community nurses are concerned that their expected input to the family is unrealistic and not related to the identified health care needs of the family, they must make this clear both verbally and in writing. Community nurses can refer and discuss their concerns with the child protection nurse specialist for their trust. This may result in negotiation at team manager level about the appropriate input from community nursing services to the family. Our experience would indicate that such an approach is usually effective in clarifying the appropriate input from the community nurse. Similarly, if a health worker is concerned about the functioning or the coordination of the core group, he or she should initially discuss this with the social worker and may then seek advice from the child protection nurse specialist who in turn may need to contact the social work team manager.

## The way forward

The authors feel it is worth reiterating the regularly called for pre-qualification multidisciplinary education for social workers, community nurses, GPs, community paediatricians, teachers and psychologists (Home Office, Department of Health, Department of Education and Science, Welsh Office, 1991). This will aid the promotion of mutual respect and understanding of roles and responsibilities. Local practice-based focus groups which meet on a regular though not necessarily frequent basis build on the joint understanding and mutual respect of each professional's role. Such groups need to be coordinated and this role is often undertaken by a child protection specialist. One function of this group could be to present and reflect on cases that have had a positive outcome for children and families through the work of the core group. Another function of the group could be to debate national initiatives, guidelines and research and how they affect local practice.

## Summary

In this chapter we have tried to outline the roles and responsibilities of health workers regarding meeting the health needs of children. Other professionals engaged within inter-agency child protection practice are often unaware of the ways in which health workers practise. As a result of this lack of awareness, these professionals often have unrealistic expectations of health staff, or they do not appreciate the various ways in which health workers can meet children's health needs and promote their welfare. We hope this overview of ways in which the different health professionals work with children and their families will raise other professional's awareness of the range of expertise that is available, thereby promoting effective working together.

# References


Appleton, J.V. (1996) 'Working with Vulnerable Families: A Health Visiting Perspective', *Journal of Advanced Nursing*, **23**: 912–18.

Appleton, J.V. (1997) 'Establishing the Validity and Reliability of Clinical Practice Guidelines Used to Identify Families Requiring Increased Health Visitor Support', *Public Health*, **111**: 107–13.

Audit Commission (1994) *Seen but Not Heard*, HMSO: London.

Barker, W. and Percy, P. (1991) 'Health Visiting Under Scrutiny', *Health Visitor*, **64** (1): 12–15.

Billings, J. and Cowley, S. (1995) 'Approaches to Community Needs Assessment: A Literature Review', *Journal of Advanced Nursing*, **22**: 721–30.

Buchan, H., Gary, M., Hill, A. and Coulter, A. (1990) 'Needs Assessment Made Simple', *Health Service Journal*, 15 February: 240–41.

Calder, M.C. and Barratt, M. (1997) 'Inter-agency Perspectives on Core Group Practice', *Children and Society*, **11** (4): 209–21.

Carney, O., McIntosh, J., Worth, A. and Lugton, J. (1996) *Assessment of Need for Health Visiting*, Research Monograph No. 2, Glasgow: Glasgow Caldedonian University, Department of Nursing and Community Health.

Cassiday, J. and Day, M. (1994) 'Breaking Point', *Nursing Times*, **90** (47): 20–21.

Cloke, C. and Naish, J. (1992) *Key Issues in Child Protection*, Harlow: Longman/NSPCC.

Debell, D. and Everett, G. (1996) 'The Role and Function of the School Nurse', *British Journal of Community Nursing*, **1** (8): 486–93.

Department of Health (1990) *NHS and Community Care Act 1990*, London: HMSO.

Department of Health (1991a) *Working Together under the Children Act 1989: A Guide to Arrangements for Inter-agency Cooperation for the Protection of Children from Abuse*, London: HMSO.

Department of Health (1991b) *Child Abuse – A Study of Inquiry Reports 1980–1989*, London: HMSO.

Department of Health (1992) *The Health of the Nation: A Strategy for Health in England*, London: HMSO.

Department of Health (1993) *Changing Childbirth. Report of the Expert Maternity Group*, London: HMSO.

Department of Health (1994) *Maternity Charter*, London: HMSO.

Department of Health (1995) *Child Protection: Messages from Research*, London: HMSO.

Department of Health (1996) *Immunisation Against Infectious Disease*, London: HMSO.

Dingwall R. (1977) *The Social Organisation of Health Visitor Training*, London: Croom Helm.

Gibbons, J., Conroy, S. and Bell, C. (1995) *Operating the Child Protection System: A Study of Child Protection Practices in English Local Authorities*, London: HMSO.

Hall, D.M.B. (1996) *Health for all Children. Report of the Third Joint Working Party on Child Health Surveillance*, Oxford: Oxford University Press.

Hallett, C. (1995) *Interagency Co-ordination in Child Protection*, London: HMSO.

Health Visitors' Association (1991) *In their Own Hands – Introducing Personal (Parent-held) Child Health Records: An HVA Guide*, London: HVA.

Health Visitors' Association (1994a) *A Cause for Concern: An Analysis of Staffing Levels and Training Plans in Health Visiting and School Nursing*, London: HVA.

Health Visitors' Association (1994b) *Protecting the Child: an HVA guide to practice and procedures*, London: HVA.

Health Visitors' Association (1995) *Legal and Professional Issues in Child Protection: a skills-based training resource*, London: HVA.

Home Office, Department of Health, Department of Education and Science, Welsh Office (1991) *Working Together under the Children Act: A Guide to Arrangements for Interagency Co-operation for the Protection of Children From Abuse*, London: HMSO.

Horwath, J. and Calder, M.C. (1998) 'Working for Children on the Child Protection Register: Myth or Reality?', *British Journal of Social Work*, **28** (6): 879–95.

Laurent, C. (1994) 'Survey. Over-worked and Under-valued', *Health Visitor*, **67** (11): 373.

Machen, I. (1996) 'The Relevance of Health Visiting Policy to Contemporary Mothers', *Journal of Advanced Nursing*, **24**: 350–56.

Mayall, B. and Foster, M. (1989) *Child Health Care. Living With Children, Working For Children*, Oxford: Heinemann Nursing Publishing Ltd.

Nettleton, R.J. (1991) 'Support and Supervision of Health Visitors Dealing with Child Abuse', unpublished MSc thesis: University of Manchester.

NHS Executive (1996) *Child Health in the Community: A Guide to Good Practice*, London: Department of Health.

Orr, J. (1980) *Health Visiting in Focus*, London: RCN.

Potrykus, C. (1990) 'The Price of a Child's Life', *Health Visitor*, **63** (7): 217.

Report of the National Commission of Inquiry into the Prevention of Child Abuse (1996) *Childhood Matters. Volume 1: The Report*, London: The Stationery Office.

Sharma, A. and Sunderland, R. (1988) 'The Increasing Medical Burdens of Child Abuse', *Archives of Diseases in Childhood*, **63**: 172–5.

Stevens, A. and Gabbay, J. (1991) 'Needs Assessment Needs Assessment', *Health Trends*, **23** (1): 20–23.

Taylor, S. and Tilley, N. (1989) 'Health Visitors and Child Protections: Conflict, Contradictions and Dilemmas', *Health Visitor*, **62**: 273–5.

# 11 Helping teachers to help children

*Anne Peake and Julie Turner*

In this chapter, consideration is given to the following:

- discussing the role of the teacher in working for children on the child protection register;
- the root of the difficulties encountered by teachers when asked to work together with social services;
- the profiles of the presenting behaviours of some children who have been identified as having experienced abuse;
- the problems teachers have in coping with children whose learning and behaviour have been adversely affected by their experiences of abuse;
- a practical view of what teachers can do to help children; and
- what help teachers need in order to help children with histories of abuse.

> Schools should contribute to a co-ordinated approach to child protection by developing effective liaison with other agencies and support services. (Department for Education Employment, Circular No. 10/95)

Viewed from a busy classroom with 30 to 34 children to teach, books to mark, dinner money to collect and the need to maintain order, 'working together' can seem much more like a goal in an ideal world than a practice which teachers can understand, willingly undertake and achieve, to the benefit of the less fortunate amongst their pupils.

**Case Study**

Joseph is six. He is thin and has a pasty complexion. At registration time he sits in a corner at the back of the room by the wall, playing with a toy clock. He plays with it the whole time, holding it close to his face, concentrating on it, making noises and humming. When the children are told to get out their reading books, all the other children do so. Joseph paces up and down the length of the classroom library shelves playing with a *Lego* truck. The teacher speaks to him firmly and reminds him of her request to get a book. He doesn't get a book but moves off to wander around the classroom, making noises. The class has become accustomed to Joseph. One or two children look at what he is doing, but he looks at no-one. The teacher approaches him and gently reminds him of her request. He shakes his head, lies on the floor and makes noises; he squirms across the floor. Without one-to-one help Joseph cannot keep on task for even the simplest things. What is most difficult is the times when Joseph spits on other pupils and staff, locks himself in the toilet and, on occasions, runs out of the classroom and hides. Joseph's name is on the child protection register in the category of 'actual emotional abuse'.

## Training Matters

> The criteria governing all courses of initial teacher training require newly qualified teachers to have acquired the necessary foundation to develop a working knowledge of their contractual legal administrative and pastoral responsibilities as teachers. Within that framework the coverage in initial teacher training (ITT) courses of awareness and recognition of child abuse and the need for the education service to work together with the statutory agencies is a matter for individual institutions. (Department for Education Employment, Circular No. 10/95)

Worker confidence to practise and develop one's skills begins with initial training. Training has to cover the theories and concepts on which the skills to practise rest. While the ideal is that the different agencies who deal with children should work together with regard to child protection issues, the reality is that the initial training of workers in the different agencies is so different that there are often few shared understandings. A brief look at some comparisons between the initial training of social workers and the training of teachers serves to illustrate the point.

It may be stating the obvious to say that teachers are trained to teach children. The emphasis of initial teacher training is on the methods of teaching children knowledge and skills. The introduction of the National Curriculum, together with the assessment of pupils (SATs), delineates the main teaching tasks. The role of teachers in child protection matters is made less of a priority as a consequence. As Circular 10/95 illustrates, the awareness and recognition of child abuse and a need for all elements of the education service to work together is not a feature of the necessary foundation to teaching; in fact, it is a matter for individual institutions. There is no agreement that child protection should be a part of all initial training of teachers.

The focus of all initial training courses for teachers is a child-centred one. Teachers receive a great deal of training in child development, theories of how children learn and ways of understanding children's behaviour. Such training is of enormous usefulness as a basis for considering children whose presenting behaviours are a focus for concern. It means that the concern about the behaviour of one child can be set by the teacher in the context of normal development for a child of that age or ability (Peake, 1996b). The usefulness of this training needs to be set against the lack of training for understanding the factors in the wider context of children's behaviour and difficulties. What is often so singularly missing is training for understanding the familial context of children's learning and behaviour in school. The training of teachers contrasts quite sharply with the training of social workers, which has an extremely wide focus, including work with children and families, mental health, older people, legal matters and so on.

Training in child abuse and child protection procedures is an essential feature of any social work training course. This is of course in keeping with the proper preparation of social workers for the statutory role they have in child protection work. While such training for teachers remains a matter for individual institutions, the result will always be that, at best, where relationships between the different agencies in a given area are good, there will be a session in the form of a lecture or turorial; and, at worst, no reference will be made to it throughout the entire teacher training course.

It is now common practice for social services departments to provide staff who work with children and families with in-service courses on basic child protection. A social worker can confidently expect that whatever child abuse training was provided on their professional training course will be supplemented by in-service training once in post. Unfortunately, again Circular 10/95 is equivocal: 'schools and local education authorities may wish to include coverage of child protection issues in their induction training for newly qualified teachers'. There is some recognition that designated teachers will need 'appropriate practical in-service training'.

The fact remains, then, that the class teacher for Joseph is unlikely to have had any training in understanding child abuse and in child protection procedures, yet she will deal with Joseph for a minimum of six hours a day, five days a week, 40 weeks a year. Given the extent of the contact teachers have with children about whom there are child protection concerns, the pressing needs of the children, and the scope and opportunities for teachers to help the children, the argument for child abuse and child protection procedures to be an integral part of all initial training of teachers and built into a programme of induction for newly qualified staff, and the continuing professional development of more experienced teachers, is a strong one.

## Roles and models of working practice

> Schools should monitor pupils whose names are on the child protection register in line with what has been agreed in the child protection plan. The plan sets out the role of the child's parents and various agencies in protecting the child. (Department for Education Employment, Circular No. 10/95)

The tasks involved in teaching groups of children necessitate a structured and consistent approach. Anyone who has watched an infant teacher bring a class of 32 five-year-olds from the hall to the classroom, ask them to change back into their everyday clothes, and settled them back into doing individual pieces of work, will have seen how important is a carefully thought out routine. The gift of teaching is of managing children and their individual needs in the structure set up in the school to promote their learning and a level of orderliness. The success of schools and teachers depends to a large extent on their capacities to set up clear routines which facilitate the management of groups while allowing for some flexibility and attention to individual children. A comparison of the roles and models of working practices of teachers and of social workers highlights how differing models of work can lead to very different reactions to the recognition of child abuse. Teachers and social workers dealing with child protection cases have the shared focus of the interests of the child. This, together with the requirement that agencies should work together coordinating action on child protection across the authority, provides much of the common ground between the two roles.

Children are compelled to attend school by law. While there are exceptions, the majority of children attend school regularly, so that the demands on teachers are to develop such working practices as are helpful to children learning in school and encourage them to learn. For child protection workers, their role is a statutory one which requires them to intervene in the lives of families at times when things are going drastically wrong. Often the only consistency to be found is that of the child protection procedures established by the ACPC. The role for the worker is to engage children and families, many of whom will actively resist such engagement.

The vast majority of teachers are in the teaching profession because they like children and want to promote their development. The role of a teacher is essentially an optimistic one in which the success of the teacher is to a large extent measured by the progress children make. This nature of the teaching task, coupled with the absence of child abuse training in initial teacher training courses, means that teachers are more likely to develop hypotheses about specific learning difficulties when encountering a child who is unable to make progress in school. The possibility of child abuse remains for many a last-ditch hypothesis, so the expectation that the role of a teacher will involve taking action in cases of child abuse is not widespread. The role and models of working practices of child protection workers and those professionals in other agencies such as education social work, the police and health visitors, include a level of preparedness to contemplate the possibility of child abuse.

Schools are highly structured places. An analysis of the structure in schools would suggest that much of the structure is concerned with the separation of tasks and responsibilities. Nowhere is this more clear than in a large, busy secondary school where there are clear structures of hierarchies and delineated roles leading to separate tasks. Any visitor to this system can be forgiven for finding it hard to grasp how such a complicated system of separate responsibilities can actually work to cater for the needs of children, in groups and individually. The social worker, accustomed to a system of line management where there is regular supervision and plans for action are routinely discussed with line managers, should be forgiven for finding the problem of who to approach to discuss the needs of an individual child with a history of child abuse a difficult one: should it be the deputy head with responsibility for pastoral care, the head of year, the form tutor, the special educational needs coordinator, the designated teacher, or the obvious head of the institution, the headteacher?

Anyone who has entered a school staff room at break time will see teachers as busy, sociable and mostly cooperative. However, this is to ignore the times when teachers teach. With the exception of open planned schools and some schools who really do practise team teaching, the majority of teaching is a solitary process for the teachers. Teachers are accustomed to working alone with groups of children and being in charge. When teachers do work with other people, it is usually with other teachers or staff from the various education support services who, in the main, come to the school at the request of the teachers or the headteacher. So the experience of teachers in terms of working with other agencies is limited. This is a far cry from the demands on social workers to establish a model of working practice which includes regular liaison with a whole range of other agencies, with the social worker initiating much of the contact and frequently going to meet workers in other agencies.

While few would doubt that the standing of teachers in our society is less highly regarded now than in previous times, teachers remain well regarded. Differentials in status and pay can lead to difficulties in decision making when communications about child protection procedures become unbalanced by local perceptions of professional standing.

> The class teacher is concerned about Kathleen who is nine years old. She is not working to achieve her potential in class and seems to lack the ability to concentrate. Her behaviour is disruptive. She spoils the work of other children, steals food and leaves taps running in the school cloakroom area. She is frequently dirty, and the other children complain that she smells with the result that they are reluctant to play with her and sit near her. Kathleen's mother seems only to complain about her. Kathleen's name is on the child protection register on account of neglect.

## Teachers and core groups

The common ground of our focus on the interests of children and locally agreed child protection procedures is swamped by the hinterland of different professional roles and models of working practices. One development which has much to offer as a way of drawing together a range of workers from different agencies to the advantage of children is that of core groups. Core groups are generally welcomed as a way of establishing and maintaining inter-agency cooperation and ensuring that child protection plans are put into action (Hallett, 1995). In areas where the setting up of core groups is part of the ACPC policy and included in local child protection procedures, they can provide a literal meeting point for front-line workers who need to work together despite the differences in their training, roles and models of working practice. Properly set up and run, these groups can do much to promote inter-agency liaison and, in particular, can help teachers to help children.

The main benefits of core groups for teachers are as follows. The core group provides a regular forum for the members to share information and keep up to date with the circumstances of the child and the family and the perspectives of other workers on the work that needs to be done. Core groups are a powerful way to help workers avoid 'being frozen in time'. Sometimes the news that the child has been the victim of child abuse and the unfolding details of their experiences are shocking to workers in agencies where the main task is not child protection. The impact of the information has such an effect that attitudes formed at the time become hard to shift: workers can find it hard to leave behind the feelings and opinions they formed when they were first told of the children's experiences. Then moving on to realise that, with time, more information and the beginnings of a working relationship with the family, can mean that the situation becomes increasingly complex. There is an urgent need to believe that people can change and that coordinated child protection intervention does make a difference. These shifts are not ones that are easy to make. Core groups mean that significant staff in the lives of children remain in touch with each other and with the developments of the case in a way which helps core group members make these shifts. Perhaps one difficulty that teachers encounter, particularly at secondary school level, is that the teacher who is a member of the core group may well make these shifts, but going back to a staff team and a group of teachers who have not had similar opportunities to develop their ideas can be difficult.

The fact that core groups meet regularly means that it is possible for the members to build up a sense of trust in their relationships with each other. Prior to the introduction of core groups it was the case that, quite frequently, workers from different agencies only met at initial child protection conferences or at child protection reviews. The formal nature of the occasion, with a designated chairman, agenda items, minute taking and the presence of parents, was such that anxieties about children on occasions spilled over into anger projected onto workers from other agencies with no time to understand and resolve differences in points of view. Core group meetings are less formal and, by definition, include those workers who are most willing and in a position to make a positive contribution to the situation. The absence of formality can nurture the build-up of mutual trust on the basis of familiarity and shared understandings.

While training and roles can drive workers apart, the opportunities for regular contact and experiences of working together can provide a forum for skill sharing. For social workers well used to having to engage families at crisis points in their lives, with the skills they have for so doing and their understanding of the wider family issues, there is much that can be passed on to the child's teacher in terms of ways of relating to parents and understanding the situation for the child. In their turn, teachers have much to offer social workers in terms of the strategies they have built up over time for motivating children and in particular what works with a child about whom there are concerns. Ideas, techniques and skills can all be shared once there is a forum in which to do so.

Core groups are not without their drawbacks. The advantages of such groups are most clear when viewed from the point of view of the child protection agencies, but the benefits are there for children whose names are on the child protection register. However, from the point of view of teachers, the fact that core groups are set up at initial child protection conferences and that the plan is that they should meet on a regular basis throughout the time that the child's name is on the register is the very basis of their limitations: a commitment to attend a core group is a commitment to set aside time to do so. We are now at a point in time where front-line workers are under mounting pressures from an ever-increasing workload, dwindling resources and scrutiny from the public and the media (see Chapter 4 of the present volume for a further discussion of these issues). Taking time to meet and discuss child protection plans can be a real struggle. Unless the group is able to meet at the end of a school day, the teacher attending to discuss the concerns about one of the pupils in his or her class has to have teaching cover for the whole of the class. When there are two or three children from one family to be discussed, the organisation of time to meet in the face of timetable teaching commitments can seem impossible.

The system of core groups is specifically for children whose names are on the child protection register. What most teachers will say is that the numbers of children about whom they have concerns, where there is the possibility that the children are the victims of abuse, are far greater than the numbers of children whose names appear on the register. There is as yet no system of inter-agency joint working with regard to the suspicions of abuse. A teacher will often have a gut feeling that something is seriously wrong for a particular child. It is the suspicion of abuse that is particularly anxiety arousing as the warning signs that a child may be the victim of abuse are frequently ambiguous. The use made by teachers of opportunities for consultation with regard to the suspicion of abuse is a clear indication of the need for a forum which provides information, advice and support to teachers concerned about individual children (Peake, 1996a).

It is only at initial child protection conferences that a decision can be made whether a child's name will be put on the child protection register. Often the decision is not to place a child's name on the register. This may be because the abuser is not a member of the child's immediate family and so a child can be protected from further contact, or if the abuser was a member of the immediate family, he has either been prosecuted or left, and remaining family members are able to believe and support the child. In such cases the child's name need not be placed on the register and there would be thought to be no need to set up a core group. However, as many teachers will attest, such children may well act out the pain and distress they have felt and continue to feel in a way which is entirely disturbing to them and to their peers in a school situation. In times when resources are scarce, a child who has been deemed to be safe from an identified abuser and with some familial support may well have minimal social work intervention and be seen as low down on any priority list for organised inter-agency cooperation. Many such children tax their teachers and would benefit from the advantages of core groups.

---

**Case Study**

Gavin was a Year 7 boy in a large comprehensive school. The teacher had a good working relationship with the social worker and had been involved from the beginning of the concerns. The first she had known about it was a call from social services asking if there were any issues with regard to child protection. This is generally what happens. Social services ring and ask if there are any issues and that is how the whole things starts. The teacher is in regular contact by telephone with Gavin's mother. Gavin has talked about what has happened at home. When the teacher went to the child protection conference she had not quite realised what was involved, but now is closely involved in monitoring the case. She has a very good link with the social services as there is a core group meeting which has been set up. Through the information from the initial child protection conference and the core planning group, she is now able to support Gavin. Gavin's name is on the child protection register on account of physical abuse.

---

What becomes clear is that, when we consider how best we can work with children on the child protection register, we need to have a breadth of vision about working for all children who have experiences of being abused. The use of core groups is a solution to one particular part of the problem – a part of the problem which is the most clear, given the context of child protection procedures. We need also to plan actively how best we can work together when there is a suspicion of abuse and how workers whose roles encompass child protection work can help teachers whose primary task orientation is far removed from child protection and yet who are the only group in regular, virtually daily, contact with children about whom there may be concerns. Similarly, we know from therapeutic work with children that the consequences of experiences of abuse remain with children, and that changes in circumstances and different developmental stages resurrect feelings of pain in new guises. There is a pressing need for continuing support for key professionals in the lives of these children, support which can go on long after the child protection procedures are deemed to have served their purposes. This is highlighted in the following examples.

**Case Study**

Paul was 10 years old. He was one of 11 children who were able to make statements about their abuse by a paedophile in the local community. Paul has a significant hearing loss and needs to wear hearing aids. He will not wear the aids. He is behind in his attainment levels across all areas of the curriculum. The effects of his experiences of being abused and the huge publicity that the case attracted are such that Paul is becoming increasingly difficult to manage. He is unable to make and sustain friendships. He adopts a loud and bullying approach to interactions with peers. His language is sexually explicit and offensive. The bribes the abuser used have now become a part of his behavioural repertoire and Paul smokes, drinks lager and has begun to steal from home and from school. Paul is becoming increasingly hard to contain in a classroom situation. Paul's name is not on the child protection register.

**Case Study**

Louisa's mum has come into school to talk to the teachers. She is distraught about her daughter. Louisa is 14. She is not eating properly and is visibly looking less well and underweight. She is also not washing herself as frequently as she has done previously. Her mother is aware of Louisa's drinking alcohol and suspects that she is also taking drugs. She is often late to school or not in school at all. Most worrying of all, she frequently does not come home on time, she can be missing overnight and on occasions her family are unaware of her whereabouts. Money has gone missing from the family home. When the concerns about Louisa were referred to social services, they were dealt with by a duty worker who visited the family home on one occasion. Louisa's name is not on the child protection register. Her mother asked the teachers to help.

## How then can we help teachers?

Teachers are in a unique position. First and foremost, their initial training as teachers includes considerable work in child development and this is a helpful basis for considering children whose presenting behaviour is a focus for professional concern. The expertise of the teacher means that the concern about the behaviour of one child can be set in the context of normal development for a child of that age and ability. Secondly, teachers are the only group in regular, virtually daily, contact with children about whom there may be concern, so a teacher is able to make a detailed observation of a child often in a variety of situations and a variety of interactions with peers and adults. Thirdly and most importantly, there is no other group which has such regular daily contact with large numbers of children of a given age group, so, as a group, teachers are able to place their observations of children about whom there are concerns in a context of training in child development and practical regular experience of the normal range of children's behaviour. Therefore the observation of a teacher that a child is different from his or her peers in specified ways is a powerful one (Peake, 1996b). Most teachers enter the profession because they like children and they feel they have a contribution to make to promoting the development and learning of children. Their primary task is that of teaching. Individually, teachers encounter child abuse rarely but, when they do, they are usually enormously troubled by the situation of the child and the consequences for that child. An informal survey of teachers revealed the kind of help the teachers need via the sort of questions they ask:

- What was the reason the child's name was put on the child protection register?
- What is the nature of the category under which the child's name is registered?
- Who is the social worker?
- Can I read the background file notes?
- Who needs to know?
- Who will be involved in the core group?
- Does the child know that the teacher has been informed about the concerns?
- What can and cannot be said to the child?
- What can and cannot be said to the parents?
- Is there any potential threat to the child?
- Is there any threat from the child's family to people helping the child?
- Who else is involved?
- What are the roles of the workers in the different agencies?
- What is the child protection plan for this child?
- What do social services want me as a teacher to do?
- How is it envisaged that I as a teacher can help this child?
- What do I do if the child is disruptive or withdrawn?
- What are the limits to the talk or behaviours that the child may produce?

- What talk or behaviours should a teacher record and pass on to the social worker?
- How should a teacher answer the child's questions with regard to what has happened in the past or what might be happening as a consequence of a recognition of the abuse of the child?
- How should the teacher respond to a child talking in some detail about what has happened?
- Should records be kept?
- Where should the records be kept?
- Do the child's family have a right to see the records?
- What support is there for the child during weekends and school holidays?
- What support is there for the teacher helping the child?
- What happens when the child's name comes off the child protection register?

Joseph, Kathleen, Gavin, Paul and Louisa are all children in our schools, and what we learn from teachers is that, when the circumstances of abuse to children become known in their class, this has a huge emotional impact on the teachers. Child abuse raises huge anxieties for staff in schools. These anxieties focus not only on what is thought to be best for the child, but also on issues of the teacher's own sense of professional and personal confidence. Teachers will frequently ask, 'Why didn't we know?' and 'Could we have done more?' The help that teachers say they need to assist children on the child protection register is as follows.

1 Teachers need information about what has happened to the child, what the child protection plans are and how information should be managed.
2 Teachers need to know who is part of the professional network around the child and what are the respective roles of the workers involved. They need to know who they can contact, how to do so and under what circumstances.
3 It is clear that teachers recognise that they need guidance if they are to help children about whom there are child protection concerns. Inter-agency training events are particularly welcome as they offer contact with other staff from different agencies, insight into the roles of other workers, information and opportunities to discuss issues and develop ideas.
4 Last but not least, teachers will need advice on resources to help the children. Resources can include additional help in the classroom, time and support to attend case conferences and core planning groups, and materials appropriate, in terms of age, gender, ability, ethnicity and culture, for work with the child.

## Teachers helping children

There is much that teachers can do to help children with histories of child abuse. The role of teachers to promote the development of children and encourage them to learn can have many facets which are helpful to abused children. For some abused children, school is such an oasis in which the routines, rules and demands are clear, that all they want is to appear to be the same as everyone else, and many gain a great deal from simply that. For others, the consequences of being abused weigh so heavily that they have no peace of mind and there is a deterioration in the child's emotions and abilities to learn and behave. Teachers can help these children in a number of ways.

First and foremost, the contribution of a teacher lies in motivating children to learn and to make progress in all areas of the curriculum. For children who have been neglected and abused and who have all too often felt worthless and a failure, success in school can be one of the means of regaining a sense of pride in one's achievements. Improved educational functioning increases a child's capacity to deal with the world around them.

Second, the ways in which teachers manage children as individuals can do a great deal to build their sense of self-confidence and self-esteem. For abused children this is a critical area. Many feel that they are the only child in the world that this has happened to and blame themselves for what has happened. Teachers can help to rebuild children's sense of self-esteem by being careful to praise the child for both efforts and achievements. They can, by giving the child appropriate responsibilities within the classroom setting, support the child to make a contribution to the class and to gain some confidence by so doing.

Third, if there are problems for children with histories of abuse, some of the problems often lie in the relationships between the child and other children and adults. A child who knows that he or she has not been safe with the people who are most close, and has been abused, will find it hard to make other relationships. Teachers can help by demonstrating to the child and to the other children in the class that they are able to make a distinction between the problems which the behaviour of the child may bring to the school situation and the child as a person, by always making it clear that the child as a person is valued. Other children will take their cues from the teacher. Teachers can, by a sensitive use of small group work and children working in pairs, do much to create situations where the child is able to cope socially with peers and perhaps begin to build relationships.

Fourth, all schools do much to teach all children basic social skills. For a child who has known nothing but abuse, the routines and rules of school can help the child become more socialised. What is important is that, when abused children do have difficulty in coping with the routines and rules, the way in which their difficulties are managed will be what makes the difference. They may need more repetition to learn basic social skills, more explanations, more help and more understanding. With all of these comes the message to the child and to other children that this child is valued.

Fifth, particularly when children's names are first placed on the child protection register, it may be the first time that the school is aware of the abuse that the child has endured. A crisis may well have participated the need to apply child protection procedures and this is often a time of heightened concern, changes and intervention in the lives of children and families. For an abused child, each day leaving home where there have been such difficulties, or leaving an alternative home placement, can be a struggle as he or she goes to school to face a high level of complex demands. Teachers can do much to help children who find coming to school difficult by the way in which the children are welcomed to the school. A few minutes of one-to-one contact aimed at welcoming the child to the classroom and orienting the child with regard to what is expected of him or her can help the child believe that he or she is welcome and that a new day has dawned and that he or she can be successful.

Sixth, some schools and teachers are able to offer children counselling. For some children it can help to have a regular and reliable time set aside when there is the opportunity to have one-to-one attention. Some secondary schools have teacher counsellors on their staff who are able to offer children regular individual sessions. It can help a child to know that there is someone in the school setting to whom they can go, who knows what they have had to deal with and is available to talk to them and most important of all, to listen to them.

Seventh, even if abused children can start each day at school with some optimism, many have such difficulties that they go through a stage where little can be achieved. For abused children whose days in school do not go well, it can be helpful to have a planned daily review for five or ten minutes with their class teacher or form tutor at the end of the school day. The child can be helped to pinpoint some successful aspect of the day and to talk about what has gone wrong. If the review can be carried out in an atmosphere which is seen by the child to be supportive of them as an individual, it can be used as an opportunity to discuss alternative strategies for the next day. The child then can go home with a sense of their teacher taking a balanced view of their performance in school and investing with them in the likelihood that they will do better the next day.

Eighth, teachers are experts on children's learning and behaviour. The assessment of a child by a teacher is worth a great deal. On the basis of the judgement of the teacher, children can be referred to specialists and education support services such as behaviour support teams, specialist teachers and educational psychologists.

Ninth, one of the sad features of the lives of children with histories of abuse is that their experience of abuse leaves them vulnerable. It can be this vulnerability that is seized upon by other abusers at other times in their lives. Sadly, a percentage of abused children go on to be abused by other people at other times in their lives. With support, some teachers are willing to work with children on prevention programmes specifically designed to free them from their sense of self-doubt and to work with them in ways which would make them less needy and less vulnerable in the future. At Key Stage 1, the National Curriculum states that children should 'know about personal safety for example, know that individuals have rights over their own bodies and that there are differences between good and bad touches, begin to develop simple skills and practices which will maintain personal safety' (David, 1993).

Finally, teachers have a key role to play in terms of monitoring children whose names are on the child protection register. Teachers can, by their daily contact with the children, be in a position to observe the child and monitor the effect of the child protection plans. These observations will be a key contribution to the work of any core planning group and to the safety of the child.

There is much that teachers can do to help Joseph, Kathleen, Gavin, Paul and Louisa. Our message is that, in order to help children, teachers need information, supportive contacts with workers from other agencies, training or guidance and resources.

## References

David, T. (1993) *Child Protection and Early Years Teachers*, Milton Keynes: Open University Press.

Department for Education Employment (1995) 'Protecting Children from Abuse: The Role of the Education Service', Circular No. 10/95.

Hallett, C. (1995) *Interagency Co-ordination in Child Protection*, London: HMSO.

Peake, A. (1996a) 'Consultation – A Model for Inter-agency Co-operation', in *Working with Sexually Abused Children*, Oxford: Oxford Brookes University, School of Education.

Peake, A. (1996b) 'Dealing with the Suspicion of Child Sexual Abuse: The Role of the Teacher', in *Working with Sexually Abused Children*, Oxford: Oxford Brookes University, School of Education.

# 12 Inter-agency training for post-registration practice

*Michael Murphy*

In this chapter consideration is given to:

- the function and responsibility of inter-agency training;
- a post-registration training strategy;
- the structure of training: blocks and pitfalls;
- planning the training;
- delivery of training; and
- suggested exercises for inter-agency post-registration training programmes.

## Introduction

This chapter will address the issues and challenges around providing positive inter-agency training to meet the practitioner training needs of those involved in post-registration work. The chapter begins by outlining the wider issues involved in understanding the proper function of training and its relationship to policy and practice. This is followed by an exploration of ways in which to establish a local Area Child Protection Committee (ACPC) training strategy. Consideration is given to structuring the training and identifying the common pitfalls that accompany training around post-registration work. The next section offers a guide for those planning inter-agency training events to assist them in their planning and preparation process. The delivery of the training is explored and facilitation, evaluation and feedback is examined. The final part of the chapter offers some suggestions about the types of exercises that might usefully be included in a training programme.

## Identifying the issues: the function and responsibility of training

Although sometimes treated as a wholly separate activity, as described in Chapter 1 of the present volume, training is in fact totally enmeshed in the whole process of child care and child protection. Training that is isolated from policy, or is introduced before policy is formulated, will not significantly affect the system. Training will be a process that involves all participants in a great deal of hard work, without always ensuring positive outcomes. The participants who attempt to put their training into practice will be frustrated by a system that is unchanged, as illustrated in the example below.

Lisa was the child protection coordinator in Northtown. Her manager indicated to her that it would be a good idea if she devised and delivered some core group training, as core groups in Northtown were working in a very spasmodic way. No policy or guidance was available, so Lisa designed the training courses with a group of practitioners from other agencies. The courses were delivered, with an enthusiastic response from participants. However, there was a low take-up of places by some of the key professionals, particularly health visitors and field social workers. One year later, in supervision, Lisa's manager suggested that the training did not seem to have made much difference: core groups were still spasmodic and of poor quality. Lisa felt very responsible, very inadequate.

If post-registration inter-agency practice is not of a high quality, or is occurring on a haphazard basis, how can training help to make a positive difference? What is the relationship of training to the proper establishment and effective running of a post-registration system? Is high-quality training the answer to the post-registration 'problem'? Is training the solution to ensuring that all practitioners and parents work cooperatively together between the initial child protection conference and the child protection review?

### The change process: the position of training

When it is established that 'something must be done' about a particular problem, training can often inappropriately figure as the immediate and convenient solution. If training is seen as the solution, future problems can be put down to the qualitative or quantitative inadequacies of the training offered, instead of the continuing difficulties within practice and management systems:

> good training will not make up for a poor system, and will not overcome major inter-agency disputes on policy or procedure. Poor quality multi-disciplinary training would in all probability exaggerate and exacerbate inter-agency problems that already exist. (Murphy, 1992: 32)

The proper role and function of training is not to provide the solution to 'something must be done', but to provide the means to inform staff about that change or solution once established: 'From a training perspective what is crucial is to establish a common set of principles about practice which then inform policy making. The aim of training is then to service and support these principles and agreements about practice' (Morrison, 1988: 21).

Although training is to do with change, training is not the vehicle to decide what that change should be, or how it should be accomplished. Neither should training be the initiator of that change once those decisions have been made. Figure 12.1 highlights the appropriate position of training for front-line practitioners within the change process. It is essential that practitioner training be allowed to maintain its proper position at stages 6 and 7, instead of being put in the 'provide solution' position of stages 2, 3, 4 and 5.

Senior managers and the ACPC have roles to play as policy makers, and middle managers as practice formulators. As outlined in Chapter 1, training can play a role in raising awareness amongst these managers of current research and guidance, enabling them to formulate policy. In the same way, training can raise the awareness amongst middle managers of current practice issues. 'Integrating training, management and practice is of particular relevance in child protection work ... where tensions between management and fieldworkers can create increased anxiety for those undertaking the face to face work' (Morrison, 1988: 21).

The role of the trainer (along with middle managers) can be to link policy and guidance to practice and to serve as a link between ACPC and practitioner. It seems clear that, if training is a vehicle to move people from actual to desired practice, that movement can only be accomplished if the training is part of a wider strategy that is rooted in a strongly mandated policy on the establishment and role of post-registration work. It is important that this policy actually makes explicit the role of the social worker and other practitioners in the core group and that this policy is 'owned' by the inter-agency system: 'training for good practice can only be effective if there is a clear framework of policy and procedures owned by the Area Child Protection Committees, not only by Social Services' (Mittler, 1997: 86).

Rather, the appropriate role of training is to complement established and agreed change by helping to energise staff's thoughts, feeling and behaviour towards that change (Figure 12.2). Training is the means by which the practitioner explores all three areas of change.

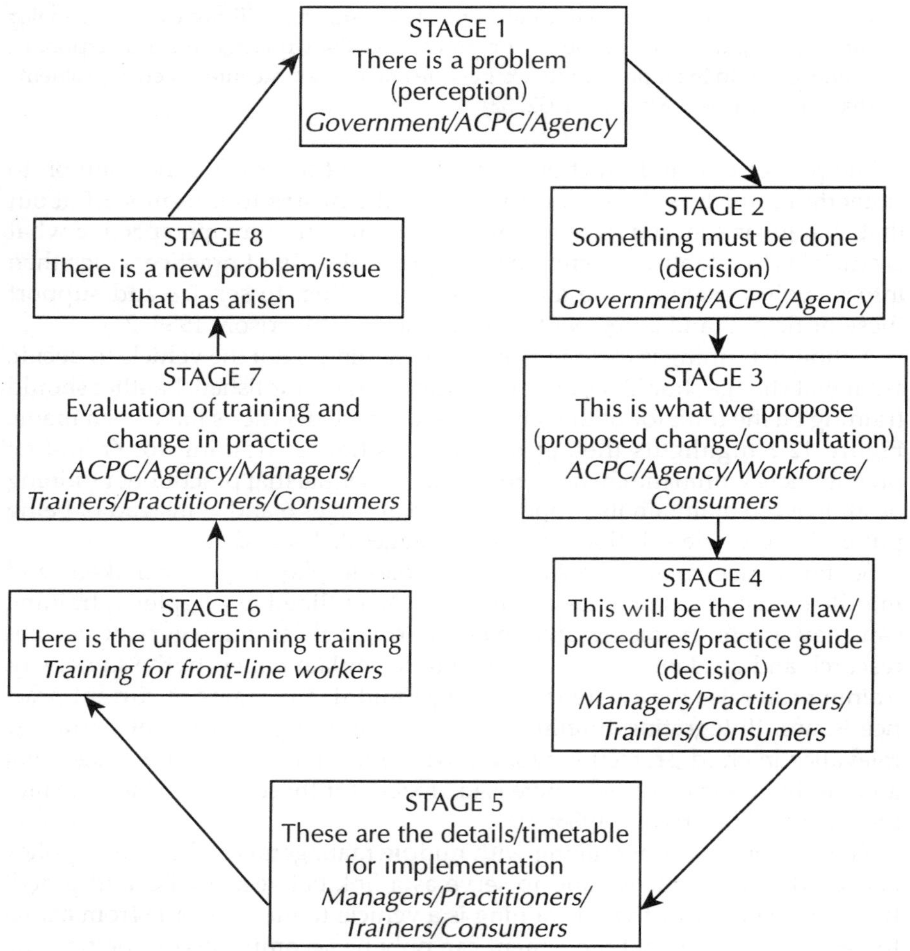


**Figure 12.1 The change process: the position of training for front-line practitioners**

# Establishing a post-registration training strategy

## The local context

In developing a positive relationship between training and the post-registration process, it is important to recognise the existence, not of a national child protection system, but of a series of highly individualised, local child protection

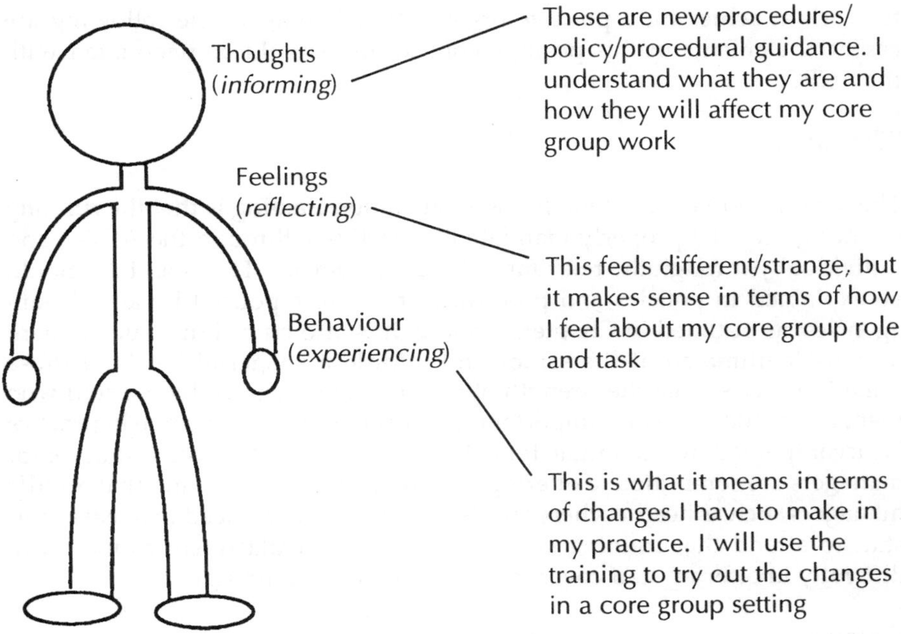
Thoughts
(*informing*)
These are new procedures/ policy/procedural guidance. I understand what they are and how they will affect my core group work
Feelings
(*reflecting*)
This feels different/strange, but it makes sense in terms of how I feel about my core group role and task
Behaviour
(*experiencing*)
This is what it means in terms of changes I have to make in my practice. I will use the training to try out the changes in a core group setting

**Figure 12.2 Training and change**

systems: 'there exists a local history, a local perspective and a local development of child protection systems, which is related to, but not controlled by, the national system' (Murphy, 1996: 131). Bingley *et al.* (1993) go further in claiming that significant differences exist even within these systems. In each of these systems, managed by its own ACPC, the post-registration process will operate in relation to local issues in a way that is different to other areas (Calder and Horwath, 1996). The relationship of training within that process will again be highly individual to each ACPC.

Is it possible to establish, in the face of such diversity, what are the common elements for positive post-registration training? It is proposed here that, even in the face of diversity of process, there are certain key areas that are held in common when organising training in this area: the organisational context, structuring the training (blocks and pitfalls), planning the training, and delivering the training. These will be dealt with individually below.

## The organisational context

When working in the training area we can focus down on training delivery and training content, but to achieve a positive training strategy it is important to work at achieving a positive organisational context. The following are essential elements in this positive context and should be negotiated with the ACPC.

### *The mandate*

The most important element in post-registration training is that the running of core groups be properly mandated, collectively through the ACPC, and individually through the relevant individual agencies. This mandate should be explained in policies and procedures that are espoused by all relevant agencies, as outlined in Chapters 1 and 2. It is also crucial that such a mandate be legitimated at the senior and middle managerial levels of those organisations, so that the strength of the mandate is agreed by the staff who manage practice. It is also important that this mandate for change in practice be accompanied by a mandate for extensive training. This means that senior managers are committed to offering training to relevant staff and that middle managers such as headteachers are also convinced of the need to release their staff to attend that training (some agencies, particularly education, have difficulty in offering staff cover for child protection training).

### *Resources*

The setting up of effective post-registration training is not a 'cheap' option for child protection systems. The training strategy ideally should consist of an incremental training programme with introductory, intermediate and more specialised courses. As well as the normal costs of venue, refreshments and training materials, there are also significant costs in terms of releasing staff for training and the cost of their cover as well as the costs of trainers.

If the training is to be planned and facilitated by members of staff, it is important that they be afforded sufficient time to plan, prepare and debrief. If external trainers are commissioned to deliver the training it is important that they be afforded the time to really get to know the system that they are working with, particularly its practice, policies and history around post-registration practice.

### *Support*

It is not sufficient for the training team to be sent away to 'get on with it'. The training must be supported by the ACPC. This means a commitment to releasing staff both to deliver and to attend the courses and ensuring that staff are prepared before the training and given opportunities to discuss the implications of the training for developing their practice. The training team need support and consultation from a training manager or coordinator, to help with difficulties in the training process, but they also need support and consultation from a practice manager with up-to-date experience of how the core group system is working.

## Structuring the training: blocks and pitfalls

### Wider strategy v. single course

As is evident from the chapters in this book, post-registration work is a complex area of practice. Practitioners require knowledge of local and national guidance, skills to apply this knowledge to practice and the attitudes that promote working together with other professionals' children and their families. Training can only be delivered effectively if the training delivered is constructed to meet the identified needs. This requires those responsible for planning and delivering the training to design a training strategy that considers ways of addressing the training needs of different workers within the ACPC. For example, a police officer may not have a great deal of involvement in core groups and may consequently require a half-day or one-day course to raise his or her awareness of the framework for protecting children on the child protection register. Other professionals may require a great deal more training. For example, social workers, health visitors and class teachers will need training regarding their own and others' roles and responsibilities, ways in which core groups operate, working in partnership with other workers, children and families, undertaking comprehensive assessments and designing and implementing child protection plans.

Below we have a suggested inter-agency training strategy for post-registration practice for front-line workers, designed by Jan Horwath.

#### *Foundation training*

*Target group* All those who are likely to be working with children and families, directly or indirectly, where the child's name is on the child protection register.

*Aims of training* To raise participants' awareness of post-registration guidelines and procedures; to enable participants to understand their own roles and responsibilities in the post-registration phase.

*Approach to training* Incorporate into inter-agency foundation courses designed to raise participants' awareness of *Working Together* (DoH, 1991).

### *Focused training*

*Target group* Professionals who have attended foundation training and are likely to be engaged directly in post-registration work with children and families.

*Aims of training* To enable participants to apply the guidelines and procedures to promote effective practice; to clarify the roles and responsibilities of the various workers engaged in post-registration practice; to develop skills in working in partnership with other professionals, children and their families; to identify methods and begin to develop skills in assessment, intervention and evaluation as part of a child protection plan.

*Approach to training* Inter-agency training courses for 1–3 days, focusing specifically on post-registration practice.

### *Specialist courses*

*Target groups* Those who have completed foundation and focused training and are regularly engaged in post-registration work.

*Aims of training* To develop knowledge, values and skills in particular areas of post-registration practice, such as (1) managing conflict within core groups, (2) working with non-compliant families, (3) working with families that show no indication of change when voluntary arrangements are not sufficient to protect the child.

*Approach to training* Inter-agency courses of 1–3 days' duration that focus on a specific topic, for example comprehensive assessments.

## The single disciplinary v. multidisciplinary debate

Even in ACPC areas that enjoy a strong commitment to multidisciplinary working, the establishment of core group policy reanimates the debate about who should control the core group process and who should do which pieces of work. A good policy should address this issue, giving clear guidelines for organising core group work.

In its wake this issue also revitalises the debate concerning the relative merits of single disciplinary and multidisciplinary training programmes. If core groups are to be a truly shared, multidisciplinary effort, the arguments for training staff together in a multidisciplinary context seem undeniable. However, because the roles of keyworker, chairman and main 'assessor' often rest with the same person (the field social worker), single disciplinary training for field social workers may also be necessary.

Though field social work staff hold specific roles within the core group, it seems preferable that they are trained in those roles whilst operating in the same multidisciplinary context that they will be working in in practice. Thus, if they find in the training that they are operating at a different level or with a different burden of responsibility than their colleagues, this is, in fact, excellent experience of the 'real' world of core groups.

## Planning the training

### Planning and preparing before the event

With any training event, an important factor in its eventual success is that the event be well planned and prepared. On the macro level, it is important that the ordering/commissioning group give some guidance on all the questions which we list below. It is important, particularly with new training, to establish a multidisciplinary training group to plan the training. Although this group needs to pay careful attention to what the 'purchaser' needs, it is also important that the 'provider' group be left with sufficient flexibility to be creative and to deal with the (inevitable) hitches and unexpected happenings that arise.

The questions below focus on areas to be considered in training preparation.

#### *What is the remit?*

What are your staff's training needs (as indicated in your Training Needs Analysis)?
What are the expectations of the ACPC and the training sub-committee about the training?
What do the policies and procedures of the ACPC need the training to achieve?

#### *Who is to be trained?*

How many courses are to run in total?
What is the ideal number of participants per course?
Who is most likely to be involved in core groups?
Which groups of staff should have priority?
Should managers be selected initially?
Which areas should have priority?
What will be the right group mix and how should we allocate available places?

### *Who is going to advertise and administer the training?*

Who is to administer, where and how, the training advertising and training nomination system?
Who is going to be responsible for the general administration (letters, photocopying, room booking) of the courses?

### *Who is to train and how many times?*

How is the group going to allocate the training work to individual members?
Are some group members going to be more involved in preparing or facilitating?
If different levels of training are planned, are different group members to be attached to different levels?

### *Where should the training take place?*

What will be the best venue for the training? Consider accessibility, price, comfort, availability and numbers to be trained.

### *How much training or planning time is available?*

If there is clarity about who should attend the training, work out the length of the events using proposed group size and trainer availability and training resources. Usually, very short training events can offer a fast throughput of staff for reduced cost. However, long-term changes in inter-agency values, beliefs and practice are not easy to achieve with this model. Long-term changes in manager/practitioner/inter-agency behaviour require longer courses, smaller groups and more resources.

### *What should the content and methods of training be?*

Before being able to work out the content and methods of the course it is important to spend some time considering and agreeing course objectives. Course objectives inform you and the participants where they should be by the end of the course; content and method are the vehicle used for the journey. It is very important that the content and method 'fit' the objectives.

### *Content*

In post-registration training, the content of the training should include the wider information and history of post-registration practice in our child protection system (Chapter 1 of the present volume can be used for this purpose); it should also encompass all the guidance, procedures, issues and difficulties around core groups from the local area. The content of the training must facilitate the exploration of the beginning, middle and end of core groups, the difficulties of forming partnerships with other practitioners, parents and children and, most importantly, must consider the whole balance between assessment, protection and therapy.

## *Ground to be covered*

Although the decision on what should be included within training must rest with the local training group, the following are areas of concentration that most groups will consider:

- what a post-registration practice is, what a core group is (definitions and boundaries);
- history and research concerning post-registration practice (the wider picture);
- national guidance (or lack of!), local policies, procedures and guidance about core group practice ('how we do things here');
- good beginnings – making a positive start at conference and the first core group meeting;
- how to include parents positively in the core group process;
- how to include the child's perspective within the core group process;
- how to deal with inter-agency and intrafamilial conflict;
- an exploration of the assessment process (why, who, what can we all contribute?);
- dealing with crises;
- reporting back to review.

## *Method*

It is important in all training events over a half-day in duration to try to achieve a balance of method. This balance will vary according to the course, but should include informing (including theoretical input, new guidance and procedures), reflecting – allowing participants to reflect on the new information and experience (often including discussion in pairs or small groups) and experiencing, which will allow participants to experience directly aspects of the process under discussion (this will normally be achieved in experiential exercises).

In core group training, the informing will be all about core groups; the reflecting will be about core groups in general and linking training material to personal experience in core groups; the experiencing must involve the group simulation of the core group process so that participants can experience being part of a core group.

### *What materials and handouts do we need?*

Materials and handouts will be suggested by the content and methods that the course uses. Traditionally, most materials will be related to the informing part of the course. These materials need to be clear, brief, attractive and easy to read and understand. They should follow the 'track' of the content in the course, but can also offer more complex material that the participant can read later.

There is an increasing appreciation that good material can also enhance the learning offered in the reflecting and experiencing parts of the course. So a good summary, quiz or a list of extra questions can help the participant to reflect, and clear, written guidance for an experiential exercise can better help the participant take on the part they have to play.

## Delivering the Training

The training team will need, as a minimum, handouts that include (1) copies of core group policy and all procedural and practice guides, (2) all the information presented at conference, on a family that is about to go through the core group process, and (3) information on the progress of core group work, preferably including a 'crisis' and a report to a review.

## Facilitating and running the course

A training course is an event where disparate groups of people come together to undertake a task. An inter-agency child protection training course brings together disparate practitioners and managers to work together in a cooperative, positive manner. In this a training course exactly mirrors child protection practice. This positive working together is not an automatic process and to a large extent is facilitated and developed by those responsible for running the course. Preparation, a good programme and good material will all prove extremely helpful, but in the end the quality and ability of the training team are also crucial. The other important factor is the training group, and the process that the group goes through in the training course.

Box 12.1 shows a checklist for trainers, to be used before and during the training event.

### Evaluation and feedback to the organisation

It is important that information about the course and what it reveals about practice be fed back to the larger ACPC and to individual agencies. Where a course is new, when a course is based on new guidance or procedures, the training will be a key indicator of how the changes will go down in practice. Feedback from courses is often used to alter positively and develop new guidance and procedures.

As well as immediate feedback after the course, consideration should be given to establishing a follow-up evaluation three to six months after the event, to establish whether the training has influenced practice in the long term.

## Suggested exercises for post-registration training

What follows is a series of training exercises that may be used flexibly to organise a one, two, three or four-day training event. As regards training for *managers*, although you may wish to consider all the following, exercises 1, 2, 4(b), 6, 10 and 11 might prove particularly useful. For *keyworkers*, all exercises may be used, but exercises 2, 4(b), 5, 7, 9 and 10 may be particularly useful.

**Exercise 1: you, me, perfect harmony**

Use: this exercise can be used at any early stage in courses over one day

Timing: 35 minutes

Aim: to explore the myths about individuals working in an inter-agency way

Materials: flipchart and pens

Structure: an exercise in three parts

Part one
Ask the participants to recall one positive interaction that they have had within the last two years with a practitioner or manager from another agency (preferably within the child protection system, but if necessary in their private lives).
What was the key element about that interaction that made it so positive?

Part two
Ask the participants to find a partner from a different team/agency and share their interaction/key element.

**Box 12.1 Checklist for Trainers**

*Before the course*

Which trainers are available?

Do they reflect the 'mix' of agencies participating in the course?

Will they work well together/complement each other's training styles?

Has a full trainer's programme been prepared?

Have the training team worked out who is responsible for which pieces of the programme?

Have the training team checked who has been nominated for the course and whether there are any problems with the venue?

Have the training team got a contingency plan in case something goes wrong (for example, a disruptive or distressed participant)?

Have the training team considered how they are going to address issues to do with diversity (such as issues of race or disability)?

Have the training team prepared the venue: chairs in a circle, equipment working, right temperature, lighting and so on?

*At the beginning of the course*

Has the participant seen or heard the course objectives?

Does the participant want to be there?

Has the participant been able to introduce himself/herself to the group?

Have the training team introduced themselves to the group?

Have the training team established a series of rules or conventions aimed at keeping the group safe?

Have the training team found out what the participants' individual training needs are?

Have the training team undertaken an initial problem-spotting exercise (preferably during the preparatory phase)?

*During the course*

How are the group's morale and levels of energy?

How much 'buzzing', laughter and smiling is around?

Is the theoretical material pitched at the right level?

Are any participants struggling personally or professionally?

Are any personality clashes developing?

Are any serious inter-agency disputes developing?

Are the training team managing to keep to time boundaries?

Are the training team being supportive of each other?

Is the balance of informing, reflecting and experiencing right for this group?

*At the end of the course*

Have participants been able to reflect on the course as a whole?

Have participants been encouraged to form a 'bridge' between the course and how the course experience will be used in work practice?

Have participants been able to comment on their future training needs?

Have participants been made aware of sources of future help?

Have participants been able to evaluate the course fully?

Have participants been able to say their good-byes to the trainers and the group?

Have the training team been able to evaluate the course, the training materials and their performance as a team?

Part three

Divide the flipchart paper into two. Ask the participants to feed back, not the interaction, but what made it so positive. Feedback usually consists of being welcomed/valued/included/listened to, and of the other practitioner being positive/sympathetic/doing what they say and so on. Write the positive elements on the left-hand side of the paper.

Ask the participants to speculate on what might be the key element to negative interactions. You will find that these negative interactions will be a mirror image of the positive ones. If helpful, list the mirror image negative interactions, in a different coloured pen, on the opposite side of the flipchart.

Key learning points

1 One of the most difficult issues in core groups is the constant need to re-establish positive relationships in multidisciplinary groups, with practitioners that we don't know.

2 One of the most powerful and pervasive myths in this area of work is that 'I will only be welcomed and valued in the core group because of my child protection knowledge and expertise.' In fact I will be valued far more for my personal skills in including, valuing and cooperating with the other members of the group than for my child protection expertise.

**Exercise 2: making a good beginning**

Use: this exercise is a useful beginning exercise, used to focus participants' awareness on positive practice at the start of the process

Timing: 45 minutes

Aim: to explore the beginnings of the core group and to locate the core group in the context of the child protection conference

Materials: a case study with information/conclusions from a 'typical' child protection case conference should be available (If real case material is used, please ensure that the identity of the real child and family are protected)

Structure: an exercise in three parts

Part one

Split into groups of 6 –10. Ask the groups to read the case study information that has been collated at the end of the conference.

Part two

Ask the groups to imagine that they are the practitioners involved in the conference:

(a) Who should be involved in the core group?

(b) What should be the main elements of the work that the conference asks the core group to do?

(c) Did the groups experience any disagreement? How did they deal with this?

Part three

Take general feedback from the groups, check differences and difficult areas for later exploration.

Key learning points

1 The key to a positive core group lies in what happens within the conference.
2 A good conference should not just spend its time sharing information, but should also spend time considering decisions, and what should happen after the conference.
3 The seeds for serious disagreement are often sown at the conference stage (as are the methods of conflict resolution).

**Exercise 3: what is this thing called 'core group'?**

Use: another early, focusing exercise

Timing: 35 minutes

Aim: to establish for the group what a core group is

Materials: flipchart and pens, information on local policy and practice guidance

Structure: an exercise in two parts

Part one
Split into small inter-agency groups. Take 20 minutes to consider:
(a) What is a core group?
(b) What is the task and function of the core group?
(c) Who should be in a core group?

Part two
Participants feed back in the main group. Trainers input relevant information from local policy and practice guidance.

Key learning points

1 The definition of a core group is not externally defined, but is defined within local practice and procedure. In the same way, the task of the core group and the details of how it should work are for local determination.
2 The membership of a core group (apart from parents, possibly child, and keyworker) is always a compromise between the need to keep numbers in the group low, and the need to include those with a crucial role with regard to the family.

**Exercise 4(a): first meeting/making the protection plan**

Use: a crucial exercise for all longer, experiential training; use early

Timing: 60 minutes

Aim: to allow the group to experience the task of formulating a workable protection plan

Materials: flipchart, pens, family case study, individual family roles, child protection plan pro forma (if available)

Structure: an exercise in three parts

Part one
In the wider group, outline the policy with regard to child protection plans. Give out copies of the policy and of the protection plan pro forma (if available). Distribute family case study and roles.

Part two
In groups of 5–10, give everyone a core group role (this should include family roles). Ask each group to 'run' a first core group meeting, including the preparation of the child protection plan.
(It may be necessary to offer assistance/instruction to the keyworker, such as 'take your time/do not feel you've got to get everything perfect', and to family members, such as 'do not over-act'.)

Part three
Ask the groups to feed back:
(a) how the process went, what were the easy/difficult/confusing tasks and interactions.
(b) the details of their plan. (This is much less important than (a).)

Key learning points
1 The making of a child protection plan is a difficult process and one that cannot be rushed.
2 The content of the plan should include the order of work from the conference, and agreements that cover the protective, assessment and therapeutic needs of the child and family.
3 The making of the plan is also an important first step in trying to ensure that the core group works together in a cooperative fashion, a positive process is as important as a positive plan.
4 Try to avoid using the words 'monitor', 'support' and 'supervise' in the plan, as these words are understood very differently by different practitioners, and can mask great differences in expectation and practice.

**Exercise 4(b): first meeting/making the protection plan (keyworker version)**

Use: a crucial exercise for all longer, experiential training; use early; this version is adapted for use on keyworker training courses

Timing: 80 minutes

Aim: to allow the group of keyworkers to experience the task of formulating a workable protection plan and to explore some of the crucial issues for keyworkers/core group chairmen

Materials: flipchart, pens, family case study, individual family roles, policy/procedure/practice guidance, child protection plan pro forma (if available); it would also be extremely useful to have very short handouts on how groups work and on chairing skills

Structure: an exercise in three parts

Part one
Remind the group of the policy with regard to child protection plans. Give out copies of the policy/procedure/practice guidance and of the protection plan pro forma (if available). Distribute family case study and roles. Distribute handouts on groups and chairing skills.

Part two
Split the large group into two (groups of 5–10) and make one group A, the other B. Ask for two (more experienced) staff in each group to volunteer to be keyworker/chairman and chairman's assistant. Emphasise the fact that they are not going to be required to do a perfect job, but are there to help the group to learn. Give everyone else a core group role (this should include family roles).
Ask each group to 'run' a first core group meeting, including the preparation of the child protection plan.
(It may be necessary to offer assistance/instruction to the keyworker, such as 'take your time/do not feel you've got to get everything perfect', and to family members, such as 'do not overact'.)
Ask the chairman and assistant in group A to concentrate solely on getting the task done (the plan finished).
Ask the chairman and assistant in group B to concentrate solely on the process of the group, ensuring that everyone feels welcome, included and committed to the group; completing the task is of secondary importance.

Part three
Ask the groups to feed back:

(a) how group A chairmen and participants experienced (i) joining the core group; (ii) being part of a group with a total focus on the task; (iii) what were the interactions between chairmen/participants/parents; (iv) the content of the plan.
(b) how group B experienced (i) joining a core group; (ii) being part of a group concentrating solely on process; (iii) what were the interactions between chairmen/participants/parents; (iv) the details of their plan.
(c) which pieces of both groups' experience would they, as keyworkers, like to save?

Key learning points

1 The making of a child protection plan is a difficult process and one that cannot be rushed.
2 The content of the plan should include the order of work from the conference, and agreements that cover the protective, assessment and therapeutic needs of the child and family.
3 The making of the plan is also an important first step in trying to ensure that the core group works together in a cooperative fashion, a positive process is as important as a positive plan.
4 Try to avoid using the words 'monitor', 'support' and 'supervise' in the plan, as these words are understood very differently by different practitioners, and can mask great differences in expectation and practice.
5 Most important for keyworkers, the core group process involves maintaining the complex balance between task and process.
  Task brings focus and organisation, and ensures that work tasks are completed. However, if we concentrate solely on task at the expense of group process, we risk promoting resistance, alienation and conflict within the group.
  Process brings cooperative working and commitment. However, if we concentrate only on process, we run the risk of not being focused, not completing the task and sometimes 'losing' the protection of the child as a focus.

**Exercise 5: being a parent in the child protection system**

Use: a very important exercise, best used in the middle order of the course; as with any exercise that includes an element of guided fantasy, extra care should be taken to try to look after the group

Timing: 30 minutes

Aim: to raise awareness of the parents' perspective on the core group process

Materials: none

Structure: an exercise in three parts

Part one
In the large group, ask the participants to recall one minor professional mistake that they have made that no one else became aware of. Invite them to imagine that they are sitting at work one day when their manager calls them into their office. Just before they enter the room, they become aware that several other managers are present and that they have learned of the mistake and are about to discuss it. What are their feelings at this time?

Part two
In pairs for five minutes, share those feelings (not the professional mistakes).

Part three
In the large group, ask the participants to share some of those feelings (not the professional mistakes).

Key learning points
1 Parental behaviour in core groups is very understandable and is common when parents feel either enraged, threatened or disempowered.
2 The aim and skill of positive core group working is to form a positive partnership despite the above.

**Exercise 6: assessment and core groups**

Use: this exercise is useful in the middle part of a course

Timing: 60 minutes

Aim: to allow participants to explore the desirability of doing family assessments in a multidisciplinary way; also to explore where assessment fits into the core group process, and vice versa

Materials: none

Structure: an exercise in three parts

Part one
It is important for the trainer to explain the definition and history of child protection assessment. This might begin with assessment's stage of low priority

(1974–85), moving through an 'Orange Book'/social services only stage (1985–95) and ending with the need to expand the assessment base to include other practitioners.

Part two
Split the participants into the same groups as for exercises 2 and 4(a) (preferably maintaining the same roles). Ask them to decide which pieces of the assessment could be undertaken by which practitioner. What are the areas of 'crossover' and what pieces of the assessment might prove difficult to organise?

Part three
Each group is to feed back how it has organised the assessment tasks.

Key learning points
1 Just as families have contact with many different agency systems, just as the core group is made up of different practitioners, so too the assessment process should be shared between the relevant practitioners from different agencies.
2 It may be that the group decides that one part of the assessment should be undertaken by a practitioner who is not part of the core group. If this is the case, it is important that a member of the group be allocated to check that it is done and the information is fed back into the core group.

**Exercise 7: working with the crisis**

Use: useful on longer courses, beyond the halfway point

Timing: 60–90 minutes

Aim: to remind practitioners that the core group process is still about the protection of vulnerable children, and about making continuing collective judgements about child safety

Materials: for this exercise you will need written material about the child care 'crisis' within the case study family (this may involve an incident of neglect, of family violence, the presence of a schedule one offender and so on); this should be brought to the core group by one or more of the practitioners involved in the case scenario

Structure: an exercise in two parts

Part one
Ask the participants to go back into their core groups. Say that, in the middle of the core group process, the family have encountered a child protection crisis. Ask them to share the information provided and hold an emergency core group meeting.

Part two
Take feedback from the groups about the process, content and outcome of their meeting. This may focus on:
(a) how this crisis affected their partnership with parents;
(b) whether the group felt comfortable challenging parents on the crisis issue;
(c) whether a 'line' was drawn about future action/further crises and, if so, how this affected the core group.

Key Learning Points
1 As well as having an assessment/family work function, the core group still holds a more important protective function. Sometimes, particularly when work with parents is going well, this function can be ignored. All serious child protection concerns must be acted upon by the core group.
2 This crisis can be very painful for both parents and practitioners, particularly if the core group felt that it was making progress.
3 Sometimes crises can be used positively. Some families react to the crisis by becoming committed to the process for the first time and by becoming interested in exploring the possibility of change.

**Exercise 8: discovering the child's voice**

Use: this exercise and the next to be used in the middle of longer courses

Timing: 45 minutes

Aim: to allow participants to discover and explore the child's experience of abusive situations
**NB** As with all exercises that include an element of guided fantasy or childhood experience, take much care with its use. Encourage people to keep safe or to withdraw from the exercise if it becomes too difficult.

Materials: paper and crayons

Structure: an exercise in three parts

Part one
Distribute blank pieces of paper and crayons. Ask the participants to imagine a time as a younger person when an adult let them down in a minor way, and to draw a picture of that event on the paper.
(a) What were the feelings of the child in the picture?
(b) Could that child have sought help from an adult about that experience? If not, why not?
(c) What response would the child have expected or needed from that safe adult?

Part two
Find a partner and share (a)–(c).

Part three
In the larger group, ask participants if they would like to share the issues brought up in the exercise. Concentrate on (b) and (c).
Do not ask participants to share their individual stories, but ask them to share the child's feelings, perceptions and, most importantly, how the child would want their perspective to be made more powerful.

Key learning points
1 We all have experience of the child's perspective; we have all been let down, as children, by adults.
2 It is normal for the child's perspective or perceptions to remain hidden or ignored by adults.
3 That perception is not likely to be simple (an either/or choice).
4 Frequently grown-ups take decisions about the best interests of children without consulting them at all.

**Exercise 9: making the child's voice powerful**

Use: mid-to-late position in longer courses

Timing: 50 minutes

Aim: 'The greatest hurt is the secondary victimisation which occurs when children find themselves both empowered and still helpless, and when their enlightened cries fall upon deaf ears' (Summit, 1983: 451). Even when the child's perspective is heard, it is very difficult for it to become powerful within the adult system; this exercise explores how to help the child's perspective become more powerful

Materials: a letter/tape/picture from the child in the case study explaining their perspective on the family situation

Structure: an exercise in two parts

Part one

In groups, get one participant (probably the chairman's assistant) to act as an advocate on behalf of the child. Ask the person to deliver the child's message and then to get the group to return to it on each occasion that they drift into an adult, ignoring style.

**NB** It is possible to combine this exercise with exercises 4(a), 4(b) or 7.

Part two

Ask the chairman and participants what difference the presence of the child's perspective made.

Ask the child's advocate (a) how easy/difficult was the task of offering the child's perspective; (b) whether the group was able to take note of the perspective or how powerful the child's voice was; (c) what would be the pros and cons for the child of being present at the core group meeting.

Key learning points

1 It is extremely difficult, even with separate representation, to make the child's voice powerful in the system.
2 The child's perspective is not simple and is frequently different from that of parents and practitioners.
3 The child's direct presence within the meeting (and this can sometimes be very painful for the child) does not equate with giving the child a voice. It is making the child's message powerful that is the key to success.

**Exercise 10: working with conflict**

Use: to be used after the halfway stage in the course

Timing: 40 minutes

Aim: to allow participants to explore the roots of and possible solutions to conflict within the core group

Materials: flipchart and pens

Structure: an exercise in five parts

Part one
Split into small inter-agency groups. Consider for 15 minutes why core groups encounter conflict, and what types of conflict are most common.

Part two
Feed back to the larger group. Expect some of the following answers: conflict between parents, conflict between parents and practitioners, conflict between chairman and practitioners, inter-agency conflict, personality clashes and so on.

Part three
Trainer input: child abuse and family violence are all to do with intrafamilial conflict. This frequently involves one or more adults using their power to get their needs met at the expense of the needs of weaker members of the family. If this conflict is an intrinsic part of the family dynamics, it is natural for that conflict to be played out in the core group. Furthermore, it is to be expected that this conflict may be mirrored in conflict that arises between practitioners in the core group. To a large extent, the core group will attempt to measure and resolve the worst aspects of conflict within the family, but to do this they will also have to deal with conflicts that arise between practitioners.

Part four
Using the family case study that you have been working with, ask course participants to volunteer to be family members and 'sculpt' the basis of their family conflict in front of the group. Then ask other members of the group to volunteer to be the practitioners involved with the family. Ask the group which practitioner would be most likely to identify with which family member. Place the practitioner behind the family member with a hand on their shoulder. Ask the practitioners to voice the possible basis of their conflict: for example, 'you're being too critical/not understanding/not protecting/not listening to my family member'. Let the practitioners voice this conflict for a couple of minutes.
Ask the family members what is happening to them while the practitioners engage in conflict.

Part five
What next? Ask the group involved in the sculpt to remain in their positions. Ask the rest of the group to explore and suggest positive ways of moving the conflict on and negative actions that might make it worse. Record both sets of ideas on a flipchart. On the positive side, suggestions may include being inclusive, being honest without being judgemental, exploring difficulties in the group (sometimes without the family being present), getting behind the

conflict to check the different perspectives, exploring compromise, and so on. On the negative side, suggestions may include doing nothing, ignoring the conflict, scapegoating a practitioner or family member, not attending the next meeting, siding with the family member against the rest of the group, and so on.

Key learning points

1 Conflict within core groups is to be expected.
2 Frequently, that conflict will mirror conflict in the family.
3 Denying, minimising or ignoring conflict is not a successful tactic.
4 Exploring/discussing/establishing the basis of the conflict may help the professional and family group reach a positive conclusion.

**Exercise 11: preparing for review**

Use: this exercise should be used near to the end of longer courses

Timing: 40–50 minutes

Aim: to help participants understand or experience the link between the core group and the review conference

Materials: original case study and child protection plan, flipchart, review conference pro forma (if available)

Structure: an exercise in two parts

Part one

Ask the larger groups to split into small groups (see exercises 4(a), 4(b), 7 and 9).

Ask the groups to run a final, pre-review core group meeting.

Ask them (with or without pro-forma) to review the child protection plan, review the work done and the progress made since their initial meeting.

Ask them to decide the key themes of a collective report back to the review conference.

Part two

In the larger group, what were the easy and difficult elements of that final meeting?

Key learning points

1 The review conference (as with the initial child protection conference) is an important part of the core group process.
2 The difficulty/skills involved in organising positive cooperative work continue right until the end of the process.

## Conclusion

This chapter has attempted to join the wish to improve post-registration practice with a full discussion on what post-registration training might have to offer the systems it serves. It has then considered the establishment of a training strategy and how those responsible for training might avoid negative or counterproductive elements in that strategy. Finally, we have outlined the key stages and elements in developing and facilitating positive training events. Although good training backed up by good procedure and policy will not guarantee positive post-registration practice, it will offer the conditions in which that practice might grow.

## References

Bingley Miller, L., Fisher, T. and Sinclair, I. (1993) 'Decisions to Register Children as at Risk of Abuse', *Social Work and Social Science Review*, **4** (2): 101–8.

Calder, M. and Barratt, M. (1997) 'Inter-agency Perspectives on Core Group Practice', *Children and Society*, **11**: 209–21.

Calder, M. and Horwath, J. (1996) 'National Core Group Sample: Analysis of Questionnaire Responses', unpublished manuscript, Salford ACPC/University of Sheffield.

Department of Health (1991) *Working Together*, London: HMSO.

Department of Health and Social Security (1988) *Protecting Children: A Guide for Social Workers Undertaking a Comprehensive Assessment*, London: HMSO.

Hallett, C. (1995) *Inter-agency Co-ordination in Child Protection*, London: HMSO.

Mittler, H. (1997) 'Core Groups: A Key Focus for Child Protection Training', *Journal of Social Work Education*, **16** (2): 77–91.

Morrison, T. (1998) 'From Theory to Practice in Child Protection', in J. Horwath and T. Morrison (eds), *Effective Staff Training in Social Care: From Theory to Practice*, London: Routledge.

Murphy, M. (1992) 'Multi Disciplinary Training: What does it Achieve?', *Journal of Training and Development*, **2** (3): 29–33.

Murphy, M. (1995) *Working Together in Child Protection*, Aldershot: Arena.

Murphy, M. (1996) *The Child Protection Unit*, Aldershot: Avebury.

Parton, N. (1985) *The Politics of Child Abuse*, Basingstoke: Macmillan.

Summit, R. (1983) 'The Child Sexual Abuse Accommodation Syndrome', *Child Abuse and Neglect*, **7**: 177–93.

# General index

# Index of authors cited